Y SWIM LESSONS

RESPECT CARING HONESTY

YMCA
Character
Development

RESPONSIBILITY

teaching
swimming
fundamentals

YMCA
We build strong kids,
strong families, strong communities.

YMCA of the USA
      Teaching swimming fundamentals / YMCA of the USA.
          p.   cm. – – (YMCA swim lessons)
      Includes index
      ISBN: 0-7360-0044-5
      1. Swimming—Study and teaching. I. Title   II. Series
   GV836.35.Y63 1999
   797.2'1'071073—dc21   98-37499
                                                        CIP

ISBN: 0-7360-0044-5
Published for the YMCA of the USA by Human Kinetics Publishers, Inc.
Item no.: Y5418
Copyright © 1999 National Council of Young Men's Christian Associations of the United States of America

Permission notices for material reprinted in this book from other sources can be found on page xvi.

Project Coordinator: Laura J. Slane
Writers: Pat Sammann and Laura J. Slane
Acquisitions Editor: Pat Sammann
Managing Editor: Melinda Graham
Assistant Editor: Jennifer Jackson
Copyeditor: Marc Jennings
Proofreader: Kathy Bennett
Indexer: Sharon Duffy
Design and Production: Studio Montage
Photo Editor: Laura Slane
Photographer (cover and interior): Tracy Frankel
Illustrators: Cindy Wrobel and Larry Nolte
Printer: Quest Graphics

Printed in the United States of America   10 9 8 7 6 5 4 3 2

Copies of this book may be purchased from the YMCA Program Store, P.O. Box 5076, Champaign, IL 61825-5076, 1-800-747-0089.

The YMCA of the USA does not operate or manage any YMCA Swim Lessons programs.

Contents

Preface iv

Acknowledgments vi

Introduction viii

**Structure of the YMCA
Swim Lessons Program** viii

YMCA Program Objectives xiii

**The Fundamentals of Teaching
Swimming Fundamentals** xv

Credits xvi

Chapter 1 *Your Role as a YMCA
Swim Instructor* 2

Starting Classes Out Right 2

Meeting Your Responsibility
As an Instructor 3

Teaching Water Skills 5

Teaching Character Development 11

Preventing Child Abuse 17

Chapter 2 *Child Development and
Skill Teaching* 22

The Developmental Perspective 22

How Children Learn 25

Stages of Learning 26

Characteristics of Children by Age Group 26

Chapter 3 *Teaching Styles and Methods* 46

Using Student-Centered Teaching Styles 46

Teaching Methods 53

Observing Skill Performance 54

Giving Feedback 55

Creating an Effective Learning Environment 56

Chapter 4 *Class Organization* 58

Session and Lesson Plans 58

Class Organization 62

Class Organizational Patterns 62

Class Safety 67

Instructional Floatation Devices (IFDs) 70

Aquatic Games 73

Class Management 74

Evaluation 76

Family Involvement 78

Chapter 5 *Working With Adults* 80

Psychological Aspects 81

Developmental Characteristics 83

Changes in Progression Between
Children and Adults 83

Adaptations for Physical Limitations 83

Using Equipment 84

Safety 84

Providing Healthy Lifestyle Information 85

Integrating Character Development 86

Motivating Adults 87

Goal Setting and Rewards 87

Working With Older Adults 88

Chapter 6 *Working With
Different Populations* 92

Working With People With Disabilities 92

Working With People From Other Cultures 100

Working With Classes of Varied Ages
or With Families 100

Working With Day Camp and Day-Care Groups 101

Chapter 7 *Teaching Strokes* 102

Stroke Progression 102

Developmental Sequences of Swimming 103

The Physics of Swimming 109

Stroke Overview 115

Front Crawl 116

Back Crawl 118

Breaststroke 120

Butterfly Stroke 122

Sidestroke 124

Elementary Backstroke 126

Appendix A: Aquatic Skills Games 134

Appendix B: Medical Advisory Committee
Statements Related to Aquatics 150

Appendix C: Value Worksheets 160

Appendix D: Child Abuse Prevention
YMCA Checklist 166

Appendix E: Health Precautions for
Swim Instructors 168

Appendix F: Stroke Observation Checksheets 170

Bibliography 183

Index 184

Art Series 190

Resources 192

Preface

Teaching Swimming Fundamentals is the text for the initial course for all YMCA swimming instructors, whether they plan on teaching school-age children and adults or preschoolers. It describes the Y's expectations for instructors, outlines their responsibilities, and provides them with the basic knowledge they need to teach aquatics.

One of the most significant changes in this text from the earlier *YMCA Progressive Swimming Instructor's Guide* is its focus on a developmental and student centered approach to teaching skills. While it may initially take more time, it pays off in more active involvement in learning and better understanding by students. It's also more fun—for students and teacher!

Teaching Swimming Fundamentals starts with a description of the swim instructor's role. It covers ways an instructor can make students comfortable from the very beginning and can conduct himself or herself professionally with students and staff. It also discusses how instructors should teach both swimming skills and positive values in each class and how they can recognize and report signs of child abuse in students.

The second chapter covers children's development, which instructors will need to understand, especially when teaching using a student-centered approach. It explains that class activities need to be developmentally

appropriate and to follow the principles of how children best learn. Charts at the end of the chapter list the developmental characteristics of children at different ages and suggested activities to encourage development.

The mechanics of teaching using a student-centered approach are discussed in chapter three. The Laban movement framework is explained as a starting point for developing skill themes and question sequences that the instructor can use to guide students in their learning. This is followed by techniques for observing students and giving clear feedback. Finally, the chapter provides ideas for creating a comfortable class environment where students feel free to explore.

Class organization is the topic of the fourth chapter. It starts with session and daily lesson plans, then moves to organizational procedures and practice patterns that allow class activities to proceed smoothly and effectively. Class safety is then considered, as well as how instructional flotation devices and games can enhance skill teaching. The next section deals with problem behaviors in children; following are suggestions for evaluating students and the class. The chapter ends with methods for involving parents in students' instruction.

In chapter five, teaching adults is considered. The chapter begins with some of the psychological and developmental characteristics of adults that affect their learning. An adapted skills progression is suggested, along with adaptations for some common physical limitations. Then, since use of equipment and safety precautions is as important to adults as it is to children, it is explained here. Additional topics for adult classes include ways to provide students with accurate health and fitness information and methods of motivation and goal setting for students. Since older adults have special needs and concerns, a separate section describes the physical and mental changes likely to occur in an older population and provides ideas for adjusting classes to meet older adults' capabilities and interests.

Ys have always welcomed all people, regardless of their differences, so instructors can expect to work with diverse groups. In chapter six, the initial section focuses on people with disabilities, covering specifics of a number of mental and physical conditions that can affect instruction. The rest of the chapter deals briefly with working with people from other cultures, groups of children of various ages or families, and day camp or day-care situations.

The final chapter provides a detailed analysis of teaching strokes. It begins with an explanation of the progression of skill difficulty that instructors should use in teaching each stroke, along with a description of the normal progression of movement for children in learning strokes as they grow up. This is followed by a special section covering 11 basic physics principles that apply to stroke development, with sample lessons that explain these principles to students. The remainder of

the chapter is devoted to descriptions of six main strokes: the front crawl, the back crawl, the breaststroke, the butterfly stroke, the sidestroke, and the elementary backstroke. Each has a stroke evaluation chart for use during student observation. Starts and turns for the strokes are also described. The progression of steps to be used in teaching each of these strokes can be found in the companion texts of *The Youth and Adult Aquatic Program Manual* or *The Parent/Child and Preschool Aquatic Program Manual.*

Six appendixes contain additional material helpful to instructors. Appendix A contains 84 aquatic skills games categorized by skill taught and age level. Appendix B includes statements from the YMCA of the USA Medical Advisory Committee that are pertinent to aquatics. Values worksheets make-up appendix C, which help instructors develop character development program activities for their classes. The Child Abuse Prevention YMCA Checklist appears in appendix D, and medical precautions for instructors regarding the pool environment form appendix E. The last appendix, F, is a group of observation checksheets, one for each of the strokes described in Chapter 7.

Teaching Swimming Fundamentals gives new instructors the basics for teaching aquatics classes, which are elaborated on in the follow-up courses for the Youth and Adult Aquatic Program or the Parent/Child and Preschool Aquatic Program. It should prepare them to conduct classes that are student-centered, values-oriented, safe, and effective in teaching aquatic skills. Most important, it should enable them to teach so students enjoy learning and take pride in developing their skills, giving them the foundation for lifetime participation in aquatics.

Acknowledgments

The YMCA of the USA would like to acknowledge the contributions of the following people to *Teaching Swimming Fundamentals*. Staff leadership for this project was coordinated by Laura J. Slane.

Candice Bishop, RN, MS, CS, FN P–C
Kennestone Hospital–Emergency
Marietta, GA

Susan Christie
Bryn Maur Rehab,
Malvern, PA

Kathi Cook
West Park, NY

Dr. Jerry DeMers
California Polytechnic
State University,
San Luis Obispo, CA

Diane Erb
South Side/Carondelet YMCA,
St. Louis, MO

Linda Garcia
Wheeler Regional Branch YMCA,
Plainville, CT

Theresa Hill
Buehler YMCA,
Palatine, IL

Marcia Humphrey
Gwinnett Family YMCA,
Lawrenceville, GA

Dr. Ralph Johnson
North Greenville College,
Tigerville, SC

Bliss Kaye
National Organization
on Disability,
Washington, DC

Keith Lands
Tuscarawas County YMCA,
Dover, OH

Dr. Stephen Langendorfer
Bowling Green State University,
Bowling Green, OH

Marianne Mackey-Smith
Bob Sierra Family YMCA,
Tampa, FL

Jan McGah
YMCA of Greater St. Louis,
St Louis, MO

Karen Martarano
YMCA of Metropolitan Detroit,
Detroit, MI

Terri Pagano
University of North Carolina,
Chapel Hill, NC

Cami Ramo
YMCA of Greater New Bedford,
New Bedford, MA

Pat Sammann
YMCA Program Store,
Champaign, IL

Stephen Smith
Schroeder Branch YMCA
Milwaukee, WI

Debby Speck
Lake County Central YMCA,
Painesville, OH

Barb Straube
Rich Port YMCA,
La Grange, IL

Al Wagner
University of Pittsburgh,
Pittsburgh, PA

John Wingfield
U.S. Diving,
Indianapolis, IN

Pat Wolfe
Southwest Branch YMCA,
Saratoga, CA

Don Kyzer
Nancy Reece
Laura Slane
Barbara Taylor
Lynne Vaughan
Mary Zoller
YMCA of the USA

We would like to thank the staff and members of Chino Valley YMCA, Chino, Ca., Crescenta Canada YMCA, Flintridge Canada, Ca., Deb Anderson, Chino Valley YMCA, Chino Ca., and Georgia Harrison, Crescenta Canada YMCA, Flintridge, Ca. for their help and assistance with our photo shoot.

We would like to thank the following companies for their donation of equipment and supplies for the photo shoot for this book.

Adolph Kiefer and Associates (Phone: 847-872-8866)

Polywog Tube (#600510), Mesh Water Polo Cap (#600028), Kiefer Synchro Nose Clip (#690200), Kiefer Kona Silicone Snorkel (#810485), Kiefer Lahaina Silicone Mask (#810815), CPR Basic Learning System (#HLS100), Visor with Lifeguard (#909500), Kiefer Fin (#810002, #810003, #810004), Workout Dumbell Waveeater (#650610), Kiefer Barbell (#650603), Vest Type II Toddler (#621307), Underwater Slalom Game Set (#643027), 3/pk Connector Water Log 9" (#650590), YMCA Rescue Tube (#620042Y), Diving Brick (#600044), Type II Child (#621107), Vest Type II Child (#621207), Vest Type II Univ Adult (#621007), #3 Water Polo Wetball Jr. Ball (#606603), Dive Toys Pool Pals Set of 5 (#651002)

Printworks, Inc. (Phone: 414-421-5400)

YMCA Staff Tee (#43071), YMCA Staff Polo (#43082), J-Collar Theme Polo (#43112), Character Development Hot Top (#43505), Character Development Tee (#43123), Y Times 4 Tee (#43125)

Recreonics, Inc. (Phone: 502-456-5706 or 800-428-3254)

Water Woogles (#94071), Catalina Boat Kit (#94059), "Freddy Fish" Funny Float 29" (94124), Rubber Duckie, Yellow (#94150), Dive F/The Tropical Fish Game (#94150), Dive Brick (#92260), Recreonics "Superboard" (Yellow #92212.Y, Red #92212.R, Blue #92212.B), Deluxe Junior Floating Fins (#92442, #92440), Advanced Tempered Glass Dive Mask and Snorkel Set (#92450), Infant's Head Ups Vest, Orange (#12284.O), Foam Type II Life Vest (#12279, #12280, #12281)

Introduction

For more than 110 years the YMCA has been a leader in aquatics and water safety. The first YMCA swimming pool was built in 1885, and the first YMCA lifesaving corps began in 1904, so aquatics has been a part of the Y from early in its history.

However, aquatics has continued to be an important program area over all these years because it has several benefits:

→ It serves the need of communities for a resource that teaches people water safety. Today, many Americans do not know how to swim, even though water recreation activities are on the increase, and thousands of people drown annually. Offering education in water skills and safety is even more important now that public schools have cut back on physical education and aquatic course offerings.

→ It offers a means for people of all ages to learn skills that build self-confidence and esteem. From preschoolers to adults, overcoming fears of the water and developing water and swimming skills is rewarding.

→ It provides a fun activity that children and families can share and enjoy.

→ It promotes better health as a physical activity that can be performed throughout life.

One of the key programs in aquatics has been the YMCA Swim Lessons Program. In this program participants are taught not only swimming skills, but also skills that will allow them to enjoy aquatic activities throughout their lives. These include personal safety and survival and rescue skills, as well as water sports and games.

Structure of the YMCA Swim Lessons Program

The YMCA Swim Lessons Program has two main parts: The Youth and Adult Aquatic Program and The Parent/Child and Preschool Aquatic Program. The first is for children who are six years old and up and, with modifications, it can also be used for adults and for people with disabilities. The second is for children under the age of five and their parents.

The Youth and Adult Aquatic Program has seven levels, and each level builds upon the one before it. The beginning level is *Polliwog*, followed by the *Guppy* and *Minnow* levels. *Fish* and *Flying Fish* are intermediate levels, and *Shark* is the most advanced skill level. In the *Porpoise* level, participants apply the skills they have learned to an ever-widening circle of aquatic activities. It also may be used as a club program for older youth.

The Parent/Child and Preschool Aquatic Program has eight levels. The first four levels—Shrimps, Kippers, Inia, and Perch—are for children under three and their parents, and within those levels they learn water orientation and adjustment skills. The second four levels—Pike, Eels, Rays, and Starfish—are for children three through five, and in those levels they learn beginning swimming skills.

The components of the YMCA Swim Lessons Program are as follows:

Personal Safety	Rules and safety tips Floating Treading Use of PFDs Boating safety Health and safety
Personal Growth	Character development Personal growth opportunities
Water Orientation/Adjustment	Water orientation and adjustment skills (First four levels of the Parent/Child and Preschool Aquatic Program)
OR	
Stroke Development	Major swimming strokes
Water Games and Sports	Synchronized swimming Springboard diving Water polo/wetball Skin diving
	Competitive swimming
Rescue	Recognizing emergencies Getting help Nonswimming rescues First aid and rescue breathing

The history of the YMCA Swim Lessons Program goes all the way back to the turn of the century. Figure I.1 shows the highlights of program development up to the present day.

The present YMCA Swim Lessons program has been developed to take advantage of the latest research available, making sure the program is as effective and efficient as possible. Through a regular review process and communication with aquatic experts and practitioners, we hope to keep the program current and to meet future needs.

YMCA Program Objectives

Because many organizations offer aquatics programs, the question may arise, "What is different about YMCA programs?" Although the YMCA has been in aquatics for many, many years, that is not what makes our programs different. What makes them different is this: Many organizations offer their programs as an end in themselves, but the YMCA uses programs as a vehicle to deliver our unique mission of putting Christian principles into practice to build a healthy body, mind, and spirit for all. It is the activities within the programs that make the difference for Y members and participants.

The goal of the YMCA Swim Lessons Program, as of all YMCA programs, is to help people grow spiritually, mentally, and physically. To accomplish this goal, all YMCA programs address seven specific objectives.

The mission of the YMCA of the USA is to put Christian principles into practice through programs that build a healthy spirit, mind, and body for all.

Figure I.1 **Highlights of the Development of the YMCA Progressive Swimming Program**

1906	William Ball of the Detroit YMCA invited George Corsan of Toronto, Canada, to come and give swimming instruction for one week. In subsequent years, Corsan continued his visits and went to other YMCAs as well. These were the first successful community Learn to Swim campaigns.
1909	Dr. George Fischer came up with the idea of a national swimming program. Buttons were developed and given to participants. The YMCA and the American Red Cross (ARC) agreed to promote first aid on a national basis and to give joint certifications.
1910	William Ball and Major Lynch of the ARC discussed the possibility of the ARC promoting instruction in swimming and lifesaving.
1911	An effort was begun to develop a National Swimming and Lifesaving Organization. That effort failed, but the work continued through the YMCA Athletic League of North America.
1916	The first aquatic institute was organized in Boston to teach and train swimming instructors and pool managers.
1925	The YMCA Athletic League of North America was replaced by the National Physical Education Committee of the National Council, and a subcommittee on aquatics was established.
1930-36	Thomas Cureton developed a program for teaching swimming to children. Dr. John Brown invited Cureton to conduct a study to adapt the program to the YMCA.
1932	Dr. John Brown reported more than a million swimmers a year in YMCAs.
1937	The first National YMCA Aquatic Conference was held in Chicago. Dr. Thomas Cureton developed an extensive questionnaire in 16 areas of aquatics that served as the basis of the reports for the conference.
1938	New literature was released, describing the first progressive program of graded aquatic tests, charts, and worksheets. It was based on extensive research and the use of scientific measuring techniques. The Progressive levels of Minnows, Fish, and Sharks were created.
	The first national plan for certifying aquatic directors and instructors on a professional basis was begun.
1939	The new lifesaving course and theoretical examination were published; a national plan was instituted for certifying directors and instructors on a professional basis.
1949, 1954, 1959	National YMCA Aquatic Conferences were called to study, revise, and implement the aquatic program.
1950s	The YMCA aquatic program was broadened to include boating, water ballet, water polo, skin and scuba diving, and programs for the disabled.
1956	The YMCA introduced the idea of Learn to Swim month nationally.

Figure I.1   **Highlights of the Development of the YMCA Progressive Swimming Program** (continued)

1964   At the National YMCA Aquatic Conference the Progressive level of Porpoise and the Springboard Diving program were adopted.

1966   The national YMCA aquatic programs were conducted by full-time employees, usually called "secretaries." The area aquatic commissioners or field agents worked with local YMCAs to promote the aquatic programs and institutes and to certify Leader-Examiners, Directors, and Instructors.

1969   Under the umbrella name Priorities for Change, 20 study groups were formed and charged with researching, developing, and forming new aquatic programs. The groups also were asked to recommend changes to existing programs. Their work was validated through field testing in local Ys. They presented their findings at the National YMCA Aquatic Conference in Ft. Lauderdale, Florida.

1972   New programs and materials were introduced at the National YMCA Aquatic Conference in Denver, Colorado. The materials included the Progressive Swimming and the Springboard Diving program manuals. Changes in the materials included the following:
- A philosophical orientation for progressive swimming instruction
- Training, certification, and recognition programs for aquatic leadership
- A preschool swimming program called Tadpole
- A swimming program for the disabled
- A synchronized swimming program
- The addition of a new Progressive level, Polliwog

The Progressive program was streamlined by combining skills and by removing some of the emphasis on testing. Program objectives were expanded from just swimming skills to endurance, personal safety, and lifesaving skills.

1981   The Guppy level was added to the Progressive program.

1982   The Camp Waterfront Director/Assistant Director training program was introduced.

1983   At the 10th National YMCA Aquatic Conference held in Indiana, Pennsylvania, 13 ad hoc committees reported the results of two years of research done in local Ys. Program updates were recommended. Priorities were given to updating the Progressive program, producing new materials for training lifeguards, and developing training for YMCA staff for a new parent/child water enrichment program.

1986   Certification courses for Aquatic Facility Manager and Aquatic Instructor Trainer were introduced at the YMCA National Aquatic Conference in New Orleans.

Three new manuals were released: *YMCA Progressive Swimming Instructor's Guide*; *On the Guard: The YMCA Lifeguard Manual*; and *Splash!* (a youth activity book).

1987   The manuals *Y SKIPPERS: An Aquatic Program for Children Five and Under* and *Parents' Guide to Y SKIPPERS* were published to support the new preschool aquatic program.

Figure I.1 **Highlights of the Development of the YMCA Progressive Swimming Program** (continued)

1989	The *YMCA Pool Operations Manual*, the text for the Y POOL (Pool Operator on Location) course, was published. The course was offered for national certification.
1994	Trainer level certifications for each specialist instructor course replaced the Aquatic Instructor Trainer certification.
	The Principles of YMCA Aquatic Leadership course replaced the Basic Aquatic Leadership course.
	New training designs for instructor courses were released for Principles of YMCA Aquatic

	Leadership, YMCA Progressive Swimming, YMCA SKIPPERS, Y's Way to Water Exercise, and the YMCA Lifeguard Instructor course.
1995	The *YMCA Splash* kit was released as the resource for the new community Learn to Swim and water safety programs.
1999	Four new books were released as the foundation for the new Y Swim Lessons Program: *Teaching Swimming Fundamentals, The Youth and Adult Aquatic Program Manual, YMCA Swim Lessons Administrator's Manual,* and *The Parent/Child and Preschool Aquatic Program Manual*.

GROW PERSONALLY—Build self-esteem and self-reliance.

→ **Develop self-esteem.** People who are involved in YMCA programs gain a greater sense of their own worth. They learn to treat themselves and others with respect. High self-esteem helps people of all ages to build strong, healthy relationships and overcome obstacles in life so that they can reach their full potential.

TEACH VALUES—Develop moral and ethical behavior based on Christian principles.

→ **Develop character.** The YMCA has been helping people develop values for 150 years. Founded originally to bring men to God through Christ, it has evolved into an inclusive organization that helps people of all faiths develop values and behavior that are consistent with Judeo-Christian principles. The YMCA believes the four values of honesty, respect, responsibility, and caring are essential for character development. Emphasis is

on building a core set of values shared by the world's major religions and by people from all walks of life.

IMPROVE PERSONAL AND FAMILY RELATIONSHIPS—Learn to care, communicate, and cooperate with family and friends.

→ **Support families.** YMCAs are embracing families of all kinds and are more flexible in responding to their needs. Not only do Ys strengthen families through their own programs, but YMCA staff are increasingly being trained to help families in need or in crisis to find other community supports that can help YMCAs plan programs and events with today's busy, sometimes frantic, families in mind. Families will also get involved in helping plan and run Y family programs. The idea is to program with families, not just for them.

APPRECIATE DIVERSITY—Respect people of different ages, abilities, incomes, races, religions, cultures, and beliefs.

→ **Reflect the diversity of the community.** The country's diversity can be seen in terms of religion, race, ethnicity, age, income, abilities, and lifestyle. YMCAs must assess their membership to see whether it reflects the diversity of their communities. Diversity is a source of strength. The YMCA will foster an environment where everyone is treated with respect and is able to contribute to the larger community. Diversity should be celebrated, not merely tolerated.

BECOME BETTER LEADERS AND SUPPORTERS—Learn the give-and-take necessary to work toward the common good.

→ **Promote leadership development through volunteerism.** The YMCA is driven by volunteer leadership, and it emphasizes providing meaningful volunteer opportunities for all kinds of people, especially youth and families. People are encouraged to move from program participation to deeper levels of involvement, including volunteer leadership. Volunteer leadership will enrich their lives, their YMCAs, and their communities.

DEVELOP SPECIFIC SKILLS—Acquire new knowledge and ways to grow in spirit, mind, and body.

→ **Build life skills.** YMCA programs help people succeed in their daily lives through programs that build self-reliance, practical skills, and good values. Such programs include employment programs for teens and programs that support activities of daily living for seniors.

HAVE FUN—Enjoy life!
Fun and humor are essential qualities of all programs and contribute to people feeling good about themselves and the YMCA.

In addition to the preceding objectives, programs should also meet the following goals:

→ **Respond to demographic trends and social issues.** YMCAs will be called upon to reach out and do more to help make their communities better places in which to live, work, and grow up. The vision is that the YMCA will be the country's leader in prevention and development programs for children and families, and a leader in community development, bringing community resources to bear on social problems.

→ **Develop cross-cutting programs.** The days of narrowly defined programs in the Y are gone. Programs must take advantage of the expertise of the staff in all program areas and combine that expertise into cross-cutting programs. One program area may be the focus, but many others will be incorporated in some way.

→ **Collaborate internally and externally.** From diverse staff groups meeting together to the YMCA working with other community organizations, the question must always be "How can we or our YMCA bring our resources to the table to make this program or initiative a success?" Staff at all levels need to learn the skills required for successful collaborative efforts, including planning, commitment, and implementation.

YMCA Swim Lessons Program Objectives

As in all YMCA programs, the ultimate goal of the YMCA Swim Lessons Program is to develop the whole person—spiritually, mentally, and physically. In order to achieve this, you, as an instructor, should have a basic understanding of and respect for the individuality and uniqueness of each student. The teaching methods that are recommended for use throughout the program are student-centered. They are designed to help develop each participant's human potential, to encourage

Concept reinforcement

YMCA Program Objectives

→ Grow personally
→ Teach values
→ Improve personal and family relationships
→ Appreciate diversity
→ Become better leaders and supporters
→ Develop specific skills
→ Have fun

participants' awareness of safety in all aspects of the program, and to assist participants in perfecting skills to the best of their ability.

Spiritual Development

As an instructor, you are an important role model for your classes. When you relate to your students and to other instructors with sensitivity, you'll probably find that they also become more sensitive. The YMCA Swim Lessons Program should serve as a context for putting the Golden Rule into practice: Treat participants (and other instructors) as you would like to be treated.

Values form an integral part of the YMCA Swim Lessons Program, with special attention being given to the potential moral growth of each student. The Y has chosen four core values to promote: caring, honesty, respect, and responsibility. As a swimming instructor, you will need to actively teach, model, and reinforce these positive values throughout your classes. Doing this is called character development, which will be discussed in more depth in chapter 1. We will provide you with descriptions of activities that you can use in class, as well as help you develop your own ideas for character development activities.

Mental Development

The YMCA Swim Lessons Program includes teaching styles that challenge and develop students' cognitive abilities. The idea is to provide students with the tools and information they need to solve problems, then guide them toward discovering their own solutions. Students who are challenged and who meet those challenges know they have accomplished a great deal.

When teaching and learning go farther than rote memorization and response, students learn to think beyond the confines of the classroom and to transcend the limits of the subject matter. They apply knowledge, formulate ideas, and create solutions. In the book

Teaching Physical Education: From Command to Discovery, Mosston wrote that the cognitive process "releases the mind, releases inhibitions to think in a given path; it calls for another solution, it seeks the different, it uncovers the unknown." The positive, personal growth that occurs from this experience may be understood through the "I Can, I Am, I Will" philosophy: *I Can* accomplish these things and achieve; *I Am* a worthy person because I have achieved success; and *I Will* be able to solve future problems, perhaps not immediately, but eventually.

Telling challenging stories that require solutions, identifying problems that arise, and discussing ideas in a friendly, pleasant place all encourage students to participate. Providing recognition, guidance, and enthusiasm are essential, as is creating an atmosphere of love and trust. Encourage students to set their own mental, as well as physical, goals. Allow each student to develop individually, competing against himself or herself rather than against others.

Physical Development

The YMCA Swim Lessons Program teaches swimming skills and aquatic sports skills, including competitive swimming, diving, and synchronized swimming. Each class session includes time for sustained swimming. While sports skills help students have fun in the water, sustained swimming can build a personal, lifelong interest in swimming for fitness. It helps students increase their strength and endurance and improve their swimming skills.

To increase beginning swimmers' confidence and to allow them to sustain a swimming effort before they have mastered breathing techniques, provide them with flotation belts, kickboards, and other instructional flotation devices (IFDs). These aids help them kick and swim lengths of the pool. When students have adequate time to practice and to develop strength, endurance, and self-confidence, they can learn new skills faster and more easily. The use of flotation devices gives students the opportunity to practice and progress at their own pace. Using the devices also makes it possible for you to work with more than one student at a time, maximizing the amount of time students spend in the water. It also allows you to vary the tasks you assign to students.

In the YMCA Swim Lessons Program, health and physical fitness are used as a springboard for building self-confidence and for practicing the Golden Rule. As swimmers learn to take care of themselves in the water, they also learn to help others, to work jointly, and to strive for excellence. It gives students the opportunity to explore the reasons for physical and moral actions.

The Fundamentals of *Teaching Swimming Fundamentals*

Having quality YMCA Swim Lessons Program instructors is crucial to the program's success. Good instructors create an environment in which participants can grow by both providing models for students and challenging them to think. As the instructor shows interest and concern, participants gain confidence; as the instructor asks questions, students struggle for individual solutions; and as the instructor exhibits enthusiasm, the class members develop a lifelong interest in aquatic activities.

As a YMCA Swimming instructor, you will need to know something about child development, kinesiology, motor control, motor learning, motor development, and teaching methods in order to work effectively with people across all ages. We hope to teach you the basics through our training course for YMCA Swim Lessons instructors.

The course contains established objectives, and the course text, *Teaching Swimming Fundamentals,* has been constructed to give you the information you need to achieve those objectives. After you've completed the course and gained some experience as an instructor, you also may be interested in pursuing other YMCA aquatic courses.

Course Objectives

The objectives for *Teaching Swimming Fundamentals* include the following:

→ To provide instructors with the understanding of key concepts that are part of the main YMCA Swim Lessons Programs for people of all ages.

→ To explain to instructors how to incorporate the Mission of the YMCA into the YMCA Swim Lessons Program.

→ To teach instructors the mechanics of swimming and how to interpret those mechanics to students.

Use of *Teaching Swimming Fundamentals*

Teaching Swimming Fundamentals is designed to help you understand your role as a swim instructor and the basic concepts of teaching instructional classes to people of all ages. It is the manual for the Fundamentals of Teaching Y Swimming course, which is a prerequisite for any of the specialist instructor courses. In your specialist instructor course, you will learn more specifically how the information in this manual relates to each of the program levels.

Other Aquatic Instructional Programs

The YMCA encourages both veteran and new instructors to learn about the other aquatic training programs available. The Program Development Division of the YMCA of the USA can provide you with information on what training programs are currently being offered. You also can find a course listing in the most recent "YMCA of the USA Course Catalog" by calling 1-800-411-9648.

Credits

Parts of "Teaching Character Development" in chapter 1, including figures 1.3 through 1.8 are adapted from *Next Steps for Implementing Character Development*, November 1996.

Parts of "Preventing Child Abuse" in chapter 1 are adapted from *YMCA of the USA Child Abuse Prevention Training*, June 1994.

Tables 2.1-2.9 reprinted by permission, from *YMCA Discovery: Facilitating the Healthy Development of Children*, (Toronto, Ontario: YMCA of Greater Toronto).

"Working With Older Adults" in chapter 5 is adapted from chapter 1 of *Active Older Adults in the YMCA: A Resource Manual*, 1992, Ann P. Hooke and Mary B. Zoller.

Understanding Aquatic Movement, Using Skill Themes, the Game Checklist, Sample Skill Theme Questions (figure 3.1), and Developmental stages of swimming adapted from S. Langendorfer, *Aquatic Readiness*, 1995, (Champaign, IL: Human Kinetics).

Text on pp 22–23 adapted, by permission, from the National Association for the Education of Young Children, S. Bredekamp and C. Copple, 1997, "Developmentally appropriate practice in early childhood programs," (Washington D.C., NAEYC), 9-15, 156-159, and 161.

The Teaching Styles section adapted, by permission, from a paper by Ron Scott, South Oakland Family Branch YMCA.

Child Development Tables adapted, by permission, from *YMCA Discovery: Facilitating the Healthy Development of Children (0-15 years)*, (YMCA of Greater Toronto).

The following adapted, by permission, from *YMCA Advanced Swimming Trainer's Guide, YMCA Advanced Swimming Instructor's Guide*, (Canadian YMCA, Toronto): Instructor Responsibilities, Stroke Overviews of the Front crawl stroke, Back crawl, Breaststroke, Butterfly, Sidestroke, Elementary back stroke, Spin turn, and information was adapted from the following overheads: 1.3, 13.1, 13.1A, 13.2, 13.2A, 15.1, 15.2, 15.3, 15.4, 15.5, 15.6, 15.6A, 15.7, 17.1, 17.2, 17.2A, 17.3, 17.4, 17.4A, pp., chapter 14 (pg. 1) and pp. 153-154.

The following adapted, by permission, from *YMCA Advanced Swimming Instructors Guide, Y Canada Institute*, 1993 (YMCA Canada): Spin turn description and Tips on skill instruction.

The stroke description for the Back Crawl Open Turn, adapted from D. Hannula, 1995, *Coaching Swimming Effectively* (Champaign, IL: Human Kinetics).

Descriptions of Forward start, backstroke start, breaststroke turn, crawlstroke open turn, crawlstroke flip turn, backstroke turn, and butterfly turn adapted, by permission, from *Rookie Coaches' Swimming Guide* (Champaign, IL: Human Kinetics), 1995.

Games

The following games adapted, by permission from, S.J. Langendorfer and L.D. Bruya, 1995, *Aquatic Readiness* (Champaign, IL: Human Kinetics): Choo-choo Train, Name Game, Over and Under, Pop Goes the Weasel, Chin Ball, Jack-in-the-Box, Obstacle Course, Ring-Around-the-Rosy, Glide and Slide, Superman (I), "Timber!", Head, Shoulders, Knees, and Toes, Superman (II), Newspaper Relay, Twenty Ways, Wave to the "Fishies", Stroke Switch, T-shirt Relay, Zigzag, Easter Egg Coloring Time, Humpty Dumpty, Jump Into my Circle, Parachute Jump, and Push Against the wall.

The following games and checklists adapted, by permission from, YMCA, 1986, *Splash!*, (Champaign, IL: Human Kinetics): Tidal wave, Over and Under Passing, Paddle push, Tube relay, Up and over, Submarine relay, Obstacle Course, and Zig zag; Understanding aquatic movement, Using skill themes, Game checklist, and Developmental stages of swimming.

The following games adapted, by permission from, YMCA, 1987, *Y Skippers*, (Champaign, IL: Human Kinetics): I make my arms go up and down, I'm a little teapot, London Bridge, and Ring-around-the-rosy.

The following games adapted, by permission from, YMCA, 1987, *YMCA Progressive Swimming Instructor's Guide*, (Champaign, IL: Human Kinetics): Can't touch me; Chin ball; Head, shoulders, knees, and toes; Kickboard push;

Baton relay; T-shirt relay; Hurray for Hollywood; Balloon relay; Cat and Mouse; Fan race; Frogmen; Marco Polo; Dives; Charlie, over the water; Brick recovery; and Obstacle course.

The following games adapted, by permission from, S. Freas, *Aquatic Games: Water fun at pool, spas, beaches, and lakes*, 1995 (International Swimming Hall of Fame): Blockade runner, Carps and cranes, Hokey pokey, Cork scramble, Frogmen, Forty ways to get there, Hoops, Hunter, Hot and cold, Red light, green light, Simon says, Newspaper race, and Fox and rabbit.

The following games adapted, by permission, from *The Junior Lifeguard Club Coaching Manual* published by the Lifesaving Society—Canada's Lifeguarding Experts: Water baseball, Plastic jug races, and Over and under passing.

The following games were adapted, by permission, from T. Elder, *Water Fun and Fitness*, 1995 (Champaign, IL: Human Kinetics): Flip flops, Porpoise dives, Kickboard stunts, Squid dwim, Corkscrew swim, Teeter totter, and Buddy swim relay.

The following games were adapted, by permission, from *YMCA Advanced Swimming Instructors Guide, Y Canada Institute*, 1993 (YMCA Canada): Water scramble, Three-legged swim relay, Hang on Harvey, Log push, and Battleship.

The following games were adapted from the Y Character Development Cards, 1997, (Champaign, IL: Human Kinetics): Honest abes, Honesty pass, Synchro chain, Pennies for respect, Scrabble, Dive sticks, Ring-around-the-rosy, Marco polo, Honest ball, Values review, Hug our baby.

teaching
swimming
fundamentals

Chapter one

Your Role as a YMCA Swim Instructor

Being a swimming instructor at the YMCA is fun and rewarding, but it also includes a lot of hard work and, most of all, responsibility.

You will be the one who will put students at ease, make them comfortable in class, and keep them safe. You also will have responsibilities to be a good staff person and instructor, one who teaches not only water skills but also positive values.

Starting Classes Out Right

First impressions are always very important. When a student or a student's parent comes to the YMCA to register, impressions are often made even before he or she walks into the building. Even the way a phone is answered may encourage or discourage a potential aquatics program participant.

Everyone in the YMCA is part of a special family. From the people at the front desk to those in the locker room, from the secretaries to the instructors, from the volunteers to the chief executive—each person affiliated with the Y leaves his or her mark. A warm smile, a word of reassurance, and a helpful manner are the Y's way.

Keep in mind that some youngsters in your program may be totally unfamiliar with swimming pools or locker rooms. The lights, noise, and unfamiliar faces can be frightening, especially for very young children.

Although you can try to ease a child's fears, it's helpful if a parent or an adult the child knows well accompanies him or her the first few times.

Your Y probably will present a special orientation for parents that covers pool rules and class procedures to help both the adults and children feel more comfortable with the program. (If the Y staff doesn't hold an orientation, there may be a packet of orientation information available at registration.) When parents know what to expect, they can convey that information to their children. Their confidence or lack of it can be communicated to their children. (A sample parent orientation agenda is in the *YMCA Swim Lessons Administrator's Manual*.)

When participants reach the pool area, give them a smile and a warm greeting. Express genuine interest in each child and adult, and give encouragement and praise often.

For young children in the first few classes, either a parent or you should take each one by the hand and lead him or her from the locker room to the swimming pool. Establish a set place to meet your students and a set routine to make younger children feel more comfortable.

Before class begins, provide a get-acquainted time for all participants, children and adults alike, when they can introduce themselves. To start participants talking, ask them their names or interests. Ask children to talk about their school, pets, or siblings; ask adults to talk about where they work. Younger children may require a little coaxing from parents or you. For example, you can ask children questions such as "Do you like taking baths at home?" "Where is your favorite place to swim?" "Do any other kids from your school take swimming lessons at the Y?" You can then use the information you've learned during class.

Make each class member feel important. Get to know your students' names; they feel great when you call them by name. If someone has been absent, greet him or her warmly upon his or her return. If a child who was afraid to get his or her face wet during the first three lessons is now willing to try a front float, be proud and encouraging. Make swimming a positive experience, especially for students who are having difficulty with a number of skills. Remember, when a student succeeds, you succeed.

When possible, promote other Y programs through your swimming classes. During the initial orientation meeting or meetings for parents held toward the end of the course, mention other aquatic programs available either at your Y or other Ys in the area. If enough people are interested, your Y may even choose to set up advanced or specialty aquatics programs not already available.

Meeting Your Responsibilities as an Instructor

As a YMCA swim instructor, you have a number of responsibilities to your participants and to YMCA members in general. These include the Be-Attitudes:

Have a Good Attitude

→ Be positive and display a good attitude.
→ Be supportive of your peers and management.
→ Be fair and treat everyone with respect.
→ Be a role model at all times, not just when teaching class. Teach and demonstrate the YMCA Character Development values.

Help Participants

→ Be attentive to your class participants.
→ Be sensitive to participants' needs and objectives.
→ Be ready to help participants develop positive self-images.
→ Be available to assist members and participants.
→ Be sure to use positive teaching techniques.
→ Be quick to react to participant feedback. Ask participants if they are satisfied with Y services and methods.
→ Be alert, to prevent accidents and ensure the safety of your students.
→ Be ready to offer participants opportunities for volunteer service.

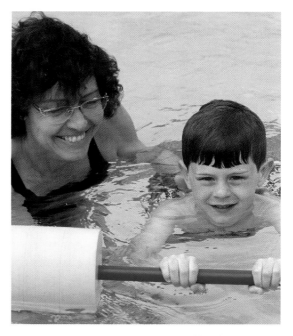

Encouraging each member of the swim class should be an important priority for a YMCA swim instructor.

Be Professional

→ Be knowledgeable about the objectives of YMCA programs.

→ Be up-to-date in your field and know your subject.

→ Be sure to follow and enforce facility rules and procedures.

→ Be sure to keep good records.

→ Be friendly and personable.

→ Be aware of the value of good public relations, especially with parents.

→ Be dressed appropriately.

→ Be reliable and punctual.

→ Be prepared and present lessons well.

→ Be able to handle emergencies calmly and correctly.

→ Be aware of your association's child abuse reporting procedures and report if you observe signs of child abuse.

You also should follow the YMCA Instructor Code of Ethics, shown in Figure 1.1.

Figure 1.1   YMCA Instructor Code of Ethics

I understand the purpose of the YMCA and its programs, which goes beyond skills and involves the spiritual, mental, and physical well-being of our participants.

I understand the YMCA program objectives, and I will strive to make sure they are incorporated into my classes.

I will set a good example in appearance, speech, and attitude.

I will be reliable, prompt, and prepared.

I will be a good role model for my students, and I will not use alcohol, tobacco, or illegal drugs.

I will speak clearly and use words whose meaning is clear to my students. I will not use profanity.

I will create a good learning atmosphere.

I will be encouraging, respectful, and considerate to students, parents, and instructors regardless of race, religion, or culture.

I will always be conscious that the safety of my participants comes first.

I am committed to keeping my certification and training up-to-date, and I will take part in learning opportunities to remain an effective instructor.

I recognize the importance of not being alone with children, except in emergency situations, nor will I ever leave a child unsupervised.

I will use positive correction techniques and will never abuse children physically, sexually, verbally, or mentally (including humiliation, degradation, or threats).

I will report any suspected child abuse or molestation according to the proper procedures.

I will refrain from socializing or associating with program participants or members under the age of 18 outside of YMCA activities.

I believe I am free of psychological or physical conditions that might adversely affect others' health, including significant fever or contagious conditions.

I will follow the Golden Rule.

I will remember how intimidating a pool can be to a nonswimmer or a young child.

You will have several tasks to accomplish as you teach:

Setting the Climate | At the beginning of the class, you set the stage and provide a framework for effective learning. Your mood and behavior make a difference in how your class performs.

Assigning Tasks | Each student may need to perform a different set of tasks to learn and improve the necessary skills. You must know a variety of ways to approach these skills and determine which ways will work best with which students.

Bridging | You need the ability to link ideas from one section of the course to another. This linking shows students how learning progresses and helps them learn by association with previously learned concepts.

Intervening | You must take steps during class to ensure that learning is taking place and is experienced positively. Such steps include motivation, discipline, and feedback on performance.

Summarizing | Close each class by highlighting the key learning concepts and reviewing the day's materials.

Teaching Water Skills

The style of teaching you choose to use can have an effect not only on how well students learn swimming skills, but also on their enthusiasm and on the devel-

opment of their ability to learn on their own. At the Y, we recommend that you choose a student-centered teaching style that will keep students actively involved in their own learning, not just following instructions. We also want you to have an organized approach to teaching swimming skills, so we offer you suggestions and ideas that have worked well for many instructors. Finally, we add some points about how the water environment affects beginning swimmers, points that you can take into account when you teach.

Teaching Styles*

Teaching style is especially important at the YMCA because we are trying not only to teach physical skills, but also to encourage growth in other areas. For instance, we are concerned with the social aspects of the class, how students interact with each other and with us as instructors. Our goal is for students to develop new friendships and to have a positive relationship with us. We also care about students' feelings. Do they think of our classes as nonthreatening and trusting environments? We want to stimulate participants to think. Instead of spoon-feeding knowledge to them, we should be challenging them and giving them time and space to explore on their own. We need to challenge their creativity. We also need to challenge them to think about their values, to consider what they do each day and whether what they believe is reflected in their actions.

This next section is meant to help you choose among several teaching styles. Each style is described and rated on a spectrum according to how well it promotes growth in all areas of development: physical, social, emotional, and intellectual. Figure 1.2 shows this spectrum, which was developed by Muska Mosston in the 1966 book *Teaching Physical Education*. The progression is toward more creativity and the development of students as independent individuals. The *cognitive barrier* is the dividing line between those

Our goal is for students to develop new friendships and to have a positive relationship with us.

* Adapted from a paper by Ron Scott, presently at the South Oakland Family Branch YMCA.

Figure 1.2 Teaching Style Spectrum

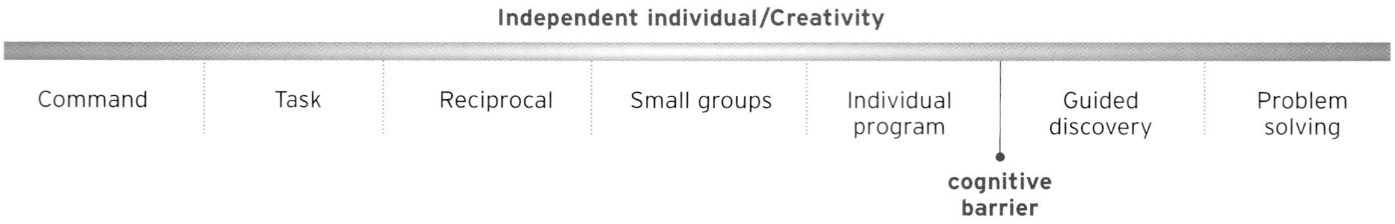

Independent individual/Creativity

Command	Task	Reciprocal	Small groups	Individual program	Guided discovery	Problem solving

cognitive
barrier

teaching styles that do and don't promote the development of students' independent ability to discover answers and solve problems.

That dividing line breaks the styles into those that are teacher-centered and those that are student-centered.

The seven teaching styles covered in the following sections are the command style, task style, reciprocal or partner style, small group style, individual program style, guided discovery style, and problem-solving style.

Command Style

In the command style, the instructor demonstrates and the participant imitates the instructor. Because the instructor is the only one who makes decisions on class activities, the instructor also establishes the social and emotional atmosphere of the class. Participants are expected to stay within the limits the instructor sets.

Task Style

In the task style, the instructor still decides on the subject matter, class organization, and lesson plan. However, participants execute the tasks themselves after hearing instructions or being given written instructions. The participants can decide when and how to do the tasks, so they are somewhat involved in making decisions. Some intellectual, social, and emotional development and exchanges can occur in this style.

Reciprocal or Partner Style

In the reciprocal or partner style, each student works with another student. They observe each other's performance and evaluate it. Participants take on more responsibility and involvement in the learning process.

Small Group Style

For the small group style, at least three people are grouped together, and each person is assigned a different function. For example, one person may perform a task, another may observe and evaluate, and the third may record the observations. These tasks are rotated from one participant to another until all have performed each role. Such a style develops greater interrelationship and cooperation within the group.

Individual Program Style

The individual program style is individual study in which a written program is provided to each student. Participants can proceed at their own pace. This style requires much more preparation by the instructor, but it offers more independence to the participants. In turn, this independence leads to more participant development.

When students are allowed to figure out what to do on their own, they are actively and creatively participating in their learning. As a result, they tend to remember what they learn better and longer. This also gives them responsibility for their own learning.

Guided Discovery Style

The guided discovery style of teaching requires a series of lead-up problems in which each solution builds upon the prior one and leads to an end point. The instructor needs to be ready to offer new problems and shouldn't be surprised if participants come up with solutions that he or she didn't think of. In this style, the instructor doesn't give students the answer, but rather allows them to discover it themselves. Beginning with this style, students' emotional and intellectual capacities are finally being challenged.

Problem-Solving Style

In the problem-solving style, participants finally are free to seek solutions by themselves. The instructor poses problems by asking questions that begin with phrases such as, "Who can…?" or "Can anyone show me how…?" (a question stem). With this style, there are no wrong or right answers. Most problems have more than one solution that fits the criteria of the problem. Instructors using this technique for the first time will notice that their class may initially seem more disorganized. This is because all participants are working more on their own. The longer an instructor works with this style, the more he or she will see the benefits as students grow and become more independent.

Teacher-Centered vs. Student-Centered Learning

As instructors, we are *agents of change*. We help students change their performance by facilitating their learning. However, changes have to come from the students themselves, and if we keep this in mind, we naturally will involve our students more in the learning process.

Traditional teaching methods often have been *teacher-centered,* giving the instructor control of what is taught. A specific skill is demonstrated by the instructor, and students are expected to try to match it as closely as possible. The instructor observes students performing the skill and corrects them, telling them exactly how to change their movements. These methods do not allow students the flexibility to adapt performance of the skill to their own bodies or to be actively involved in discovering how to best perform the skill.

Teaching approaches that keep students actively involved in their learning often are called *student-centered.* Student-centered teaching uses methods such as guided discovery or problem-solving in which instructors act as facilitators, play leaders, or learning guides. They set tasks or ask questions that elicit open-ended responses from the students, rather than telling students *directly* what to do, so these techniques are called *indirect teaching methods.* When instructors use these methods, they are constantly observing, asking questions, setting tasks, and modifying the use of equipment, keeping the students at the center of the learning process.

Although we may try to involve students more by using indirect teaching methods, such as asking students guiding questions or helping them solve problems, it's easy to slip back into direct, teacher-centered methods such as giving students directions or pointing out exactly how their performance differs from the ideal. This happens because teacher-centered methods seem to take less time to set up and use. When we use those methods, though, we are the ones determining how the skill should be performed, and we are the ones doing all the thinking and talking. Such methods lessen students' opportunities to explore and to learn what works best for their bodies. When students are allowed to figure out what to do on their own, they are actively and creatively participating in their learning. As a result, they tend to remember what they learn better and longer. This also gives them responsibility for their own learning.

As instructors, we are agents of change.

What we need to do as instructors is concentrate on giving students more learning opportunities over the long run. Give them the chance to explore each skill fully and discover for themselves the most effective method of performance for them individually. It is our job to guide students in their exploration and to assist them in refining the skill. It may take a little longer initially, but it pays off eventually with better and faster learning for students. And it's much more fun for them!

A Student-Centered Approach to Teaching Skills

The following student-centered approach to teaching skills is one that has worked for many instructors. It follows these four steps:

1. Preparation
2. Presentation
3. Practice (observation and developmental analysis of student performance)
4. Feedback

Let's look at each of the steps, plus some tips for making your class run smoothly.

Preparation

When you prepare for each lesson, keep these points in mind:

→ Know your topic well.
→ Know your students and take their abilities and personalities into account.
→ Prepare objectives for your class.
→ Select the skill or information you want to present.
→ Using the information from this text and *The Parent/Child and Preschool Aquatic Program Manual* and *The Youth and Adult Aquatic Program Manual*, plan how best to present it using questions or tasks (see chapter 3).

→ Choose which teaching tools, such as flotation devices, you want to use.
→ Plan how to arrange your class when you present and demonstrate so students can hear and be safe. Do the same to plan for practice time, trying to maximize the amount of practice (see chapter 4).
→ Take into account the number of swimmers in your class and the amount of space, equipment, and time you have.
→ Decide how you will check to see if your lesson succeeded and objectives were met, such as determining the movement patterns and performance students should have achieved by the end.

Presentation

When you present a skill, arrange the class so everyone can see and hear you, and try to minimize distractions such as noise or other swimmers.

Your presentation should consist mainly of question stems. Question stems are questions such as, "Who can (perform a certain task)?" or "Can you (perform a certain task)?" that ask students to solve creatively a task they are presented. In your presentation you should

→ get everyone's attention before you ask questions,
→ be brief,
→ stress only one thing at a time, so you avoid overloading students with too much information at once,
→ use short, descriptive phrases for the important parts of the skill (cue words),
→ use language appropriate to the students' age group and experience (not jargon),
→ refer to skills students already know (called *bridging skills*), such as relating the back float to sleeping in bed,

→ speak clearly,

→ make sure everyone in the class can see and hear you, making eye contact with everyone in class at least once, and

→ ask questions of increasing difficulty, extending the task.

Before students begin each task, ask them questions to make sure they understand the task, and allow them time to ask their own questions.

As students perform the task you set, observe them. Point out to the class those students who are performing the skill closest to the desired movement, and ask the others to observe and try to imitate it. This type of peer demonstration can be very effective in helping students understand what you are asking them to do.

Practice (Observation and Developmental Analysis of Students)

Students need to repeat skills over and over in order to develop technique, endurance, strength, and speed. Try to vary the ways they practice to keep it interesting, and use games when possible (see appendix A for aquatic skill games). Organize your class to maximize the amount of time spent practicing, rather than waiting for a turn, and use as little class time as possible on routine tasks such as roll call.

For the practice session, choose a formation appropriate for the skills to be practiced (see chapter 4 for more on possible formations). It should be one that is safe and that allows swimmers the maximum amount of practice time. Start practice as soon as possible, and check the water formation to make sure it's working as planned.

Once you have the practice session under way, your job becomes observing how each of the students is moving. Give feedback, using guided discovery and problem-solving techniques (described in chapter 3). Check students' individual performance one at a time,

allowing the others to continue practicing safely.

To analyze student performance, you need to be able to do the following:

→ Know what each developmental level of each skill looks like.

→ Distinguish between effective and ineffective movement.

→ Understand the principles of movement and hydrodynamics that apply.

→ Understand what outcomes result from the student's movement.

→ Be able to observe the performance as a whole, break it down into simple parts, and help the student work on one part at a time. Don't overload the student with more than one correction.

→ Ask questions that will lead the student to discover a different, more effective performance.

Chapter 7 in this manual and the instructions in *The Youth and Adult Aquatic Program Manual* and *The Parent/Child and Preschool Aquatic Program Manual* provide more detail on the performance of specific skills, developmental levels, and principles of movement in the water.

Feedback

Whenever you give feedback to a student, you provide not only feedback on movement patterns and performance, but also about that person (even if it is only implied). Thus, you must be positive and constructive when you give feedback. Reinforce particularly what the student did right, then guide the student with questions to discover what he or she needs to do to change and improve. Present your feedback in a simple, clear, and friendly manner, working on only one thing at a time.

"Giving Feedback" in chapter 3 provides more information on how to deliver feedback.

Concept Reinforcement

The four basic steps in the student-centered approach to teaching skills:

1. Preparation
2. Presentation
3. Practice (observation and developmental analysis of student performance)
4. Feedback

Tips on Skill Instruction

Here are some ideas to keep in mind when organizing and teaching classes:

→ Check the pool area for safety hazards each session and plan class activities with safety in mind. Have a certified lifeguard on duty during each class.
→ Start class on time, and get the class in the water and swimming quickly; don't delay. Use as much class time as possible for swimming.
→ Keep your lessons student-centered.
→ Use tasks, activities, and games to improve specific skill elements.
→ Avoid giving lectures, holding land drills, or spending time doing administrative paperwork in class.
→ Remember that anxiety and fatigue detract from students' performance.
→ Continually guide each student's performance by providing alternative tasks for him or her.
→ Plan your lesson following *The Youth and Adult Aquatic Program Manual* or *The Parent/Child and Preschool Aquatic Program Manual*. Use your lesson plan as a guide, but adapt it as necessary throughout your lesson.
→ Use the whole pool.
→ Keep accurate, up-to-date records of attendance and achievements.
→ Be patient, positive, and polite.
→ Know your swimmers by name.
→ Listen carefully to your students.
→ Understand your students' different learning styles and arrange your skill instruction accordingly.

Give students your personal attention and acceptance. Help them succeed by keeping them active and at the center of learning, and praise them for success.

Doing this improves students' motivation and performance, gives them a sense of responsibility, and highlights how much they have learned, which bolsters their self-esteem.

Show your enthusiasm as you teach. Gesture to emphasize points, change voice levels, and speak in a conversational tone (instead of shouting or using a monotone). Use eye contact and smile at students; be encouraging. When possible, move among students as you teach; when you observe, watch students from the deck.

Working With Beginners

It's probably been a long time since you were introduced to the water, so it might be helpful for you to think back to what a new student is going through when he or she comes to class for the first time. Swimming is a unique experience. The water environment has a number of unique qualities that may create anxiety or tension in students:

→ *Pressure on the body.* Water is a dense fluid that has more weight than does air, so it creates added pressure on the body. Beginning swimmers initially can feel the pressure, and it may make them uneasy. Their breathing and heart rate may increase.
→ *Balance.* As swimming skills are usually performed in a horizontal position, new swimmers may find it hard to recover from this position and regain their balance to the standing position.
→ *Buoyancy.* An individual's buoyancy in water is determined by lung volume and by the amount of fat in the body. Thin students who may have negative buoyancy (a tendency to sink) will initially have more difficulty floating near the surface of the water.
→ *Vision.* When students are learning a stroke with the face in the water, their vision is distorted and

images are blurred. Impairment of vision may make it harder to learn.

→ *Hearing.* With the head in the water while swimming, students' hearing is impaired. They may not be able to hear your feedback clearly. Even when first raising the head from the water, it takes a few seconds for the water to drain from the outer ear canals.

→ *Touch and smell.* The senses of touch and smell are changed somewhat in water. Although these senses are not significant to learning to swim, they are additional sensory changes.

→ *Body position.* On land, we usually relate to our environment in an upright position. However, when we attempt to swim strokes, our bodies must be horizontal to move efficiently. All external stimuli must then be interpreted from that new position, which is a radical change from previous learning experiences in the upright position on land.

→ *Resistance.* Movement requires more effort because water resistance is higher than air resistance. Fatigue may occur more rapidly than if the same movements were done on land, especially if the water is cool.

→ *Propulsion.* On land, our primary form of propulsion is using our legs to push our feet against the ground. With a few exceptions, movement in water depends on the use of our arms as well as our legs to create enough force to move through the water's density.

→ *Breathing.* Breathing through the nose and mouth during land activities is unrestricted and done naturally. To breathe while swimming, students must learn to breathe in through the mouth and exhale through the nose and mouth. Also, inhalation and exhalation often must be synchronized with arm movements. Finally, water may get into the nose and mouth, causing discomfort.

→ *Fear of drowning.* Learning to swim is one of the few motor skills in which the possibility of drowning is always present. Some students will come to class having had bad experiences in the water or having been told about them by a friend or relative.

Nonswimmers and novice swimmers must adjust to all of these factors, ones that experienced swimmers take for granted. If you keep these factors in mind, it will help you better work with beginners.

Teaching Character Development

Values are the cornerstones that make our society safe and workable. They are the principles of thought and conduct that help distinguish right from wrong and provide a foundation for decision making. Values, which are sometimes referred to as *character,* are the basis of who we are, how we live, and how we treat others. Living with and acting on good values contributes to the development of a healthy self-esteem and overall personal happiness.

If we believe that values are what makes society good, then it seems likely that inadequately defined values or a lack of values could be the source of many of today's problems: poor work ethics, lack of personal responsibility, lack of trust in our leaders and public officials, crime, violence, and substance abuse. In the long run, character development is an effective strategy that can help solve these problems and help develop self-esteem. It fits the Y's continuing long-term goal of helping people develop their spirit, as well as mind and body.

The YMCA believes that self-esteem and values are closely related, and that honoring our values is a key way we can build our self-esteem.

Values, which are sometimes referred to as character, are the basis of who we are, how we live, and how we treat others.

The Y has chosen four core values to promote: caring, honesty, respect, and responsibility. These character development values are defined as follows:

Caring: to love others; to be sensitive to the well-being of others; to help others

Honesty: to tell the truth; to act in such a way that you are worthy of trust; to have integrity, making sure your actions match your values

Respect: to treat others as you would have them treat you; to value the worth of every person, including yourself

Responsibility: to do what you ought to do; to be accountable for your behavior and obligations

The Y defines *self-esteem* as the positive valuing of oneself. The Y helps children and adults develop self-esteem by providing opportunities for them to become more capable and worthy. By *capable* we mean having practical abilities and competencies. The more capable a person is, the more confident that person is in his or her ability to think and to cope with life's basic challenges. By *worthy* we mean being able to act in a manner that is consistent with those principles a person has been taught are important, such as doing one's best or doing the right thing. As a person becomes more worthy, he or she also becomes more confident of the right to be successful and happy. It makes the person feel more deserving and entitled to assert his or her needs and wants, achieve his or her values, and enjoy the fruits of his or her efforts.

Because we have free will, we always have three choices when we act:

1. We may choose to act in ways that we know will earn and support our self-esteem.
2. We may choose to act in ways that will not earn and support our self-esteem.
3. We may close our eyes to the necessity of maintaining our self-esteem and proceed through life blindly, choosing at random.

Building self-esteem and developing character (values) are connected. When we behave in ways that conflict with what we judge to be appropriate, we lose face in our own eyes and our self-esteem suffers. We feel less worthy.

The higher our self-esteem, the more apt we are to strive to make principled choices. Doing this makes us feel more worthy, increasing our self-esteem. We cannot earn self-esteem without values, and we cannot act consistently on our values without being influenced by our self-esteem.

For a YMCA to help youth and families develop self-esteem and values, it must provide participants with

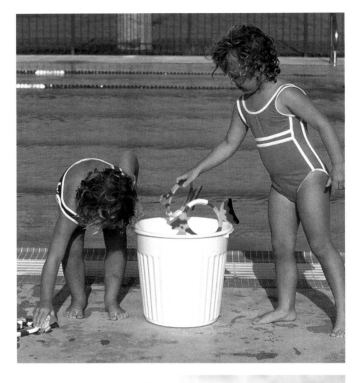

Encouraging responsibility in children requires positive reinforcement and rewarding relevant behavior.

sustained relationships with adults, such as YMCA staff members. The YMCA and its staff must convey consistent messages about values, attitudes, beliefs, and behaviors. (Values are not situational; the same values apply in all situations.) To do this, staff behaviors must be consistent with the values, attitudes, and beliefs that they preach.

Character development is an element that is woven into all YMCA programming, so it is, of course, part of YMCA aquatics. As an instructor, you will need to do the following:

→ Communicate to students that character development is an important part of the course.
→ Teach the four values to participants so they know what those values mean.
→ Include the values in each lesson.
→ Consistently model those values with your behavior so students can see what those values look like.
→ Celebrate those values and hold them up to students as what is right in order to help them learn to believe in the values.
→ Ask students to practice those values over and over again.
→ Consistently reinforce and reward behaviors that support the values, using the specific value word that is relevant.
→ Consistently confront a child whose behavior is inconsistent with the values, doing it in a productive way that does not devalue the child.
→ Be prepared to talk to parents about the character development portion of your classes.

Teaching children values requires a somewhat different approach than teaching skills. First, it requires that you yourself be a good role model. You must exemplify the four values in your words and actions. Second, you must understand at what level children are capable of understanding and applying values. Younger children do not think about moral decisions in the same way as adults. Children gradually develop the ability to understand values as they grow. Third, you need to learn to identify situations in class that relate to the four values. Many everyday occurrences provide a chance for you to demonstrate to students that values are relevant to their daily lives. Finally, you will have to develop the ability to create activities for your classes that emphasize values and make students think about them.

Checking Your Own Behavior

Most of us believe in the YMCA's core values of caring, honesty, respect, and responsibility, but we don't always follow our own beliefs. To assess how well our behaviors fit our values, we can consider how our students or our supervisors would see us if we were following the four core values. Use the worksheet in figure 1.3 to describe what behaviors you think they would expect.

Character development will continue to be an important part of your student's lives for years to come.

Figure 1.3 Personal Values Worksheet

In my job, what would my behavior look like if I acted on the Y's core values?

From the perspective of my students

Caring: _____

Honesty: _____

Respect: _____

Responsibility: _____

From the perspective of my supervisor

Caring: _____

Honesty: _____

Respect: _____

Responsibility: _____

Understanding Children's Moral Reasoning

According to Kohlberg (1971, 1980), children's approach to determining what is right or wrong gradually develops over time. Children under the age of seven often consider actions to be right or wrong based on whether they are rewarded or punished for those actions and on the authority of the rule enforcer: "We do what is right because Mommy says so." They don't think abstractly, so judgments tend to be black or white, with no middle ground.

As children become older, moral decisions are made on the basis of what pleases others or what authority or society says is acceptable or not acceptable: "We do what is right because people expect it." They are more able to think abstractly, and so can see some shades of gray in their decision making.

Teens and adults may reach a stage in which the rightness of their actions is seen in terms of society's individual rights or standards or, possibly, in accord with individually chosen ethical principles that seem to be logical, universal, and consistent.

Given this progression, you probably should follow these guidelines in discussing values with children:

→ For children seven and under, keep values activities simple and clear. Use concrete examples and tell stories that have morals. Repeat examples of values frequently. Talk about consequences of actions, but keep the discussion very simple and concrete.

→ For children older than seven, ask them what the right thing is to do. Guide them to understand the reasons actions are acceptable or not acceptable, and talk about the consequences of actions. Label acceptable behaviors as reflecting specific values and explain why those behaviors are important. Also talk about how following or not following values makes them feel, labeling those emotions.

→ For teens, try describing moral dilemmas to them, then asking them what the acceptable behavior is and why. Have them role-play situations in which they have to make value decisions.

Using "Teachable Moments"

During class games and activities, you may find a situation arises that gives you a chance to point out how values apply. This type of situation is known as a *teachable moment,* and it might be something like one team's behavior toward an opponent, one student's behavior toward another, or a violation of a class rule. This moment can be triggered by either good or bad actions; you can praise an individual's or group's supportive, fair behavior or stop an activity briefly to talk about negative behavior. The following are some examples:

→ If a child splashes another child, talk to the child about respect.
→ If a child gets in the pool before the lesson starts, talk to the child about responsibility.
→ If a child brings another child a kickboard, talk to the child about caring.

Try to balance positive and negative instances; don't use just negative situations. Teachable moments illustrate to students what values look like beyond the words and how values are a part of our everyday lives.

Developing Values Activities

You can create activities that will challenge participants to accept and demonstrate positive values. Such activities should meet the following criteria:

→ Be age-appropriate and developmentally appropriate
→ Account for varied personal backgrounds and differing views on values
→ Attempt to change people's attitudes as well as actions
→ Focus on long-term results
→ Be planned and intentional
→ Fit logically with what you are doing
→ Be positive and constructive, not putting participants down
→ Be inclusive and reflect diversity
→ Be significant, not trivial or corny
→ Be fun

Don't feel that you must force character development into most activities. In fact, that might turn students off. Rather, use character development to supplement the program, and integrate activities into the program when they fit.

Before you begin thinking of activities, take into account the factors in your aquatic program that might affect your choice of activities and their presentation. Figure 1.4 on the following page is a worksheet that will help you sort out what factors to consider.

After you have completed the worksheet, turn to page 160 in Appendix C for all of the Four Values Worksheets. Each of these addresses one of the core values. Use these to help you develop program activities that will fit into your classes.

Besides developing activities yourself, you can use the character development games in appendix A of this manual or the activities available in the *Character Development Activity Box* available from the Y Program Store.

> Teachable moments are occasions on which you can hold up the right value and explain why it is the acceptable thing to do.

Caring Worksheet

Caring
To love others.
To be sensitive to the well-being of others.
To help others.

YSWIM LESSONS.

Ask yourself what you can do with your program participants.

1. What can I do to teach them about caring?

2. What can I do to remind myself that my behavior and attitude should reflect my caring at all times?

3. What can I do to celebrate caring and hold it up as the appropriate thing to do?

4. What can I do to give them opportunities to practice caring for others?

5. What can I do to reinforce and reward their attitude and behavior each time they demonstrate caring?

6. What attitudes and behaviors are currently being reinforced and rewarded? What adjustments, if any, need to be made?

7. What can I do to remind myself of the importance of consistently confronting behavior that is not caring?

An example of a Values Worksheet

Figure 1.4   **Factors Worksheet**

Answer these questions to see what factors might affect your selection of values activities and their presentation.

The target audience: Who is the recipient of the values education? An adult, a child, parents, or families?

_____

_____

Activity considerations: For the program activity being conducted, what type of character development exercise would be most effective for the circumstances? (For example, an exercise appropriate for a day camp discussion circle might not work in a swim class.)

_____

_____

Staff considerations: Are you older or younger than your target audience? Given your age relationship, which activities do you think you can deliver most effectively?

_____

_____

Facility considerations: Where will program activities be delivered—in the pool, in a classroom, on a sports field? Which activities will work most effectively in this setting?

_____

_____

Other factors: Are there other factors, such as the amount of time you have spent with the target audience, that you should consider before selecting or building character development activities for your program?

_____

_____

Preventing Child Abuse

One important responsibility you will have as a Y swim instructor is helping to prevent child abuse. This means being alert to signs of child abuse in your students and reporting such signs to the proper authorities if you observe them. It also means taking care not to put yourself in any situation in which you could be suspected of abusing a child. Your YMCA should offer you training in child abuse prevention.

Recognizing Signs of Child Abuse

Four types of child abuse have been defined:

→ *Physical.* An injury or pattern of injuries that happen to a child that are not accidental. These injuries may include beatings, burns, bruises, bites, welts, strangulation, or broken bones.

→ *Neglect.* Neglect occurs when adults responsible for the well-being of a child fail to provide for the child. Neglect may include not giving sufficient food, clothing, or shelter; failing to keep children clean; not supervising children; or withholding medical care.

→ *Emotional.* Any chronic and persistent act by an adult that endangers the mental health or emotional development of a child, including rejection, ignoring, terrorizing, corrupting, constant criticism, mean remarks, insults, and giving little or no love, guidance, and support.

→ *Sexual.* The sexual use of a child for an adult's pleasure:

 – *Nonphysical:* indecent exposure, obscene phone calls, or Peeping Toms

 – *Physical:* long and intimate kissing, genital or oral stimulation, fondling or sexual intercourse

 – *Violent:* forcible rape, beatings, or other physical abuse

 – *Pornography:* forcing children to view pornography or using them in pictures, films, or tape recordings

A list of possible indicators of abuse can be found in the document "Child Abuse Identification and Prevention: Recommended Guidelines for YMCAs" from the YMCA of the USA's Medical Advisory Committee in Appendix D. Watch for these, but don't overreact. Look for combinations of these indicators; do they form a pattern? See if they occur more than once, unless the indicators obviously are the result of abuse. Keep in mind that some of these indicators may also be signs of stress that is not related to abuse.

Reporting Abuse

As an instructor, you have a legal obligation to report suspected abuse. Know your local association's procedures for reporting child abuse, and follow those procedures when necessary. Under the procedures recommended by the YMCA of the USA, you would notify the program director if you had probable cause to believe that child abuse had occurred. The director would then review the situation and make a report in accordance with the state child abuse reporting act, cooperating to the extent of the law with any legal authority involved. These actions would be taken immediately and carried out promptly, as the YMCA takes all allegations or suspicions of child abuse seriously.

In all cases in which you report child abuse, you should not talk to anyone about what you have observed other than those individuals involved in the reporting procedures; this information should be kept confidential. You may be asked to make a written report of what you observed or to assist a staff member in doing so. You probably will be asked to document the following information:

As an instructor, you have a legal obligation to report suspected abuse.

Who

- → Who is completing the report?
- → Who reported the observations?
- → Who is involved in the incident?
- → Who else witnessed the incident or who else can verify information?
- → Who is assigned to follow up, and how?

What

- → What signs or symptoms did you observe? (Take photographs, if possible.) List specifically what you saw, and don't speculate.
- → What happened before, during, and after the incident?
- → What caused you to become concerned or to document the information?

When

- → Date, time observed
- → Activity child was engaged in, if the incident occurred at the Y

Where

- → Facility or program area, and specific place within the area, if the incident occurred at the Y
- → Places on the child's body where you observed signs

Try to document the information as soon as possible after your observation, while the facts are still fresh in your mind.

Taking Precautions

Although you may know that you would never intentionally harm a child, you also must be careful not to become involved in any situation that might be interpreted as being abusive to a child.

First, never use any of these inappropriate disciplinary techniques with children:

- → Verbal or emotional abuse
- → Shaming
- → Withholding food or rest room privileges
- → Confining children in small locked rooms
- → Physical punishment, such as pulling hair, striking, biting, kicking, or squeezing

Use of these will not be tolerated in the YMCA.

Second, you may appropriately touch children to express affection, but you also need to be sensitive to each child's need for personal space. Some children may not want to be touched or hugged, and you must respect that.

Third, to protect yourself from suspicion, follow these guidelines:

- → Never be alone with a single child unobserved by other staff. If you find yourself in this situation, make sure you report it to your supervisor.
- → Don't become involved with the children in your program in non-YMCA activities, such as babysitting or weekend trips, or socialize with them outside Y program activities without obtaining approval from your YMCA executive.

Your Y may ask you to sign a Code of Conduct that specifically outlines your responsibilities as a YMCA employee. It may look like the one in figure 1.5, which is from the YMCA of the USA's Child Abuse Prevention Training.

Figure 1.5   **Sample Code of Conduct**

1. In order to protect YMCA staff, volunteers, and program participants, at no time during a YMCA program may a staff person be alone with a single child where he or she cannot be observed by others. As staff supervise children, they should space themselves in a way that other staff can see them.

2. Staff shall never leave a child unsupervised.

3. Staff will make sure the restroom is not occupied by suspicious or unknown individuals before allowing children to use the facilities. Staff will stand in the doorway while children are using the restroom. This policy allows privacy for the children and protection for the staff (not being alone with a child). If staff are assisting younger children, doors to the facility must remain open. No child, regardless of age, should ever enter a bathroom alone on a field trip. Always send children in pairs and, whenever possible, with staff.

4. Staff should conduct or supervise private activities in pairs—diapering, putting on bathing suits, taking showers, etc. When this is not feasible, staff should be positioned so that they are visible to others.

5. Staff shall not abuse children, including
   • physical abuse—striking, spanking, shaking, slapping;
   • verbal abuse—humiliating, degrading, threatening;
   • sexual abuse—inappropriate touching or verbal exchange;
   • mental abuse—shaming, withholding love, being cruel; or
   • neglect—withholding food, water, basic care, etc.

   Any type of abuse will not be tolerated and may be cause for immediate dismissal.

6. Staff must use positive techniques of guidance, including redirection, positive reinforcement, and encouragement rather than competition, comparison, and criticism. Staff will have age-appropriate expectations and set up guidelines and environments that minimize the need for discipline. Physical restraint is used only in predetermined situations (necessary to protect the child or other children from harm), is only administered in a prescribed manner, and must be documented in writing.

7. Staff will conduct a health check of each child, each day, as the child enters the program, noting any fever, bumps, bruises, burns, etc. Questions or comments will be addressed to the parent or child in a nonthreatening way. Any questionable marks or responses will be documented.

8. Staff respond to children with respect and consideration and treat all children equally regardless of sex, race, religion, or culture.

9. Staff will respect children's rights to not be touched in ways that make them feel uncomfortable and to say no. Other than diapering, children are not to be touched on areas of their bodies that would be covered by a bathing suit.

10. Staff will refrain from intimate displays of affection toward others in the presence of children, parents, and staff.

11. While the YMCA does not discriminate against individuals' lifestyles, it does require that in the performance of their jobs they will abide by the standards of conduct set forth by the YMCA.

12. Staff must appear clean, neat, and appropriately attired.

Figure 1.5 **Sample Code of Conduct** (continued)

13. Using, possessing, or being under the influence of alcohol or illegal drugs during working hours is prohibited.

14. Smoking or use of tobacco in the presence of children or parents during working hours is prohibited.

15. Profanity, inappropriate jokes, sharing intimate details of one's personal life, and any kind of harassment in the presence of children or parents is prohibited.

16. Staff must be free of physical and psychological conditions that might adversely affect children's physical or mental health. If in doubt, an expert should be consulted.

17. Staff will portray a positive role model for youth by maintaining an attitude of respect, loyalty, patience, courtesy, tact, and maturity.

18. Staff may not be alone with children they meet in YMCA programs outside of the YMCA. This includes babysitting, sleepovers, and inviting children to their homes. Any exceptions require a written explanation before the fact and are subject to administrator approval.

19. Staff are not to transport children in their own vehicles.

20. Staff may not date program participants under the age of 18.

21. Under no circumstances should staff release children to anyone other than the authorized parent, guardian, or other adult authorized by the parent or guardian (written parent authorization on file with the YMCA).

22. Staff are required to read and sign all policies related to identifying, documenting, and reporting child abuse and attend trainings on the subject, as instructed by a supervisor.

I understand that any violations of this Code of Conduct may result in termination.

Employee signature _____

Supervisor signature _____

Date _____

Other precautions taken in most YMCA programs are these:

→ Administrators prescreen all instructor candidates before hiring to try to identify those who might be likely to abuse children.

→ Parents can visit any program their child participates in unannounced.

→ Administrative staff make unannounced visits to observe staff performance.

→ Young children are never allowed to be unsupervised in bathrooms, locker rooms, or showers.

→ Staff communicate frequently with parents about their child's day-to-day activities, and parents are encouraged to report anything their child shares with them that seems unusual.

→ Staff are taught how to discuss sensitive issues with children such as toileting, sleeping, and questions about sex.

→ Staff are taught how to identify parents who are stressed and offer them support and referrals for help.

The Child Abuse Prevention YMCA Checklist in Appendix D lists ways that all Ys can help prevent child abuse.

If you became involved in an incident in which you were charged with child abuse, you probably would be suspended from the YMCA, regardless of whether the incident happened on or off YMCA premises. You would be reinstated only after all allegations were cleared to the satisfaction of those involved in the reporting procedures.

Chapter two 2

Child Development and Skill Teaching

Your success at teaching children to swim will depend in large part on your understanding of children's development.

First, what and how you teach should be tailored to each child's abilities; the Y encourages the use of developmentally appropriate activities. Second, understanding the principles of how children learn best and the stages of learning will help you decide how to structure your lessons for maximum effect. Finally, knowing the language, physical, cognitive, and social/emotional capabilities of children and their interests at different ages will guide you in choosing activities that help them not only learn to swim, but also to grow to their potential.

The Developmental Perspective

The skill progressions used in the current YMCA Swim Lessons program and the Parent/Child and Preschool Aquatic Program are based on children's physical, social, emotional, and cognitive development. You will need to understand some of the typical behaviors—and their variations—of children in the age groups you work with if you are going to effectively and efficiently teach them to swim. To enhance learning, we want to be able to match what we do as instructors with what the children would normally do.

Some principles for promoting developmentally appropriate practices have been established by the National Association for the Education of Young Children in the

book *Developmentally Appropriate Practice in Early Childhood Programs* (Revised Edition, 1996):

1. *Domains of children's development—physical, social, emotional, and cognitive—are closely related. Development in one domain influences and is influenced by development in other domains.* As children become more mobile, they receive more input that stimulates their cognitive development. As they learn to speak, they are better able to socially interact with others.

2. *Development occurs in a relatively orderly sequence, with later abilities, skills, and knowledge building on those already acquired.* Knowing developmental sequences allows us to observe, assess, and teach more realistically and effectively.

3. *Development proceeds at varying rates from child to child as well as unevenly within different areas of each child's functioning.* Age is only a rough indicator of developmental progress. Use age only to get a general sense of what a child might be expected to do.

4. *Early experiences have both cumulative and delayed effects on individual children's development; optimal periods exist for different types of development and learning.* Frequent positive or negative experiences, or a lack of experiences, can weigh heavily in determining whether a child succeeds or fails in a particular area. The effects may also not be seen immediately. In addition, some fundamental motor skills may be more easily learned during the preschool years, so children who don't have those opportunities then may have more difficulty learning them later.

5. *Development proceeds in predictable directions toward greater complexity, organization, and internalization.* Concrete behaviors, knowledge, and simple skills precede the ability to use abstract symbols or representations and more complex skills.

6. *Development and learning occur in and are influenced by multiple social and cultural contexts.* As instructors, we need to try to understand the culture of the children we teach if it differs from our own. We also should ask children to learn to function well in the society as a whole and move comfortably among people of similar and dissimilar backgrounds.

7. *Children are active learners, drawing on direct physical and social experience as well as culturally transmitted knowledge to construct their own understandings of the world around them.* We can enhance their learning by helping them to reflect on what they experience and by using references to experiences outside the pool.

8. *Development and learning result from interaction of biological maturation and the environment, which includes both the physical and social worlds that children live in.* The child's physical maturation and the environment influence each other in complex, subtle ways.

9. *Play is an important vehicle for children's social, emotional, and cognitive development, as well as a reflection of their development.* Child-centered play experiences are optimal safe places to try out new ideas and skills, and to practice them.

10. *Development advances when children have opportunities to practice newly acquired skills as well as when they experience a challenge just beyond the level of their present mastery.* With your support and guidance as an instructor, children can be challenged to do more and succeed often. Exploration, guided discovery, and problem-solving teaching techniques are optimal means for helping children advance their development.

11. *Children demonstrate different modes of knowing and learning and different ways of representing what they know.* They may have different preferred ways of learning concepts and skills, so we as instructors should offer information and structure learning environments using diverse methods.

12. *Children develop and learn best in the context of a community where they are safe and valued, their physical needs are met, and they feel psychologically secure.* The YMCA of the USA provides programs and core values that promote this principle.

These principles can and should be used to guide our decision making in teaching.

Taking a developmental perspective gives the student credit for what he or she is able to do instead of pointing out what the student can't do.

Motor development can be observed to occur as children get older, but it doesn't happen automatically with the passing of time. Instead, it is the product of the interaction of inherited general abilities, experiences, and specific instruction. Motor development changes aren't attributable just to increased physical size or abilities; they also include differences in how movements are performed and the results of those movements. For example, over time a child may throw a ball faster or farther, but this is due not only to the fact that the child is larger and stronger, but also to the use of a more refined pattern of movement than earlier.

Patterns of movement usually match task demands more closely and efficiently as development proceeds. Researchers who have studied children to determine the sequence of movements through which various skills develop can reliably predict which type of movement a child will be able to perform next, given the one he or she can perform now. Each change in movement builds on previous ones. Running is built upon walking. Throwing with a turn of the trunk and a step is built upon an "arm dominated" toss with no step. Children's movement generally changes toward becoming more skilled or adaptive, although it can also regress to earlier levels if the task is too difficult or challenging.

The rate of motor development change depends on a number of factors, such as the child's strength, flexibility, sense of balance, perceptual abilities, or motivation. It will differ from individual to individual, and although it is loosely related to age, age does not guarantee a certain rate of change. Biological growth differs widely between children of the same age; so do children's opportunities to experience and practice skills. Understanding and motivation levels also may differ.

The core idea behind taking a developmental perspective is to start instruction wherever the child is. Whatever movement he or she is presently capable of performing is acceptable, and you find ways to build

upon that to the next movement in the sequence. This is quite different from looking at a movement and comparing it to the way an adult would perform it, then giving the student "error" corrections based on that comparison. Taking a developmental perspective gives the student credit for what he or she is able to do instead of pointing out what the student can't do. This can give the student more self-confidence and encourage him or her to try new experiences and take on harder challenges.

To teach this way, you will need to understand the components of each skill and know how to assess children's present skill levels. Once you know each child's abilities, you will need to break up your class into smaller groups that can work on specific, possibly different, tasks or use different equipment. You may even have to assign different tasks to individual students in order to meet their specific needs.

You also will need to learn to observe how children are performing and to think about what features of the task might be making it more difficult. You then will have to modify those features so students can perform more successfully. For example, a child learning to swim in a prone position can use many possible arm and leg motions, body positions, and breathing patterns. A number of factors contribute to the difficulty of this task and may prevent a child from being successful. If the child is thin and floats poorly, arm recovery over the water might be a very difficult action. If the child is not comfortable putting the face into the water, rotary breathing, timed tightly with arm motions, might also be very difficult. Cool water, cool air, or relatively deep water likewise provide a less-than-optimal learning environment. Conversely, providing the child with an instructional flotation device or goggles, or with shallower and warmer water, or not requiring an arm recovery over the water all might enhance the child's prospects for success. You can adjust any one of these factors and then observe to see if the child's performance improves. Part of using indirect teaching methods is progressively altering key tasks and environmental factors to help the child succeed or to challenge the child and help him or her progress.

How Children Learn

Some principles hold true for all children's learning. The following concepts, based partly on Jean Piaget's work, can help you plan children's classes effectively:

→ **Children learn best in a step-by-step, sequential pattern.** To teach this way, you will need to understand the general growth and development patterns of the age group you work with. You will want to build on each child's previously learned skills.

→ **Children learn from concrete to abstract, simple to complex.** Show them a basic skill, then have them try it a number of times. At this initial point, especially for children younger than seven, it's not necessary for them to develop a mental image of the skill. That will come later in the process.

→ **Children learn through reinforced repetition.** After you have introduced a skill, let the children explore it, trying it in a variety of ways. Through practice and with your guidance and feedback, they will gradually change the form and effectiveness of the skill. As the children progress, be sure to recognize and reinforce their accomplishments.

Within the YMCA Swim Lessons program, children will practice or work on some complex skills over several levels. We begin by teaching the whole stroke at one level. Once the students achieve some benchmarks, they move to the next level, where they continue working to improve and refine the skill to a more advanced level.

→ **Children learn through hands-on experiences.** Remember the saying "When I hear, I forget; when I see, I remember; when I do, I learn"? As an instructor, you need to first ask the children to explore a particular task or skill using a well-designed question stem, then guide them to explore the skill under different conditions. Be sure to use words they can understand. As they practice, they also will increase their endurance, and you will be able to guide them to improve the skill.

→ **Children learn through play.** Play is important for children. It helps them develop socially, emotionally, intellectually, and physically.

→ **Children want classes to be fun.** Games that develop new skills or practice old ones can be an important part of your classes. In chapter 4 we will talk about how to use games to improve specific skills and how you can choose games to help students master particular aspects of skills. Using games, songs, and other such activities keeps classes fun and exciting for students.

→ **Children absorb new information when they are developmentally ready.** When children are developmentally ready, they have a foundation for absorbing what you tell them. Their thought processes are developed enough that they can understand the new information, and they can learn the skill quickly. When children are not ready, they will not be very successful at learning the skill and may become frustrated.

You need to match the skills you teach with each child's present abilities. The skills in this program have been reviewed carefully to match the developmental readiness of most children.

→ **Children learn best in child-centered environments.** A child-centered environment is one in which children can explore and create, in which they are not frustrated by unnecessary limits. It also is an environment in which they feel (and are) safe.

Stages of Learning

According to motor learning theory (Langendorfer, German, and Kral, 1988), swimming skills are learned in three general stages:

1. Getting the idea of the movement (extension)
2. Practicing the skill until it can be performed consistently (refinement)
3. Mastering the skill and being able to use it in different situations (automatic mastery)

During the first stage, the student tries to understand what the skill requires and attempts to perform it. This includes taking into consideration the environmental conditions, such as thinking how motor skills learned on land will transfer to the water. At this stage, the student must consciously think about what he or she is doing. Performing the new movement sometimes feels awkward, and the student may become tense and frustrated or be slow to learn. It takes your assistance and reinforcement during the student's practice for him or her to reach the point at which the movement can be performed reflexively.

Once the student grasps the basis of a movement, he or she moves to the second stage. Here the child practices until the skill can be performed repeatedly the same way. He or she then feels more relaxed and confident, and you can help the child refine the skill through drills and similar activities until he or she reaches the final stage—mastery.

Expect your students to progress through these stages at very different rates. Also expect that students may start out with rapid initial improvement, then plateau for a while before showing additional improvement. The time it takes each student to move through a skill to mastery varies widely, and some students may never completely master a skill.

The ability to learn and the speed at which children learn to swim depends on many factors (*Looking at Physical Education*, (n.d.)). Physically, the child's size, strength, and body type will play a role, as will any physical disabilities he or she may have. Mentally, the child's cognitive abilities and motivation will make a difference. Fears of—or experiences with—swimming and social expectations may have a positive or negative effect. The characteristics of the swimming facility and the water environment, and even the personality and experience of the swimming instructor, can affect the results.

Characteristics of Children by Age Group

To work with different age groups of children, you need to know the general behaviors common to most children of those age groups. These behaviors can be classified as falling under language development, motor/physical development, cognitive development, and social/emotional development. The charts in this section (tables 2.1-2.9) show the development of children from the ages of 0 to 6, 7 to 11, and 12 to 15. They also include suggested activities to help promote children's development in each of the charted areas.

Please keep in mind that age group charts provide **only** a very general, approximate method of identifying children's behaviors. Many children within each age group may be either less or more developmentally advanced.

Table 2.1 Development of Children from 6 to 12 Months Old

Development Behaviors

Language Development	Activities to Promote Language Development	Motor/Physical Development	Activities to Promote Motor/Physical Development
• Babble a lot. • Find that sounds and intonation of native language are reinforced. • Understand language better than speak it. May shake head for "no," point to dog, etc. • Cry and point to try to get needs met. • Respond to sounds, music, airplane, own name, etc. • Like to be held on lap and look at books and hear rhythm of words. • Like interactive games (peekaboo).	• Provide opportunities to read and talk to them, play games such as peekaboo, point-and-name, etc. • Reinforce sounds they make, such as "ma" for "Mommy." • Try to understand them and meet needs to keep frustration to a minimum. • Sing action songs, such as "The People on the Bus" and "If You're Happy and You Know It." • Use simple aquatic terms: kick, paddle, bubble.	• Continue to wave arms and kick. • Can hold head steady. • Reach toward hanging mobile. • Sit with support. • Pull self up to stand, with support, to upright position, important for getting leg muscles ready for walking. • Crawl and creep. Reach, explore. May crawl up stairs. • May pull self up from sitting position. • Walk, holding onto objects. • Enjoy action games. • Is relaxed when held close in the water; at 9 to 12 months, when in front tow or back cradle positions. • Can blow bubbles; later can blow on command. • Can put mouth in and out of water when chin is held at water level; at 9 to 12 months can spit on command. • Remains stable while in towing position with minimal parental support; at 9 to 12 months can let go of parent's arms and move own arms while being towed. • Can turn 180 degrees while wearing an IFD by turning head; at 9 to 12 months can maintain stable vertical position in IFD without support. • Can kick or wiggle legs while being towed; at 9 to 12 months can focus on parent's face to remain stable. • Can change position while cradled in the water. • Can wet face and arms. • At 9 to 12 months can balance on parent's knee without support. • At 9 to 12 months can climb out of pool with some assistance.	• Provide balance bar at children's level for them to walk while holding on to bar. • Provide lots of opportunities to walk, crawl, explore, climb in a safe environment. • Play action games, such as crawling and barking like a dog. • Ensure environment is childproof, with small toys, chemicals, and sharp objects out of children's reach, as they love to explore. • Provide gates at doorways, stairs, etc. • Provide push-pull toys. • Blow bubbles, spit, or splash so they can mimic.

Table 2.1 **Development of Children from 6 to 12 Months Old** (continued)

Development Behaviors (cont.)

Cognitive Development	Activities to Promote Cognitive Development	Social/Emotional Development	Activities to Promote Social/Emotional Development
• Imitate facial expression. • Look for objects when they are dropped. • Are egocentric, view everything from a personal point of view. • Explore objects through smell, touch, and taste. • Establish tastes. • Demonstrate likes and dislikes in food.	• Provide sensory experiences: water, sand, rice, Play-Doh, with pails, measuring cups, shovels, etc. • Provide toys that make sound: squeeze toys, music boxes, instruments, etc. • Introduce a variety of foods that they enjoy. • Put floating toys in the water, allow to kick and paddle for toys.	• Enjoy being held and cuddled at times other than feeding and bedtime. • Enjoy new experiences and objects. • Become social beings. • Love interaction. Enjoy attention. • Show preference for parents. • Are scared around strangers, may cry when parents leave. • Smile at self. • Enjoy simple games (pat-a-cake). • Become upset if toys are being taken away, needs are not being met. • Establish a routine and need one.	• Have sit on lap when read to. Provide variety in toys, activities. • Ensure parents stay with children prior to leaving. Children should see parents leave and say good-bye. Give proper orientation. • Provide an unbreakable mirror at children's level; they love reflection of self. • Sing songs, say rhymes. • Warn before moving on to different activity, such as, "We are going to take a bath soon." • Avoid frustration as much as possible. Soft lights and music before bed, nap after lunch. • Play simple games with partners or a group. • Stay with the same songs each class. • Praise everything they do. • Use caution when taking the children from the parents.

Disclaimer: Age group charts should be used only as general approximations for identifying children's behaviors. Many children may be either less or more developmentally advanced.

Table 2.2 Development of Children from 12 to 18 Months Old

Development Behaviors

Language Development	Activities to Promote Language Development	Motor/Physical Development	Activities to Promote Motor/Physical Development
• Speak first words, continue babbling. Speak new words daily. • Love rhymes, one-word page books. • Use words to attract adult attention. • Use two words together first time (telegraphic speech). • Indicate verbal and nonverbal needs.	• Reinforce new words. • Introduce cloth and vinyl books so can turn pages by themselves. • Listen to wants to eliminate frustration and reinforce new words learned. • Call things by their proper names. Child: baba Parent: You want your bottle? • Understand and possibly repeat words. • Sing songs. Change words to water terms.	• Climb stairs, stand alone, walk, climb tables, get under counters. Bounce on furniture. • Pick up small objects. • Use both hands freely but may favor one hand. • Expand range of exploration, empty cupboards, poke into shelves and drawers. Pull out pots and pans. • Nest toys, pull, push. • Can turn from 180 to 360 degrees while wearing an IFD. • Can kick or move arms on request. • Can move intentionally toward a target. • Can get to various locations independently while wearing IFD. • Can climb out of pool with assistance. • Can move cautiously on deck while entering/exiting pool. • Can put face in water and blow bubbles. • Can maintain stable vertical position in IFD without support.	• Provide lots of opportunities to move climb, explore, in a safe environment. • Give small objects to pick up. Make sure objects are large enough to avoid choking. • Ensure toys, plastic pots are accessible on lower shelves. • Give push-pull toys, soft blocks, pop-up toys, nesting toys, size sorters.

Table 2.2   **Development of Children from 12 to 18 Months Old**   (continued)

Development Behaviors (cont.)

Cognitive Development	Activities to Promote Cognitive Development	Social/Emotional Development	Activities to Promote Social/Emotional Development
• Get frustrated when learning new skill. Express frustration by throwing tantrum. • Have short attention span. Often get distracted when pursuing goals. Get frustrated with own limitations. • Begin to develop skills in problem solving. Can match simple puzzle pieces in a form board. • Begin developing imagination. • Understand the concept of more. • Begin to sort by colors, size, etc. • Can count two objects. • Begin to understand consequences of actions.	• Provide opportunities to repeat activity and new skill. • Assist with expressive language by acknowledging frustration. Do not get angry with tantrums. • Give simple wooden three-piece puzzles with knobs. • Provide Busy Box for them to operate. • Ask them if they want more milk, lunch, etc., and respond accordingly. • Count with them to three or four. • Sing songs.	• Show an interest and preference in toys and clothes. • Play with dolls and animals as if they were real. • Run to be picked up and cuddled. • Love affection and demonstrate affection. Enjoy roughhousing. • Enjoy tossing games. • Will obey "no," say "no" a lot. • Are possessive. • Like to be within sight and earshot of parents. May stop playing for a while to ensure parent is nearby. • Have a sense of humor. • Want a security blanket. • Need daily routine. • Enter pool eagerly from sitting position on side at parent's request.	• Respond to wants by offering some choice, no more than two: "Do you want to wear the blue shirt or the yellow one?" • Provide stuffed animals (dolls with props, baby bottles, bowls and spoons, etc.) • Have them run to you and pick them up and cuddle. • Provide lots of opportunities for conversation. • Provide soft ball or sand bean bags for tossing. • Do not force to share—not ready for that yet. • Do not let parents sneak out. Ensure they say good-bye and leave quickly. • Provide toys, blanket that they are attached to. • Have bed, meals, baths at regular times. Keep changes in routine to minimum. • Do partner and group activities.

Disclaimer: Age group charts should be used only as general approximations for identifying children's behaviors. Many children may be either less or more developmentally advanced.

Table 2.3 Development of Children from 18 to 24 Months Old

Development Behaviors

Language Development	Activities to Promote Language Development	Motor/Physical Development	Activities to Promote Motor/Physical Development
• May use the word "no" a lot. Use two to three words in sentence. • Can name familiar items in pictures, such as a cat, ball, etc. • Can follow simple directions: "Get your shoes," "Pick up the ball," etc. • Can call self by name. • Enjoy rhymes, chants. • Sometimes use biting as expression of frustration. • Language is limited. • Can imitate simple sounds, and everyday noises, etc. • Has basic understanding of and can use simple words hot, cold, high, low.	• Introduce books with two to three words on each page with illustrations of familiar objects such as a cat, ball, or car. • Give simple instructions, one at a time. • Provide opportunities to sing. • Keep frustrations to a minimum. • Intervene before children get really frustrated. 	• Can walk, jump down, climb up, primitive throw. • Can build small towers. Can do primitive kick of large ball. Can open and close small containers. • Use crayon marker to scribble on paper, walls, and other available surfaces. • May be ready for toilet training (through 36 months). • Can be held in front and back positions in water by adult. • Will allow another adult to hold them in the water. • May inhale and blow out, forming bubbles in water on request. • Can change positions and directions while in IFD. • Show basic body position control in water by putting face in water. • Can stand without aid in shallow water (<3 feet). • Can move specific body parts on request, including simple flutter kicking and paddling arm motion. • Can enter and exit the pool by climbing out with minimal help. • Will walk 10 feet to target in waist-high water without help. • Can climb onto a boat or hold onto a floating safety object. • Can float wearing an appropriately-sized PFD (Class I, II, III). • Can move to various locations independently while wearing IFD.	• Provide opportunities to run, dance to music, climb, and throw soft balls or bean bags. • Provide nesting and stacking toys, jars, etc. • Provide washable markers, paper, crayons, etc., to write with. • Introduce the toilet and let them see other children use the toilet.

Table 2.3 **Development of Children from 18 to 24 Months Old** (continued)

Development Behaviors (cont.)

Cognitive Development	Activities to Promote Cognitive Development	Social/Emotional Development	Activities to Promote Social/Emotional Development
• Are curious and starting to explore. • Strive for autonomy. Show independent streak. Continue to be egocentric. • Can identify size and relationships such as which ball is bigger. • Can recognize similarity and differences in objects. • Usually see objects in terms of only one prominent feature. • Demonstrate short-term memory, has object permanence, remembers and will look for objects when they are out of sight.	• Provide opportunities for accomplishing simple tasks for self, such as eating or putting toys away. • Sing songs and play number games and games using matching and comparing opposites and similar objects, memory games, etc. • Introduce a print-rich schedule. • Use guided discovery to develop skills. • Have them put away toys and equipment after use. • Keep changes in routine to a minimum to enjoy predictable day.	• Play in parallel near other children, but not with them. • May imitate simple parent behaviors. Resist demands of parents both playfully and seriously. • Are affectionate, yet can be rough. Treat other children like objects, not meaning to hurt them or realizing they are. • Need concrete limits and close supervision, yet lots of room to explore. • Do not like unexpected change. Prefer regular routine. • Biting is part of normal development.	• Have other children around. • Give choices: "Do you want to play outside with your doll? Inside or outside?" • Avoid frustration by encouraging expressive language, warnings, etc. • Have a consistent class routine. • Give opportunities to share things, such as playing ball by passing it.

Disclaimer: Age group charts should be used only as general approximations for identifying children's behaviors. Many children may be either less or more developmentally advanced.

Table 2.4   Development of Children from 24 to 36 Months Old

Development Behaviors

Language Development	Activities to Promote Language Development	Motor/Physical Development	Activities to Promote Motor/Physical Development
• Expand vocabulary to 1,200 words, use two- to four-word sentences. • Enjoy singing, rhythm instruments, repetitive tunes, and clapping. Use silly language, jokes, and riddles and memorize simple rhymes. • Express artistic ability. • Develop language through reading. Spend time alone looking at books. Will ask for specific books to read. Role-play favorite stories, make pictures of favorite characters and events. May recreate personal experiences. • Read familiar signs and symbols (pre-reading skills) • Experiment with swear and toilet words.	• Introduce storybooks with more words, musical instruments, action songs, silly stories, jokes, and riddles. • Provide opportunities to draw and represent characters and events by providing markers, crayons, and paints. Adult could add descriptive words on children's pictures. • Provide road signs and logos for use in play. • Give directions to children rather than parents. • Can express wants. Asks "why?" frequently. • Talk to self during play.	• Ride tricycle. • Insert shapes, pegs into board. • Can work five- to six-piece puzzles. • String large beads. • Develop skills such as eating and pouring. • Walk down stairs. • Learn bowel control and toilet training. • Run. • Stack, build tower, climb.	• Provide tricycles for outdoor play, pegboards, five- to six-piece wooden puzzles. • Encourage serving of food portions to self. • Encourage going to the bathroom before class. Continue toilet training. • Provide blocks and accessories. • Encourage horizontal kicking in the water. • Can move through water short distance without help.

Table 2.4   **Development of Children from 24 to 36 Months Old**   (continued)

Development Behaviors (cont.)

Cognitive Development	Activities to Promote Cognitive Development	Social/Emotional Development	Activities to Promote Social/Emotional Development
• Enjoy and need activities that develop and challenge fine motor skills. • Can copy simple shapes. • Can represent the world with mental images. • Can classify objects, puzzles on the shelf, trucks on the carpet. • Has an understanding of time concepts: "After lunch, we will go to the park." • Understand the concepts of more, less, empty, full, up, or down. • Begin to learn to print name.	• Provide opportunities to print (primary pencil, paper, etc.) • Use print-rich labels; for example, a picture and word on a label will assist the child in cleanup. • Play "Simon Says." • Give clear directions, one at a time. • Begin to get numbers one to 10 in sequence. • Begin to use toys and objects to represent people.	• Are outgoing, lives in extremes of love, hate, etc. • Use physical aggression if frustrated, tired, angry. Can become brash, disobedient, over-demanding. Cry less, but whine a lot. • Identify with superheroes. May develop imaginary friends. • Fearful of the dark, monsters. May have disruptive sleep and act out aggressive feelings in nightmares. • Possessive of playthings. Watch and imitate play of others, but seldom join in. • Have difficulty taking turns. • Begin to separate from parents more easily.	• Provide opportunities for dramatic play. • Set very clear limits. • Keep waiting to a minimum. No lining up. • Supply enough toys for each child to have one. • Keep classes moving. • Promote independence, but encourage instructor/child relationships.

Disclaimer: Age group charts should be used only as general approximations for identifying children's behaviors. Many children may be either less or more developmentally advanced.

Table 2.5 Development of Children from 3 to 4 Years Old

Development Behaviors

Language Development	Activities to Promote Language Development	Motor/Physical Development	Activities to Promote Motor/Physical Development
• Have approximately 3,000 words in vocabulary. May not pronounce all words clearly. • Can carry a simple tune. Find singing enjoyable. • Participate in shared reading experiences. Will pretend to read to other children. May create unique stories while playing in the block or drama center. Role-play favorite stories, make pictures of favorite characters and events. • Enjoy extremes in voices (whisper, loud). May use gestures, voice, and facial expressions to enhance personal statements.	• Provide opportunities to sing and read. • Encourage children to draw and talk about their pictures, then have staff label the pictures. • Provide props, musical instruments and an environment that promotes creative expressions.	• Have lots of energy. Enjoy running, galloping, jumping, dancing. • Continue to develop fine motor skills such as cutting, hand washing, and eating. • Master the tricycle at age three. • Enjoy throwing balls, bean bags, etc. • Use and obey road signs.	• Provide equipment for physical activities: tricycles, balls, skipping rope, etc. Include throwing activities such as playing Frisbee, throwing a ball, bean bag, ring toss, or bowling. • Provide opportunities for lots of handwork, such as cutting out pictures, tracing, sewing cards, etc. • Provide lots of variety in swimming activities. Use barbells, kickboards, etc.

Cognitive Development	Activities to Promote Cognitive Development	Social/Emotional Development	Activities to Promote Social/Emotional Development
• Recognize some letters and numbers. • Develop pre-reading skills by recognizing familiar signs, labels, names, etc. • Are imaginative. • Show appreciation for diversity, uniqueness in children. • Can complete larger puzzles. • Can recognize and print own name. Can write numbers, may be able to recognize names of others. • Can recognize signs and logos. • Understand and appreciate other children's individuality.	• Give larger puzzles. • Provide sorting, classifying activities.	• Demonstrate parallel play that evolves into cooperative play. • Develop friendships and may develop a special friend they seek for play. • Begin to develop more focused preferences. • Show pride in achievements. • Have increasing awareness of and sensitivity to nature. • Develop turn-taking skills through positive successful play experiences. • Have a sunny disposition, are pleasant to be around. • May develop imaginary friends and fears. Egocentricity disappears.	• Provide opportunities to get together with friends. • Play cooperative games with rules. • Give housekeeping responsibilities. Allow them to get toys out and put the toys away. • Conduct or encourage classes in which parents do not participate.

Disclaimer: Age group charts should be used only as general approximations for identifying children's behaviors. Many children may be either less or more developmentally advanced.

Table 2.6 Development of Children from 5 to 6 Years Old

Development Behaviors

Language Development	Activities to Promote Language Development	Motor/Physical Development	Activities to Promote Motor/Physical Development
• Enjoy participating in shared reading experiences. Will pretend to read to other children. May create and role-play unique stories. • Are talkative and enjoy using extremes in voices (soft whisper, loud). May use gestures, voice, and facial expressions. • Take things literally. For example, if you said, "You can't have your cake and eat it, too," They would look around for cake. • May have aptitude to learn to read. • Enjoy humorous books and factual books that tell them about the world.	• Provide opportunities for reading, dramatic play, writing (pencils, erasers, chalk, and chalkboard). Can make own books. • Introduce joke books, dictionaries, encyclopedias, maps, etc.	• Are very energetic. Master skipping, throwing a ball, but not catching it. By this age, it's evident whether they are right- or left-handed. • At five years of age, have poise and control of body. • Will develop certain interests in sports, dance, etc. May take lessons in some. • Development of physical skill relates closely to development of self-esteem.	• Provide gross motor activities with learning skills, such as skipping, throwing a ball, or dancing lessons. • Provide endurance-building activities.

Cognitive Development	Activities to Promote Cognitive Development	Social/Emotional Development	Activities to Promote Social/Emotional Development
• Know all letters (upper and lower case) • Count accurately to 100. • Need to begin to make some of their own decisions by planning and managing their own time.	• Provide opportunities to have input in planning activities such as menus or snacks. • As word recognition has begun, provide books and games to help develop reading skills. • Ask them to assist with layout of environment, classroom, bedroom, etc. • Provide opportunities to learn about nature, why things happen, etc.	• Have a pleasant disposition to five-and-a-half years. Then can become brash and disobedient, overdemanding, and explosive. Need patience and understanding. • Enjoy helping and receiving praise for doing so. Show pride in achievements. • Are influenced by peers (peer pressure). • Have increasing awareness of and sensitivity to nature, small animals, plants, cloud formations, etc.	• Introduce responsibilities for pets, plants, etc. • Provide opportunities for science experiments and observations. • Provide assistance with conflict resolution. • As they need to feel successful and industrious, give lots of praise.

Bibliography

Beaty, Janice, J. 1990. *Observing the Developing Child*. Merril.

Carnegie Corporation of New York. 1994. *Starting Points: Meeting the Needs of our Youngest Children.*

Hohmann, Mary and David Weikart. 1979. *Young Children in Action*. Ypsilanti, MI: High/Scope Press.

Premier's Council on Health, Well-Being, and Social Justice. 1994. *Yours, Mine, and Ours*. Government of Ontario.

Santrock, John W. 1995. *Children*. Dubuque, IA: Brown.

Disclaimer: Age group charts should be used only as general approximations for identifying children's behaviors. Many children may be either less or more developmentally advanced.

Table 2.7 Development of Children from 7 to 8 Years Old

Language

Development Behaviors	Activities to Promote Development
• Are curious, asking "Why? What for? How?" questions. They are beginning to understand objects, actions, and events serve purposes. • Are beginning abstract thinking. • Have increased verbal understanding and can communicate their own thoughts more objectively.	• Provide opportunities for children to problem solve. Listen and facilitate learning, provide ideas for further discovery. • Provide opportunities for children to create activities, games, stories that stretch their imagination and test ideas. • Ensure that children are part of the decision-making process through use of guided discovery and problem solving.

Motor/Physical Development

Development Behaviors	Activities to Promote Development
• Have slow and steady physical growth. Characteristic to play actively, and children become more fatigued by sitting for long periods than by physically moving. • Begin to lose their baby teeth. Permanent teeth continue to arrive until children are 11 or 12. • Eyes are still immature in size and shape, with a tendency toward farsightedness that corrects itself by age 8 to 10. • Begin to understand consequences of actions and try various solutions. • Begin cursive writing, prefer the use of a pencil to a crayon. • Play vigorously in one activity, but will quickly drop it for another. • Enjoy active games and team sports with an emphasis on skill development and lots of opportunity to practice. They understand and accept rules, but will change them depending on the group. They have a belief in fair play.	• Provide opportunities for children to skip, run, jump and cycle to assist in development and practice of new skills. • Take them for regular dental visits to ensure the healthy development of new teeth coming in. • Provide large-print books, which are easier to read. Provide opportunities for children to practice reading. • Provide activities for children that require problem-solving and teamwork. Allow children time to learn skills and practice them. • Practice cursive writing by introducing journals, signing in for activities. Encourage use of handouts such as Family Huddles. • Provide a variety of activities in which the number of participants varies from solitary to team and the skill level changes to include endurance, agility, concentration, coordination, and movement. • Provide games and sports that focus on enjoyment rather than winning. Give everyone an opportunity to play.

Table 2.7   Development of Children from 7 to 8 Years Old (continued)

Cognitive Development

Development Behaviors	Activities to Promote Development
• Are learning the relationship of money and work.	• Introduce an allowance based on family values. Introduce philanthropy and philanthropic activities.
• Understand the concepts of time and space.	• Outline the time available to complete tasks to allow children the ability to plan activities to ensure they accomplish what they want to do.
• Realize that other people see things differently.	
• Begin to understand that nature has purpose, for example that the sun provides warmth.	• Provide opportunities for group discussions in which children can practice problem solving and listening to other points of view.
• Learn best in concrete terms.	• Provide science activities where children can practice their learning, such as planting seeds, starting a terrarium.
• Prefer to participate rather than just watch.	
• Have increased memory.	• Introduce new activities using props to increase understanding. Demonstrate an activity providing opportunities for children to practice individually before moving into groups or teams.
• Like field trips and question all they see. Like to talk about the past, history, far-off places, and ways of communication.	
• Developing a sense of moral judgment, right and wrong. Developing confidence and feelings of self-worth with a growing awareness and acceptance of strengths and shortcomings.	• Provide activities in which all children can participate and the waiting time is limited. Have them practice sustained swimming.
	• Give several directions to children with successful follow through.
• Learn some degree of self-control. Learn to live and cope with frustration.	• Provide information prior to an excursion, allow children time to research, then be available to answer questions or have group discussions. Introduce projects that include children researching and discovering. If children in the group speak other languages, have them teach their peers.
• Have increased independence as they make friends away from home, become interested in external events and experiences, and begin to want decision-making capabilities in keeping with what they learn other children have.	
• Children's personalities are affected by people and how they react to the children.	• Create rules that have been agreed to by the group with a clear understanding of consequences.
• Are able to envision a concept of self regarding particular physical, social, and emotional characteristics.	• Acknowledge the accomplishment or task with positive reinforcement and encouragement. Avoid negative labels.
	• Allow opportunities for children to plan and implement daily activities.
	• Encourage feedback about outcomes.
	• Be aware of obsessive concern regarding appearance, particularly weight.
	• Give praise, encouragement, and positive reinforcement. A positive self-concept enables people to feel good about themselves, leading to self-respect and increased self-confidence.
	• Focus on health and a healthy lifestyle.

Table 2.7 **Development of Children from 7 to 8 Years Old** (continued)

Social/Emotional Development

Development Behaviors	Activities to Promote Development

- Peers take on greater importance and are typically same-sex "best friends." Peer group begins to influence the child's behavior and growth.

- Their play is influenced by gender roles.

- Are curious about the differences between the sexes.

- Settle most conflicts verbally.

- Begin to be self-critical and like to do things well.

- Like to assume some responsibility.

- Are very talkative, using language to direct, report, reason, and speculate.

- Will play fairly well with others, but will spend some time in solitary activity.

- Get along well with parents, but better with friends.

- Allow opportunities for group work, problem solving, sharing ideas, and roles (leading, following, listening). Provide activities for groups of children to participate together, choosing their own groups.

- Provide variety in dramatic activities, including puppetry, mime, role-playing, and improvisation, having the children direct the activity.

- Answer questions truthfully, but not in great detail.

- When conflict arises, allow children time to listen to one another's point of view and to reach a mutually agreeable solution.

- Provide activities that emphasize participation, skill development, and fair play, ensuring all children feel good about their accomplishments.

- Provide opportunities for children to demonstrate responsibility. Ideas include mentoring programs, signing in/out, setting up/taking down activities, or chores at home.

- Allow opportunities for children to express themselves and share their thoughts. Encourage them by providing feedback and facilitating group discussions.

- Balance group and solitary play activities by providing opportunities and choice.

- Parents and adults are still considered the authority. Develop rules and guidelines with the children's participation, demonstrating respect for the child's opinion while maintaining safety and values.

Disclaimer: Age group charts should be used only as general approximations for identifying children's behaviors. Many children may be either less or more developmentally advanced.

Table 2.8   **Development of Children from 9 to 11 Years Old**

Language

Development Behaviors	Activities to Promote Development
• Can listen critically (detects flaws in reasoning of others, questions validity of conclusions, evaluates). • Can appreciate the values and feelings expressed through prose, poetry, and music. • Ability to argue increases with ability to take another point of view. • Use more complex sentences, with words such as when, if, because, and since used more frequently. Can consciously appraise and improve own speech habits. • Are much more aware of choosing words to share feelings. • Rate of silent reading increases and surpasses rate of speech. Oral reading may become difficult because of this.	• Provide time for discussion and "debriefing" experiences. • Provide opportunities to express reactions to art forms. Stories that take place in different time periods are helpful for creative outlets. • Provide creative opportunities to examine other sides of an issue, which is helpful during group conflict. Issues of character development and safety can also be discussed. • Provide opportunity for self-evaluation and "cause-and-effect" discussions. Useful when dealing with results of individuals or group actions (on feelings, for example). • Talk about the "weight" of such things as compliments or putdowns. • Be patient and explain the natural process that is occurring. Be sensitive to situations that might be very uncomfortable.

Motor/Physical Development

Development Behaviors	Activities to Promote Development

• Consume tremendous energy (often hungry). May give little thought to other body needs except when hurt or tired.
 	
• Body growth slows down until just before puberty, when it accelerates (ages 10-11).
 	
• Girls are 12-15 months ahead in development.
 	
• Right/Left dominance established and manipulative skills increase.
 	
    • Hand/eye coordination well developed. Now children are ready for skill building.
 	
    • Late in phase, boys and girls may be very fidgety, squirmy.
 	
    • Generally very healthy.
	• Be very careful to ensure that proactive health measures are taken (eating, liquids, sunscreen). Ask for feedback often.
	
	• Be aware that children may be unsure of what is happening to them. Offer support and explanation that different and changing rates of growth are natural.
	
	• Be sensitive to changing peer relations as physical changes create differences. Talk about natural differentiation in development.
	
	• Introduce games and activities that give practice in fine motor skills.
	
	• Begin introducing activities and skills requiring more complex movements and thought patterns.
	
	• Be sensitive to activity lengths and amount of variety in format.

Table 2.8 Development of Children from 9 to 11 Years Old (continued)

Cognitive Development

Development Behaviors	Activities to Promote Development
• Beginning to distinguish difference between private and public life (realize privacy of own thoughts). • Show an understanding of reason/consequence. • Ability to argue increases with ability to take another point of view. • Able to sort and organize ideas as well as objects. • Can conduct more complex, controlled experiments because of ability to deal with an increasing number of variables. • Early in phase may have some difficulty distinguishing between own ideas (based on personal perception) and fact (based on reason). • Make and carry out plans. • Understand change. For example, can reason about adaptation to environment and interdependence of living things. • Can use models, graphs, and symbols to solve problems.	• Can begin to talk about the meaning of personal values and conflict with peer norms. • Debriefing "negative" group experiences through examination of cause-and-effect rather than focusing on the people involved. • Provided opportunities to discuss ideas and examine issues. • Provide activities involving classification and healthy debate. • Revisit routine things while making observations, such as the physical principles of swimming. Make finding cause-and-effect a game. • Help group set clear ground rules during "brainstorming" to ensure that creative ideas are not "shot down." Allow a group-centered process for eventual evaluation based on reason. • Give group challenges, initiatives, or projects. • Begin to give opportunities for children to see changes and learn about natural processes. • Encourage making written plans, using maps for exploration, and diagramming ideas.

Social/Emotional Development

Development Behaviors	Activities to Promote Development
• Are eager, enthusiastic, and anxious to win. • Are developing perseverance, but interests may be short-lived. • Are interested in finding out how things work (by examining and manipulating). • Are becoming more skilled at evaluating own ideas. • Begin to doubt and become sensitive about self. • Are learning about individuality through peers. By end of this phase, physical changes may cause outbursts, fighting, and tears.	• Channel competitive energy into activities that require the group to "win" without an individual or another group "losing." • Praise small victories and slowly build up to larger (or more complex) goals. • Provide tools for creative exploration of the environment. • Encourage "brainstorming" and creative problem solving. • Provide activities that illustrate the value of people with different skills. • Ensure activities provide for success regardless of physical stage. Games emphasizing precise coordination can hurt self-esteem.

Table 2.8   **Development of Children from 9 to 11 Years Old** (continued)

Social/Emotional Development (cont.)

Development Behaviors	Activities to Promote Development
• Gang spirit and influence strong. Want to be like others. • Looked up to by younger children. • Organize activities and develop own rules. Realize need for cooperation and mutual understanding.	• Emphasize the responsibility that comes with freedom to make choices. • Provide opportunities for leadership such as peer instruction. • Facilitate groups through processes that encourage positive group decision and norm making.

Bibliography

Baker, Cowan and Bonnie., 1979. *For the Love of Kids.* Canadian Living.

Cole, Michael, and Shiela Cole., 1990. *The Development of Children, Second Edition.*

Miller, Karen., 1995. *Ages and Stages.*

Reschly, Barbara., 1994. *Supporting the Changing Family: A Guide to Parent to Parent Model.*

Disclaimer: Age group charts should be used only as general approximations for identifying children's behaviors. Many children may be either less or more developmentally advanced.

Table 2.9 Development of Children from 12 to 15 Years Old

Language

Language Listening

- Can listen critically to reports and views and make positive contributions.
- Become more sensitive to implied meanings.
- Can appreciate the feelings and values expressed through prose, poetry, and music.
- Use language to maintain self, to direct, to report, to imagine, to reason, to predict, to project.
- Use language to maintain group relationships.
- Practice discussion techniques.
- Able to discuss and support alternative ideas.
- Able to reexamine and refine conclusions.
- Interested in discussing and clarifying ideals and abstractions, such as power.
- Developing interest in techniques of argument and debate. May use metaphors.

Activities to Promote Development

- Provide opportunities for small group situations, such as problem solving, debates, group discussions, cooperative games.

Intellectual Growth

Cognitive Development

- Able to perceive and analyze relationships (still needs "hands-on" materials).
- Think more objectively.
- Can reason about things never experienced. Can reflect about own thoughts.
- Can see and test situations from another point of view.
- Can see many alternatives in solving problems.
- Can generate "What if..." scenarios.
- Able to think of probability.
- Able to verify a hypothesis using controls, that is, holding some variables constant.
- Able to look back, recheck thoughts, correlate ideas, and recognize when own ideas need rethinking.
- Can think abstractly about cause-effect relationships.
- Developing understanding of historical past and future time.
- Construct ideals and reason about own future.
- Develop schemes to aid memory.

Activities to Promote Development

- Provide small group work experiences.
- Provide problem solving and cooperative games.
- Inform them of the how's and why's of what they are thinking about or experiencing.

Table 2.9 **Development of Children from 12 to 15 Years Old** (continued)

Social/Emotional Growth

Behavior/Self-Image

- May experience rapid physical changes that produce strain. May need privacy to reflect and gain perspective.
- Seek identity, trying out many roles.
- Uncertain and self-conscious about image.
- Need to integrate self-image with opinions of others.
- Responsible, self-critical and/or self-admiring.
- Construct ideals and compare with reality.
- Experience mood fluctuations.
- Become more secretive about thoughts and discreet about opinions.
- Have difficulty making decisions, as are aware of so many possibilities.

Activities to Promote Development

- Educate and praise.
- Provide leadership opportunities.
- Provide opportunities to set goals and plans to achieve these goals.

Relationship to Adults

- Critical toward adults but need adult approval and support (select significant adults).
- Need to separate from adults to develop own identity.
- Fluctuate between dependence and independence.
- Understand rules as mutual agreements for the social good.
- Abhor double standards.
- Can be rebellious and uncooperative.
- Test limits.

Activities to Promote Development

- Provide small group experiences, including adults in the group.
- Ensure that adults are positive role models.

Relationship to Peers

- Require close and trusted friend.
- Find group acceptance important (may have positive or negative effects).
- Peer groups less random and longer lasting (based on special interests with recognized leaders). Groups become mixed by end of phase.
- Have great interest in opposite sex.
- Anticipate group reaction to self.
- Like to discuss social issues.

Activities to Promote Development

- Provide small group experiences and discussions on topics such as values, life skills training, sexuality, social issues, environment, and social justice.
- If interest is shown, provide team games and group activities. They may be more competitive now.

Table 2.9 **Development of Children from 12 to 15 Years Old** (continued)

Physical Growth

Rate of Growth

* Have rapid and uneven growth (usually between 12 and 16).
* Have increased concerned about body image.
* Growth may alter their swim strokes until they can adjust to the new body build.

Activities to Promote Development

* Concentrate on gross motor skills. For example, teach proper technique, practice repetition individually, practice in game/real situations, provide specific feedback.
* Help them feel less self-conscious about changes in their appearance, especially in swimwear.

Body Growth

* Body type becomes more evident (endomorph, mesomorph, etc.).
* Undergo dramatic changes in weight and height.

Activities to Promote Development

* Move to fine motor skills after mastery of gross motor skills.

Organic Growth

* Onset of puberty (timing is unique to each individual).
* Hormone changes result in physical and sexual maturation.
* Maturation of the central nervous system usually incomplete until 15-16.
* May be awkward and clumsy due to the inability to adjust to rapid growth and redistribution of weight.

Activities to Promote Development

* Educate them in regard to what is happening to their bodies.
* Be patient and understanding
* Identify successes, not failures.
* Draw out discussion.

Energy (Concentration/Motivation)

* Growth rate may result in fatigue, lethargy, and restlessness.
* Glandular changes contribute to mood swings.
* Tremendous energy consumed, appetite increases.
* Range of individual differences increases in, for example, flexibility, agility, and physical abilities.

Activities to Promote Development

* Educate and provide coping techniques.

Bibliography

Bates, Ames, Louise Sidney, and Frances Lig, Gesell Institute of Human Development. *Your Ten-to Fourteen-Year-Old*. New York: Dell Publishing Group Inc., 1988.

Board of Education for the City of Toronto. *Observing Children Through Their Formative Years*. Toronto: City of Toronto, 1980.

Steinberg, Laurence, and Ann Levine. *You and Your Adolescent: A Parent's Guide for Ages 10–20*. New York: Harper Collins Publishers, Inc., 1990.

Disclaimer: Age group charts should be used only as general approximations for identifying children's behaviors. Many children may be either less or more developmentally advanced.

Chapter three

Teaching Styles and Methods

In chapter 1, we talked about why involving students in the learning process was the most efficient way to teach in the long run.

Here we talk more specifically about the best teaching styles and methods to use to accomplish this. We also discuss how to observe performance and provide effective feedback. Finally, we cover how to create an atmosphere in which students feel comfortable learning at their own pace.

Using Student-Centered Teaching Styles

Student-centered teaching is based on the assumption that people can learn to swim through a process of guided discovery, problem solving, and developmental task setting. Student-centered teaching styles initially take more time and require you to use additional skills, but they can improve communication between you and the learners, and they are more motivating to students than simply being told what to do. Students will derive a lot of satisfaction out of finding the solutions themselves—as will you!

Your job as an instructor in these styles is to be a facilitator or guide in the students' aquatic adventure. You do this by asking refining or extending questions, posing easier or harder tasks to help students explore, or providing different types of equipment for students to try. What and how you facilitate and guide is based

on what you observe in your students and your understanding of teaching principles and students' developmental abilities. Effective student-centered teaching usually doesn't look like traditional teaching (lecturing, demonstrating, and telling), but it is teaching in the best sense of the word. Students almost always respond to student-centered teaching with enthusiasm, creativity, and involvement—even joy!

To carry these styles off effectively, you need to try to be nonjudgmental. Listen to what the students say and take it seriously. Watch how you look as well as what you say: A look of disgust, disdain, or boredom can discourage a student as much as an unkind word. When you respond positively to a student's attempt to explain a principle, answer a question, or demonstrate a new skill, that student is motivated to continue practicing and striving. If you respond negatively, or even passively, he or she may withdraw and give up.

Remember to praise students for efforts as well as skills mastery. Your praise doesn't have to be lavish, but it should be given for small as well as large accomplishments. Doing a good job often is its own best reward.

When learning is an active, not passive, process, and you work with each student regardless of his or her skill, all students are likely to participate more and have more fun.

Student-centered styles of instruction also teach students not only swimming skills, but also how to respect each other's ideas and abilities—and their own. They can learn and grow at their own pace and reach the goals they set for themselves.

In the rest of this section, we present you with an organized scheme for thinking about movement in the water, ideas for using skill themes in your teaching, and an example of how to combine the two in question trees. With these tools, you can lead students to explore skills and identify the movements that work best for each skill.

Understanding Aquatic Movement

It's easier to use a student-centered approach for teaching when you have a framework from which to think about movement in the water. The one we will use is based on Rudolf Laban's movement description (Logsdon and Barrett, 1984), in which a person's movement is divided into four areas:

→ What the *body* is doing
→ Where or in what *spaces* the body is moving
→ How much *effort* or force the body is exerting during the movement
→ What *relationships* occur as the body moves

Although Laban's movement framework was originally designed for dance, it works well for aquatic movement, too. It does require a radically different approach to swimming instruction. With this, learning is the exploration and manipulation of different dimensions in the water.

The following descriptions translate Laban's dimensions into aquatic terms (Langendorfer and Bruya, 1995):

→ The *aquatic body dimension* involves exploring the specific body actions a person uses, where and how body parts move, what activities the body performs, and what shapes and positions it takes.

→ The *aquatic space dimension* requires exploring different areas in the water; moving in varied directions, levels, pathways, and planes; and moving with different limb extensions (such as paddles, fins, or kickboards).

→ The *aquatic effort dimension* relates to the time (accelerating or decelerating), weight (heavy or light), space (limited or expansive), and flow (smooth or jerky) of movement characteristics.

→ The *aquatic relationship dimension* pertains to the timing among body parts, how individuals and groups interact (such as in games or practice patterns), the use of equipment, or swimming to music or rhythms or for different purposes such as SCUBA or competition.

Use these dimensions to organize students' exploration of movement through the questions or tasks you put to them. These also can be linked to the use of skill themes, discussed next.

Using Skill Themes

Guided discovery and problem-solving teaching styles can use skill themes effectively (Langendorfer and Bruya, 1995). One example of a skill theme is to ask students to show different ways they can put their faces in the water, with the skill theme being "breath control." By the end of the lesson, students will have explored a wide variety of ways to put their faces in the water. This is in contrast to the traditional teach-

Learning to swim is really learning how to move within the unique water environment.

creative
thinking

By asking the students to show how many different ways they can do something, you are presenting them with a problem to work out. Your job is to ask the right guiding questions so the children can solve the problem, then coach them to your goal for the lesson.

ing approach, in which the instructor demonstrates blowing bubbles in the water, then tells the students to put their faces in the water and blow bubbles. In the more traditional way, the children only experience one way to perform the task, which may not work well for them individually.

When the students are involved in the process, they begin to understand which movements are more effective. By going through the options, they select on their own which way is most efficient to meet the goal.

Understand that there will be many ways to solve

any swimming movement problem you present. However, you also may have some students who have trouble coming up with any solution. Give those students short prompts or cues after you've presented the main problem, such as, "How about using your chin?" "Could you try to…." or, "What if you…."

Once you have introduced the initial broadly stated problem and it has been explored, you can present more specific problems or questions that are harder: "What if you tried…." "Suppose you…." or, "Who else can try it like Jane?"

Figure 3.1　**Sample Skill Theme Questions**

Initial Problem

Problem-Solving Style

- How many different ways can you get into the pool?
- Which ways can you float while holding on to the wall?
- Show me how you push off from the wall.
- Who can get his or her face wet with water a different way?
- How many ways can you make your arms move through the water?
- Who can make the biggest splash with his or her legs?
- How many ways can you move through the water— show me!

Guided Discovery Style

- Which way gets you into the water without getting your face wet?
- Which is the easiest way to float with your face in the water?
- Who can push off the wall and go the farthest?
- How many times can you bob your face and make bubbles?
- Which arm movement makes you go backward?
- Which leg movement makes you go forward easiest?
- How far can you swim without touching the side?

Combined Skills

Problem-Solving Style

- Which of you can jump in and come up floating on your back?
- Which of you can push off, glide, and then roll over and float?
- Which of you can hold your breath and glide underwater?
- How can you move your arms and keep your head up?
- Which of you can kick your feet without splashing while you glide?
- Which of you can jump in and swim to the other side without touching?

Guided Discovery Style

- Which jump lets you start swimming sooner?
- Which body position lets you kick with less splash?
- Which arms and legs are easiest to use together?
- Which arm movement lets you breathe easiest?
- Which kick lets you glide farthest and easiest?
- How many breaths can you take while you float on your back?

A key to using indirect teaching methods such as movement exploration, problem-solving, and guided discovery effectively is to have a thorough understanding of the concept or swimming movement problem you are presenting. You need to know how to begin by posing a very broad problem at first in order to evoke a wide variety of responses. Then, after the students have fully explored the many "solutions" to your initial problem, you can ask a more specific question that will elicit a narrower set of solutions. Your approach should be one that not only allows the students to fully explore different solutions, but also starts them on excluding solutions that require unnecessary energy (are inefficient) or that don't solve the stated problem.

When the students have the concept of the skill, you can start refining the skill and combining it with previously learned skills in order to build to the next level of difficulty.

Figure 3.1 is an example of how to present an initial problem and how to present a problem that combines skills. The example shows questions for both guided discovery and problem-solving styles.

Creating Question Trees

When you seek to teach a skill, you will want to develop a *question tree,* a list of questions that will help students to discover how to perform the skill effectively. In a question tree, the beginning questions are broad, open-ended, and indirect, with a large number of possible solutions. The questions gradually become narrower, with students selecting the appropriate responses.

The question tree combines the aquatic dimensions discussed earlier with skill themes. Table 3.1 on the following page shows a sample question tree for developing water entry skills (climbing in, jumping, and lead-ups to diving).

Table 3.1 Sample Question Tree for Water Entry

Question	Common responses	Instructor	Dimension
We are going to learn how to get into the water safely. Does anyone know how deep the water is here?	Responses such as 2′, 3′, 4′ or shallower, etc.	Instructor can show the class where the depth markers are located or show where the water hits him or her, then climb out of the water and show where the waterline comes to on students.	Space and relationship
To be safe in shallow water, what parts of our body should enter the water first?	Feet, legs, lower body, or bottoms, but not hands, arms, or heads.		Body and relationship
Can each of you show how you can get into the water safely?		Observe various ways children choose to get into the water, as well as nonverbal reactions. Intervene gently if an unsafe way is used.	Body and relationship
My, what a lot of different safe ways you all used to get into the water. Who can climb out and show me another safe way to get into the water that uses a different body part first?		Observe again.	Body and relationship
Wonderful! Can each of you think of another safe way to get into the shallow water with yet a different body part getting wet first?		Observe, assure safety, and particularly note any unique or different ways used.	Body and relationship
What parts of your body did you use when you got in safely?	Expect various responses related to the first discussion	Encourage appropriate responses and modify incorrect or unsafe responses.	Body part aspect of body dimension
Can you show me other safe ways to climb into the pool over the edge?		Observe techniques, particularly body positions.	Body position aspect and relationship
Well done! Can you climb back out and show me another safe way to climb into the pool?		Observe and note different body positions.	Body position aspect and relationship
Great! Let's sit on the side for a second. Did anyone notice how Jane got into the pool? It was a particularly safe way. Jane, can you show us all how you just climbed in?	Jane climbs in by turning stomach toward deck/gutter and slides feet first in.		Body position aspect and relationship
That's very nice, Jane. Can everyone try the way Jane climbed in, with her tummy toward the deck?	Students try getting in as Jane did.	Observe.	Body position aspect and relationship

Table 3.1 **Sample Question Tree for Water Entry** (continued)

Question	Common responses	Instructor	Dimension
Can you all sit on the side again? Now, how else might we climb into the shallow end of the pool safely? Are there other places to get in? Who can show me another place to enter the pool?		Observe for safe use of climbing on a ladder, steps or ramp in shallow end.	Area aspect of space
Who can show me safe ways to use the (ladder, steps, ramp) to get into the pool?		Observe for appropriate positioning, maintain safety.	Body, space, and relationship
Can anyone show another safe way to climb in using the (ladder, steps, ramp)?		Observe and note any particularly creative, safe, or undesirable methods employed.	
Did everyone see how Joe got in? It was particularly creative, but was it safe? Can anyone think of another creative way to climb in using the (ladder, steps, ramp)?		This is limited-indirect content structuring, because Joe is directed not to use a particular method.	
Has anyone thought of doing it like this? Does anyone want to try it that way? Show me how you can do it!		Demonstrate an obvious way. This also is limited-indirect content structuring.	
You certainly have thought of a lot of different ways to climb into the shallow end of the pool. What a creative class you are! I wonder if there are still other safe ways to get into the shallow end of the pool. Can each of you show me another way to get into the pool that is not just climbing in? Go ahead and show me.		Observe for safe stepping in or jumping.	Body activity aspect and relationship
Wow, how did you think of doing that? You jumped in and you just stepped in. Can you show another way to step or jump in?		Observe hesitant swimmers or unsafe practices.	Body activity aspect
That looks like fun! Can everyone climb out on the deck for a minute, please?	Class gathers on deck around instructor.		Body shape aspect

Table 3.1 **Sample Question Tree for Water Entry** (continued)

Question	Common responses	Instructor	Dimension
What does the body look like if it is straight? Yes, the arms and legs are held close together, like Sam is doing! How else can the body be straight? Yes, like Suzi—with the arms straight over her head!		Observe for everyone involved; look for novel straight body shapes.	Body shape aspect
How about a curved or round body shape—what does that look like? Another curved shape? How about a bent body shape? Who can show me that shape? How about a wide flat body shape? What does that look like?			Body shape aspect
(Perform this only in deep water.) Who can step into the water and make your body very straight and thin?		Observe for straight body shapes.	Body shape aspect
Who can make a step with a straight body in a different way?		Observe for other straight body shapes.	Body shape aspect

If anyone is uncomfortable or fearful about stepping in or jumping in, have him or her wear a bubble, float belt, or PFD. Use of a flotation device can be incorporated into the questions as follows:

Question	Common responses	Instructor	Dimension
What happens if we use a float (IFD) when we jump in? Yes, it slows us down going under water and helps us pop back up! Does anyone want to try to wear a belt when you jump in?		Put IFDs on those students who want them.	Body activity aspect plus relationship to equipment aspect

Instructors can then explore the various aspects of the aquatic body dimensions, such as what body actions (bending, twisting, curling, straightening) are used in entry; what body activities are involved in entry (climbing, stepping, and jumping feet first); what body parts are used as well as which enter first; and finally, what body shapes the body can make while entering. The space, effort, and relationship dimensions of water entry can all be explored systematically as well.

Teaching Methods

Swimming skills are complex motor skills (Christina and Corcos, 1988). As such, you as the instructor must decide how best to present each skill to promote learning. Some skills are too difficult to learn as a whole; they must be broken down into smaller components and presented in a logical order. Other skills or parts of skills may be so short or simple that they are better taught as a whole. Combinations of the presentation of whole versus parts are also appropriate, depending on the type of skill and the students' ability to learn.

Teaching a skill as a whole requires that students learn the skill as a single unit. For instance, the crawl stroke could be considered to be one whole skill. Teaching a skill by parts requires students to learn several components of the whole skill before attempting the entire skill. Parts of the crawl stroke could be the flutter kick, arm stroke, and breathing. Defining the whole is up to you as the instructor, as long as what is defined can be seen as an independent skill on its own. The definition of a part depends on how you define the whole; a part is any necessary component of the whole. You can use whole or part instruction in a number of ways:

→ *The whole* or whole-cognitive part method is teaching the entire skill without practicing the parts separately. The instructor describes the skill simply, demonstrates it, then has students practice the skill as a whole while mentally focusing on one part of the skill. This technique can be used for any skill at any level. The advantage to this method is that students continue to improve their coordination and efficiency as the skill is refined. Coordination is inherent in the learning process, rather than an afterthought.

→ *The whole-part-whole method* is first presenting the skill as a whole, then presenting each of the separate parts. After each part is mastered, the whole is practiced again. This method is useful because some students may grasp the whole skill right away without having to see the separate parts. Those who don't can try to understand each of the smaller parts. Some students may need to practice only those particular parts that they didn't learn through the demonstration of the whole.

→ *The part-whole method* is first teaching separate parts of the skill and practicing them in isolated drills, then combining them into the whole skill. Use of this method ensures that each part of the skill is well learned prior to execution of the whole skill, although sometimes students can execute the parts but cannot combine them. The part-whole method may also be best for skills in which the parts don't seem to fall into a meaningful sequence so the order in which they are practiced doesn't matter. In such a case, each part can be practiced separately in any order and, once mastered, can be incorporated into the whole skill.

→ *The progressive part method* consists of practicing the initial two parts of a skill separately. Once those parts are mastered, students then practice them together. They progressively add new skill parts, first in isolation and then in combination with those already learned, until the whole skill has been covered. For instance, to teach the crawl stroke, you might first teach the arm stroke and leg kick separately, then combine them. You would then have the students practice breathing as an isolated skill, and once they mastered it, you would add it to the arm stroke and leg kick.

In this course we will show you how these methods are used in swimming instruction. Most of the skill progressions we will present use the overall concept of whole learning because research has shown that students taught by this method learn to swim sooner and can swim farther and faster than those taught using part methods. However, you can use the other methods to refine the performance of skills.

Observing Skill Performance

One of the most important skills you can have as an instructor is the ability to observe. Observation is an acquired skill that requires some learning and lots of practice (Allison, 1985; Barrett, 1979). You need to learn what to look for, how to observe it, and what factors make it harder or easier to observe.

First, you must narrow down what you will be looking for when you observe. Generally, these should be the parts of the movement and the environment that make the biggest difference in the student's performance at this point, known as *critical features*. Developing an observation checksheet for a particular skill can help you with this. It shows you the components of the skill so you can decide what to focus on, and it allows you to write comments about specific skill components. The worksheet at left shows an example of such a checksheet. Checksheets for the most common strokes can be found in Appendix F.

However, knowing what you want to watch for is not enough; you need to develop a systematic plan for observing it, as well. You can choose various ways to arrange the people or divide up the space you are observing by physical space (front half, then back half of the pool), by student groupings (pairs, small groups), or by the structure of the activity itself (such as touching the wall before a turn). Just make sure that your plan includes time to observe the class as a whole, as well as individuals, for both safety and educational reasons. Also, determine when you will observe each critical feature, and for how long. It may take some experimentation to discover when the feature is best observed and how long you must observe to be able to critique it.

Breaststroke Observation Checksheet — YSWIM LESSONS.

Class: _____　Time and Date: _____　Instructor: _____

N A M E

Component Observed	Observation Criteria
BODY POSITION	Is the body in a **prone** position?
	Are the body and legs vertical?
	inclined?
	level?
	Does the swimmer glide with arms extended?
	Is the body near the surface during the glide?
	Does swimmer not move consistently left or right?
ARM ACTION	Is the arm action symmetrical and simultaneous?
	Do the forearms scull out, in, and back, tracing an inverted heart-shape underwater?
Recovery phase	Do arms recover underwater?
	Do elbows tuck to chest during recovery?
	Does a glide follow the arm recovery?
	Do arms and body stretch and streamline during the glide?
Propulsion phase	Does catch sweep outward first?
	Do palms turn slightly outward?
	Do the elbows stay high until the hands are aligned with the shoulders?
	Does the arm pull not travel back below shoulders?
	Do elbows tuck inward at finish?
	Do arms accelerate during finish?
LEG KICK ACTION	Do legs kick symmetrically and simultaneously?
	Are the knees about shoulder-width apart prior to the start of the kick, with feet flexed toward the shin (not pointed)?
	Do legs circle up, out, backward?

Sample Observation Checksheet

Finally, it helps to know what factors might influence your ability to observe. These might include the following:

→ Your level of concentration (and the distractions around you)
→ Your expectations for the types of movements you will see
→ The ability level of the students
→ The number of students you must observe
→ The speed or number of repetitions of a movement
→ The complexity of the skill

It also is important to try to find the best place or places from which to observe. The side angle generally gives you the best view, but try watching from in front, beside, and behind the swimmers—or even from underneath—as well.

When you observe, watch for both effective and ineffective movements. Be able to tell the swimmer what he or she is doing well. Also, think about what is caus-ing the movement to be ineffective, so you can ask the swimmer questions that will guide him or her to explore what he or she is doing and improve upon it.

When you see the swimmer's motion, try to relate that to the principles of physics that apply to aquatics (see chapter 7). If what you see when you observe is the result of an inefficient action, you need to tell the swimmer which action to take to create the desired reaction, rather than focusing on the ineffective reaction.

Giving Feedback

Students need feedback, both from their own perceptions and from you, to better their skills. Students get their own feedback from sensory cues of sight, sound, or feel. However, they may need your help in noticing how what they sense relates to their performance. You also can help them understand what is wrong by asking them questions and letting them explore. Watch while they try different alternatives, and make suggestions

as necessary. Then let them practice and see how they integrate change into the stroke as a whole.

Give corrective feedback by first telling the student
→ what he or she did ineffectively, and
→ how his or her ineffective motion affects performance.

Then
→ encourage the student to try different ways to make the motion more effective, and, if necessary,
→ suggest how to improve it.

For example, to correct the crawl stroke, you might say this:
→ You are rolling back and forth a lot.
→ This means that you're putting a lot of your energy into going sideways rather than forward.
→ What do you think you could do to stop the rolling? (Student makes a suggestion.) Why don't you try that?

If the student tries several ways and doesn't succeed, make a suggestion:
→ Let's see if you roll less when you put your hand straight in front of your shoulder.

Your role is to interpret what you observe and explain its meaning to the students. Use your understanding of child development, motor development, the mechanical principles underlying human movement, and the principles of learning to decide how students need to change their movements and how to express those changes to them. Develop appropriate questions, tasks, and suggestions that will help students understand their performance.

To give feedback in a way that will best be accepted by students, follow these guidelines:
→ Give feedback as soon as possible after the performance, while the experience is still fresh in the student's mind.

→ Show warmth and acceptance of the swimmer as a person.
→ Speak to the person individually, and start by praising what he or she did right (try giving three positives for each constructive criticism).
→ Focus on only one problem at a time.
→ Ask questions that will guide the student to find a better way to execute the skill. Be patient, giving him or her enough time to discover it.
→ Explain things simply and precisely, in words the student can understand.
→ Allow the student to practice the new method.
→ Don't talk about what movements the student should not perform—this will not be effective and will discourage the student. Emphasize what he or she should do, instead.
→ Don't ever shout, attack the student as a person, be punitive, or show impatience.

Creating an Effective Learning Environment

One of the tasks of an instructor is to set the climate of the class. To create the proper class atmosphere, follow the statements of this Bill of Rights:
Students have the right to
→ participate at a level commensurate with their maturity and ability,
→ have qualified leadership,
→ play as a child when a child and as an adult when an adult,
→ share in the leadership and decision making,
→ participate in a safe and healthy environment,
→ have proper preparation for participation,
→ be treated with dignity,
→ have equal opportunity to strive for success, and
→ have fun!

For guided discovery and problem-solving approaches to be effective, students must feel comfortable working at their own level. Some ways you can encourage students to do this are the following:

→ Provide a variety of equipment.
→ Use a variety of organizational patterns in which students can work alone, with others, or with different equipment.
→ Assign tasks that require students to make decisions, such as, "How far can you go without stopping?"
→ Assign different tasks to different students based on what they need.

You will reach all students better if you offer information in various ways, so each student has a chance to learn in the manner that's most effective for him or her.

→ Use all the pertinent senses (seeing, hearing, feeling) to teach a skill.
→ Present the same information in different ways.
→ Keep comments simple.
→ When working with children, explain concepts at their level of understanding, and use images and cues that they can comprehend, such as animals or a game.
→ Keep distractions to a minimum.

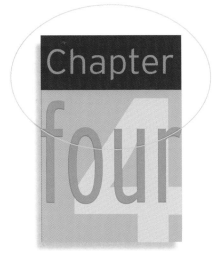

Chapter four 4

Class Organization

ood organization and preplanning of your classes will make teaching easier for you and more effective for your students. Begin by writing session and daily lesson plans before each new session.

Use consistent procedures in organizing your classes, and choose organizational patterns for practice that maximize students' opportunity to practice skills. Keep safety elements in mind, and consider how instructional flotation devices and games can enhance your skill teaching. Finally, know how to manage children's classes, so inappropriate behavior doesn't become a problem.

At the end of the session, you will have the opportunity to evaluate your students, and they (and their parents, if the students are children) will have the chance to evaluate your class. For children's classes, you also should keep parents involved throughout the session, beginning with a class orientation and continuing with periodic discussions of students' progress with the parents, and Family Huddle and Parent handouts.

Session and Lesson Plans

In the YMCA Swim Lessons program, each session consists of a set number of classes, usually six to eight. These are referred to as *closed-end classes* because the number is set at the beginning of the course. Having

closed-end classes means that the students and instructor remain the same throughout the session. This helps in maintaining a consistent lesson progression. It also allows the instructor to learn the abilities of each student and gives students time to build relationships with the instructor and other students.

Most YMCAs use the progression of skill levels and level names suggested by the YMCA of the USA. These levels are shown on page 60.

Knowing the number of classes you will be teaching, you will need to look at the skills to be taught at the level at which you are working (such as Guppy) and decide which skills will be taught during which weeks. Use the Session Planning Form on page 59 to help you with this task.

YMCA Swimming Session Planning Form

Y SWIM LESSONS.

Level: _____   Number of students: _____   Session: _____   Instructor: _____

	Personal safety	Personal growth	Stroke development	Water sports and games	Rescue
#1					
#2					
#3					
#4					
#5					
#6					
#7					
#8					

YMCA Parent/Child and Preschool

Shrimp	6–8 months
Kipper	9–12 months
Inias	13–18 months
Perch	19–36 months
Pike	3–5 years
Pike, Eel	Beginners
Ray, Starfish	Continuing beginners

} Developmental levels

YMCA Youth and Adult

Polliwog	Beginners
Guppy	Continuing beginners
Minnow	Advanced beginners
Fish	Intermediate
Flying Fish	Advanced intermediate
Shark	Advanced
Porpoise	Usually a club in which various aquatic activities are learned and performed

All skill levels are described in more detail in the manuals for the Youth and Adult Aquatic Program and the Parent/Child and Preschool Aquatic Program.

You also will need to prepare for each lesson by designing a well-thought-out, organized lesson plan. A lesson plan is necessary to ensure that all of the following happen:

→ Students are exposed to all important skills and concepts in the course of each session.
→ An appropriate balance of time is spent on each class component.
→ Class time is used efficiently, providing maximum student participation.
→ A varied, yet balanced mix of class organization patterns and creative learning techniques is used.
→ Safety is built into each component of the lesson.

A good lesson plan keeps your classes consistent, even when you're absent and someone else has to lead the class. A lesson plan has the following parts:

→ **Greeting.** Start each class with a warm, friendly word to each participant and questions about special events in participants' lives. Take a few minutes to tell them what you plan to cover that day.

→ **Warm-up (series swim).** The first part of each class should include a period of continuous kicking or swimming called a *series swim*. Use the appropriate number of lengths or widths for the level you are teaching, and begin the warm-up with stretching exercises.

→ **Review.** Reviewing skills is crucial. Besides reinforcing those skills, a review provides the opportunity for both further group instruction and individual refinement of skills.

→ **Introduction of new skills.** Teach the day's new skills at this point. Be sure you cover all necessary skills for the program level during the session.

→ **Practice.** New skills must be practiced to be perfected. Design this portion of the lesson to maximize movement for the entire class and still provide individual feedback.

→ **Conclusion (fun activity).** This is a time for organized games and sports skills. Choose activities that emphasize fun and participation for all. You also can use this time to discuss stroke development principles or character development values, or to demonstrate physics principles applied to aquatics.

→ **At-home activity.** Assign your students an activity or discussion topic to try at home. The assignment should reinforce the skills or concepts taught during the day's lesson. (Try using the Family Handouts from the *YMCA Swim Lessons Administrator's Manual,* which are described later in this chapter.)

Once you begin your class, use the lesson plan to guide you through it. Make your plan flexible enough to allow you to adapt to the progress of your students. After class, evaluate your plan and make notes about what worked and what should be modified.

The headings across the top of your lesson plan should include the amount of time to be spent on each activity, the method of teaching or a description of the skill or activity to be taught, the class organizational pattern to be used (see "Class Organizational Patterns"), the equipment needed, and any special notes you want to remember. Use the Lesson Planning Form on page 61 to help you with your task. It includes all the essential lesson plan parts and heading information.

YMCA Swimmng Lesson Planning Form

Instructor: _____   **Day:** _____   **Date:** _____

Class (level): _____   **Session:** _____   **Class time:** _____

Today's learning objectives: **Safety considerations:**   **Material/equipment:**

1. _____   1. _____   1. _____

2. _____   2. _____   2. _____

3. _____   3. _____   3. _____

	Time	Description of activity/ method of teaching	Class organization pattern	Equipment needed	Notes or explanation
Greeting					
Warm-up/series swim					
Review					
Introduce new skills					
Practice					
Conclusion— fun activity					
At-home activity					

Always review your lesson plan for safety factors:

→ Is the equipment to be used appropriate for this age group at this level? Will we be using the equipment in a safe way?
→ Are there any pool rules that should be emphasized before the class performs each activity?
→ Where can I stand during each activity to make sure all students are in my view?
→ Will the appropriate depth water be available during the lesson for the activities I have chosen?

Be sure to check the pool area and any equipment you plan to use for hazards before you begin any lesson.

Class Organization

You will make teaching much easier for yourself, as well as more effective, if you start by establishing procedures for your class. Once students have learned these procedures, they can carry them out automatically. Here are some suggested procedures:

→ Have a signal to "stop and listen," such as a hand raised in the air, a hand cupped to your ear, or a finger raised to your lips.
→ Start instructions or directions only when everyone is looking at you and is quiet.
→ Give clear and complete directions—indicate who goes where, how many in a group, how long you exercise, what to do when you finish, and other relevant information.
→ Have the equipment for the activity ready and available, usually before class.
→ Have the students practice getting into various formations, such as a line, circle, or square, so they can do it quickly.

Organize your classes so your students get the maximum amount of activity:

→ Select some simple and some challenging activities.

→ Encourage students to master all tasks, but allow each to progress at his or her own pace.
→ For children, choose activities and games that they like in order to stimulate interest and participation.
→ Use those organizational patterns that will allow the most practice while still being safe for students. (See "Class Organizational Patterns.") Make sure you have a full view of the entire class throughout the activity, with no student out of your direct vision.

Class Organizational Patterns

You can arrange students in a number of patterns or formations for practice and other class activities. Using a variety of class organizational patterns helps keep the class interesting and fun. However, some patterns are more appropriate for certain skills or ability levels than others. In this section we'll discuss the advantages and disadvantages of various formations.

When you plan your lessons, be sure to look at the flow of your class to determine how and when you use each pattern. Consider the following factors in choosing a pattern:

→ The task you're working on
→ Class safety
→ Students' skills
→ Ability of all students to see and hear clearly
→ Opportunity for personal attention
→ Maximum opportunity to practice

No matter what pattern you use, make sure that you position yourself where you can see all of your students **all the time.** Be close enough to see and hear each student and to be able to control or stop activity when necessary. Avoid any glare that keeps you from seeing students clearly.

Before beginning any formation, make sure you space the swimmers so they don't run into one another, and review the entry and exit rules with them. Also give your students instructions on how to pass other classes in the pool.

Here are some commonly used aquatic patterns or formations: the wave, the stagger, the corner swim, the single lane circle swim, multi lane practice swim, the circle swim, and the single line pattern.

Wave

Use this formation with intermediate and advanced swimmers. It is an effective pattern for students working on skills with or without instructional flotation devices (IFDs). This formation allows a large number of students a considerable amount of practice.

To form the wave, divide the class into two or more groups. Have all members of the first group (referred to as a wave) start together and swim in a line abreast. Have the second group start either after the first group has finished or far enough behind the first group (usually 3 to 10 seconds later) that they won't interfere with each other (see figure 4.1).

Figure 4.1   Wave Formation

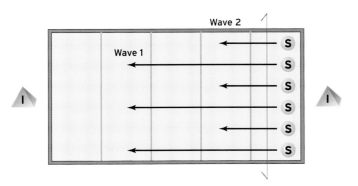

With this formation, you can give general comments to the class at the ends or sides of the pool, but you may need to move around to observe for individual

Figure 4.2   Stagger Pattern

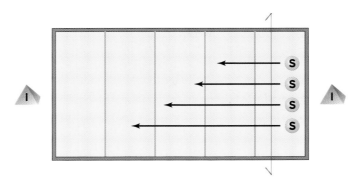

evaluations. This formation makes it more difficult for you to provide individual attention to students without interrupting the flow of the pattern.

Stagger

You can use the stagger pattern with advanced beginners on up, to provide practice time as you observe each individual.

The characteristics of this formation are similar to those of the wave. Stand in the pool or on the side of the pool and have the swimmers line up on the deck or along the side. The first swimmer swims to a predetermined mark, at which time you signal the next swimmer to start (see figure 4.2).

In this formation, as opposed to the wave, it's easier to provide students with individual attention as they reach the end or side of the pool.

Corner Swim

This pattern can be used for all class levels, but it is especially good for short distances for beginning and intermediate swimmers, because the size of the circle can be varied based on students' abilities. It also allows you to easily see students at all times, primarily from the front and back. You can give students individual attention when they reach you before swimming back

Key

 Instructor

 Student

Figure 4.3 Corner Swim Pattern

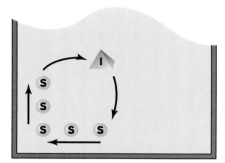

to the wall, and the students get a fair amount of swimming time.

Have students line up along the pool wall, with the line ending in a corner of the pool. The student at the head of the line swims out from the corner to you, then swims to the adjacent wall and continues swimming until he or she finishes at the end of the line in the corner. Meanwhile, the line has moved up so the next swimmer is in the starting position (see figure 4.3).

Space students so they can keep moving and not get stacked up. Let them know where the beginning and ending points are and what objects are being used as markers (such as safety cones or kickboards) if they are swimming across the width of the pool.

Short Course Practice Swim (Length Circle Swim)

This pattern, which is a shorter version of the corner swim, allows students plenty of practice time. You can position yourself to see front, side, and back views of the students. It's easiest to give individual attention at the end of the pool.

Have the class swim down one lane or side and back the other (see figure 4.4). Start the students by ability, so pacing can be controlled. You also may want to try having half the class on each end of the lane. Allow 5- to 10-second starts between swimmers, depending on their ability. Let them know whether to swim clockwise or counterclockwise.

Before students begin swimming this pattern, remind them to follow these guidelines:

→ Don't hang onto the side.
→ When you are finished, line up against the wall on the last side.
→ If you want to pass, tap the swimmer in front of you on the foot. Stay in the inside of the circle when you pass.

→ If you have long hair, tie it back or wear a swim cap.
→ You may want to wear goggles, which will help you see the others swimming around you. (Don't allow students to wear goggles while diving from the deck, doing surface dives, or swimming underwater. The pressure differential between the inside and outside of the goggles could cause injury to the eyes.)

Long Course Practice Swim

This pattern has the same characteristics as the short course practice swim, but it allows for the maximum amount of practice using the entire pool. It is especially useful for intermediate and advanced swimmers and

Figure 4.4 Single Lane Circle Swim Pattern

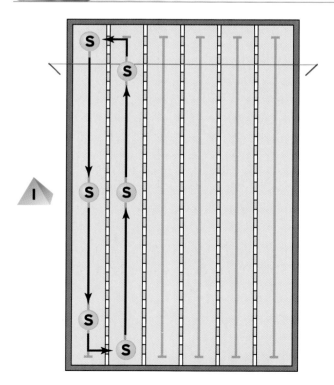

Key

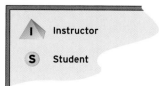

I   Instructor

S   Student

is beneficial for those working on endurance.

Have the class swim down one lane and back the next until all lanes have been covered. Students should try to swim at the same pace and keep a safe distance apart (see figure 4.5).

Figure 4.5 Multi Lane Practice Swim Pattern

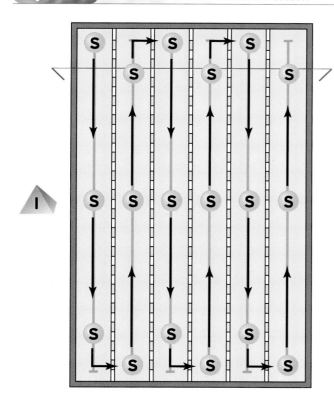

To correct individual swimmers, stop them one at a time. Pace them so they can get back into the line smoothly.

Circle Swim

The circle swim pattern lets you observe each student's performance.

Have students line up along a pool wall. As the student at the head of the line swims out to you, the rest of the students move up so the next swimmer is in the starting position. After that first student reaches you, he or she swims back to the end of the line. The next student swims out as the first student swims back (see figure 4.6).

Single Line Pattern

The single line pattern is similar to the circle swim pattern. It is used primarily for teaching new skills, especially with beginners. The single line pattern is the best pattern for providing personal attention to students, but it shortens the amount of time each student spends practicing.

Have students line up against the wall, then have each one swim out to you and back to the wall where he or she started (see figure 4.7).

You can give individual correction as each student swims out to you. Watch students from the front and back to evaluate their performance. When possible, give students who are waiting to swim another task until it's their turn. Ask them to practice a skill such as a flutter kick, rotary breathing, or arm circles in place.

Other Patterns

Other organizational patterns can be used for class activities. Figure 4.8a shows some possible patterns for class demonstrations. Patterns shown in figure 4.8b can be used for water practice. The patterns shown in figure 4.8c are good for group discussions, and those in figure 4.8d are for series swimming and instruction.

Figure 4.6 Short Circle Swim Pattern

Figure 4.7 Single Line Pattern

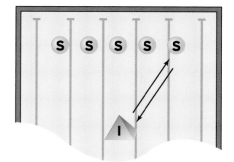

Figure 4.8 Organizational Patterns for Class Activities

ⓐ Class Demonstrations

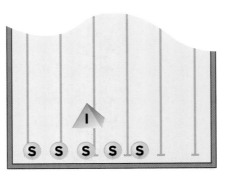

Half circle

Single line formation

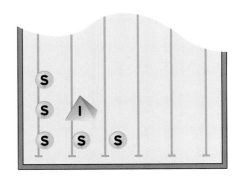

"L" formation

ⓑ Water Practice

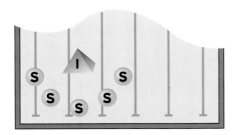

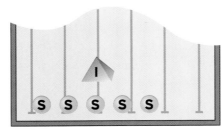

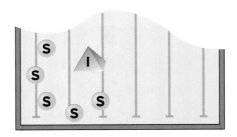

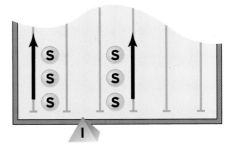

ⓒ Class Group Discussion

Key

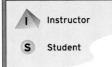

I   Instructor

S   Student

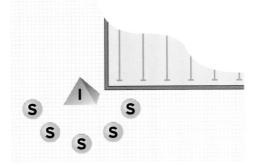

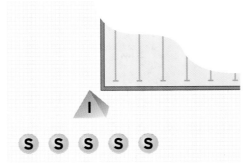

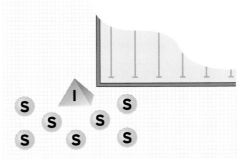

Figure 4.8 Organizational Patterns for Class Activities (continued)

d Series Swim and Instruction

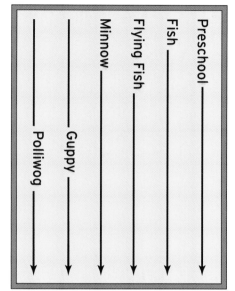

Series swim

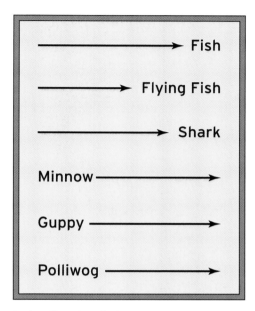

Instructional period A

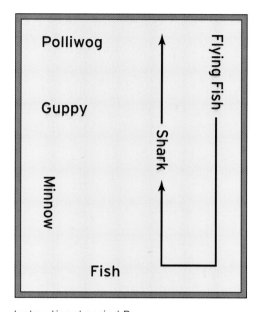

Instructional period B

Class Safety

An important part of your job as an instructor is to provide a learning environment that is safe for participants. Having appropriate instructor/participant ratios and the help of an assistant makes it easier to watch over students. Giving new students an orientation to the pool area and setting up class rules can help prevent dangerous situations from arising.

You also need to be aware of your risk management responsibilities. Finally, you need to be aware of some health risks common to aquatic environments and how they affect your students. (For information on taking precautions for yourself to avoid health problems due to the pool environment, see appendix E.)

Instructor/Participant Ratios

The ratio of instructor to participants should be based upon a number of factors:

→ The age of the participants
→ The program being offered
→ The size of the facility
→ The other programs being held in the pool at the same time
→ The number of assistants available
→ The number of lifeguards on duty

However, the YMCA of the USA has set the following generally recommended ratios for swim classes in addition to one or more lifeguards on deck:

Parent/child classes	1:10 to 12 pairs
Preschool classes	1:6

Youth classes

Polliwogs and Guppies	1:8
Minnows and up	1:10

Adult instructional classes
(depending on the type of class and
the skill level of the participants)   1:8 to 12

Aquatic Assistants

Class assistants can really help instructors and students alike. They provide students with additional individualized attention and aid in working with groups of

Familiarization with the pool area is especially important with very young swimmers.

students on different tasks. Assistants can be adult volunteers or teens from your Y's Leader or Porpoise Club.

If you have an assistant, plan how you will have him or her help you. Guide your assistant on how to work with students and what to do. Never give an assistant the responsibility for the entire class, only for specific tasks. You are responsible for supervising both the class and the assistant, as well as for ensuring class safety.

First-Day Orientation

A thorough orientation on the first day of a session will prevent safety problems from arising and make students feel more secure. Cover the following information the first day:

→ Pool rules
→ The need to stay with the instructor
→ Where to wait or line up, before or after class
→ Expectations for behavior, including the following:
  • Listen to your instructor and classmates.
  • Obey the lifeguard's instructions.
  • Be honest about your feelings.
  • Respect others.
  • Be responsible for your own learning.
  • Enter the water only when a lifeguard is on duty and when told to by your instructor.
  • Throw away chewing gum before entering the pool.
→ Hygiene, including the following:
  • Wear proper swimming apparel.
  • Take a soap shower and a warm rinse before entering the pool.
  • Wear nonslip water shoes on deck and in the locker room.
→ Proper pool entry
→ Pool tour

Risk Management

As a YMCA instructor, you are responsible for knowing your association's aquatic policies, as well as the YMCA of the USA aquatic guidelines. Be aware of these guidelines and ask for a copy of the aquatic policies that have been developed by your local Y. Review these policies and be aware of your responsibilities in maintaining them.

In addition, you should do the following:

→ Know and be ready to implement emergency procedures.
→ Attend all in-house training sessions.
→ Be aware of safety inspections for equipment. Report any problems and close down or remove unsafe equipment.
→ Communicate with other instructors if you move your class to another part of the pool, so pool organization can be managed.
→ Clean up materials resulting from accidents (such as blood, spills, or vomit) immediately according to your facility procedures, or make sure it is done right away.
→ Keep instructional equipment organized. Make sure the deck is not littered with equipment or personal items.
→ Be aware of and adhere to state and local bathing codes.
→ Report any concerns to your director so appropriate action can be taken.

If an accident or incident does occur during your class, you will need to complete an accident/incident report as soon as possible. Make sure you supply all information requested on the form.

Health Issues

Aquatic environments, both the water and pool area, can offer some viruses and bacteria methods of transmission from one person to another. Here are possible health problems that you may encounter in working with students, and the conditions under which they may be contagious:

→ *Intestinal disorders.* At the first sign of a person having an intestinal disorder, do not allow him or her to get into the pool. He or she cannot return until the condition has completely cleared up. People who regularly cannot control their bowels must wear plastic pants or swim diapers when in the pool.

→ *Bloodborne pathogens.* As you learned in your YMCA Lifeguard or Aquatic Safety Assistant course, practicing the universal precautions is your best defense against exposing yourself and others to bloodborne pathogens. Be sure to follow the exposure control plan of your facility. Also, if a child has an open, draining wound, do not allow him or her to swim.

→ *Poison ivy, oak, and sumac.* Contact with any of these plants can cause an allergic reaction that results in a skin rash. It usually takes between two hours and two days for the rash to appear, and washing the affected area immediately with soap and water may decrease the severity of the rash. If students come to swim class before the rash is fully healed, you don't need to worry about their spreading the irritation; it cannot be spread to others by contact with the rash.

→ *Warts.* Warts are benign skin tumors that are caused by a virus. They commonly occur among children and young adults. People can develop warts after frequent exposure to locker room floors or the pool deck, especially if they are barefoot. Plantar warts usually are found on the feet and are transmitted through direct contact with floors. To avoid spreading or catching warts, students should wear water shoes or sandals in the locker room and on deck. Students can be allowed to swim when they have warts.

→ *Rashes.* A rash can be caused by any one of a number of possible agents: bacteria, fungus, parasites, or viruses. Students who have a rash from an unknown cause or who develop a rash suddenly should be seen by a health care professional to be cleared prior to swimming or to exposure to other children.

→ *Chicken pox.* Chicken pox is a common viral illness accompanied by a rash that appears primarily on the face and trunk. The rash consists of small fluid-filled bubbles that break, weep, and then scab over. Other symptoms include fever and itching. The incubation period for the illness is 10 to 21 days. The illness is contagious from one to two days before the rash appears until all the blisters have scabs. Dry scabs are not contagious.

→ *Childhood diseases.* Do not allow any child with a communicable disease such as measles or chicken pox to swim or be around other children. A child who has a fever also should not be allowed to swim.

→ *Conjunctivitis (pink eye).* Conjunctivitis is a contagious infection of the eye. The symptoms are red, itchy eyes, yellow or watery discharge, and pain. It is contagious. The redness is due to inflammation, which can be present whether the infection is bacterial, viral, or an allergic reaction. If the drainage is watery, the infection most likely is a viral conjunctivitis, and it should resolve without treatment. However, if the drainage is pus or yellow, the infection is likely to be bacterial, and it will require medical treatment. Keep in mind that prolonged exposure to chlorine also can cause eye redness, which should clear up with time away from exposure.

→ *Ear pain/ear tubes.* If a student is experiencing ear pain, do not let him or her swim until a medical opinion is sought. If a student has an ear infection, do not allow him or her to swim until the infection has cleared. If a child has tubes in the ears, the parent should consult with the child's physician as to when the child can swim.

→ *Nasal discharge.* A child with clear discharge can be allowed to swim, but a child who has yellow or green nasal discharge may have an infection **and probably should not.** A child with any kind of discharge may feel mild discomfort when submerged in even four to five feet of water, because of the inability to equalize ear pressure. For this reason, children who have asthma, allergies, or colds may want to avoid swimming underwater or going to any depth. If they do swim, tell children with these problems that if they feel any discomfort, they should surface immediately.

Instructional Flotation Devices (IFDs)

Many types of instructional flotation devices (IFDs) are available: float belts, kickboards, barbells, water logs, pull buoys, and more. They provide a wonderful opportunity for you to help your students learn more quickly and develop endurance.

IFDs also help beginners by supporting them without their having to put their faces in the water before they learn how to coordinate their arms and legs and breathe while swimming (although students will need to learn all this eventually). They can develop some strength and endurance before they master a stroke and can swim without an IFD for a short distance during each class. By the time they need to put their faces into the water, they will be comfortable with being in the water and will be on the way to developing swimming techniques.

Another advantage to using IFDs is that they allow learners to explore the deep end as well as the shallow

end of the pool. Students then become comfortable with the deep end (although they still must be watched carefully). IFDs also allow you to work with more than one student at a time.

Finally, you can use IFDs to assist students in concentrating on specific parts of a stroke. For instance, a Guppy swimmer might wear a float belt to remind him or her to turn the head to the side, rather than lifting it. A Minnow or Fish swimmer might use a water log while practicing the breaststroke kick in order to focus on the kick.

Although IFDs have many benefits, students should not become dependent upon them. Always use them for a specific purpose, and watch for improper use so students don't develop bad habits. Whenever students practice a skill while using an IFD, also have them try the skill without one. This demonstrates to students

the differences between performing the skill with and without an IFD and challenges them to try the skill without it.

Always take safety into account when you use IFDs. Check the IFDs before passing them out, making sure that the belts or straps are stitched securely, the belt buckles are not broken, and the fasteners are in good condition. For younger children, make sure you or an assistant put them on and take them off; tell the children not to do this for themselves. Also teach elementary forms of nonswimming rescue to all students at all levels.

Table 4.1 lists some common IFDs with descriptions of how each might be used at particular levels. These are just some suggestions; you probably can come up with others.

Beginners can learn to move through the water on their own more quickly with the aid of an IFD. This accomplishment gives them confidence and a desire to learn and explore.

Table 4.1 Uses for Common IFDs

Equipment	Program Level	Supports	Primarily Develops	Activities
Kickboard	All levels	Upper body; using the board on the long edge provides a greater base of support for balance, especially for beginners	Legs Endurance Body position	Kicks for each stroke Stroke drills Work on breathing
Pull buoys or leg floats	Intermediate and advanced	Legs	Arms	Arm isolation drills Arm action
Barbells	All levels	Upper body; used primarily as a kickboard, but provides more balance	Legs Endurance	Kicks for each stroke Arm isolation drills Games and relays Reaching and throwing assists
Water logs	All levels	Upper body; used like a kickboard or held under the arms for vertical support	Legs Breathing Endurance	Kicks for each stroke Arm isolation drills Treading water Playing water polo Relays
Float belt*	Beginning levels	Midsection of body	Arms Legs Breathing Floating	Arm drills Kicking drills Breathing drills Treading water Games
Three-jointed bubble	All levels	Midsection of body	Arms Legs Breathing Floating	Kicking drills Treading water
Water wings**	All levels	Upper body	Legs Breathing	Relay races Diving games

*Note. When used too long, the float belt becomes an emotional crutch and can impede the development of proper body position. Explain to students and their parents how the float belt is used as a tool to help students enhance their skills, so they eventually can stop using the IFD.

**Note. If water wings are inflatable, they should have at least two air chambers.

Aquatic Games

Aquatic games are enjoyable activities all children can participate in that also improve specific skills (Langendorfer and Bruya, 1995). They should not be just fillers for free time, but rather an important part of any lesson.

Games are part of children's play, which is one important way children learn. Games structure play, to help children reach certain learning goals. They should be age-appropriate, developmentally appropriate activities that allow children to try out new skills or refine those they've already learned. Sometimes they help the child understand the essence of a skill.

Games also make practice a lot more fun. They give children a purpose for doing the practice, and it is motivational to try to win or do well. This also offers children the chance to try different variations on skills, to adapt them to specific situations, which helps them learn faster and more flexibly.

Games provide good opportunities for you to teach children values and sportsmanship. Games often have "teachable moments" (see chapter 1) in which you can take advantage of real-life situations to illustrate how values such as fair play, loyalty, or respect can be applied. You also can choose or design games specifically to teach or highlight certain values.

Finally, games allow children to work together for a goal and to learn more about each other. Playing games helps them socialize.

To help parents understand why games are included in the YMCA program, share this information with them. Let them know that games are a legitimate part of your teaching program.

The rest of this section provides guidelines to help you choose and present developmentally appropriate games that meet your instructional goals.

Choosing Games to Enhance Skills

Games can be good learning experiences, but only if you think about how to use them to teach specific skills. Follow three main steps to choose appropriate games.

First, when you select a game, choose one for which the children already have the requisite skills. Check the game to see if it in fact reinforces those skills you want by asking yourself these questions (Langendorfer and Bruya, 1995):

→ Are you practicing a well-learned or recently learned skill?
→ Are you actually learning a new skill?
→ Are you increasing students' motivation for an activity?
→ Are you distracting certain swimmers from their fears?
→ Are you filling time so you can evaluate or provide individual attention, or even avoid teaching?

Second, make sure that your class is developmentally ready for the game. Not only do they have to have the physical skills, but they also must have the appropriate perceptual, cognitive, social, and emotional abilities. Many games have rules that require children to think abstractly and to interact with other children.

If the game is too complex, you may have to modify it. Some options for modifying games are these (Roberton, 1977):

→ Simplify the tasks, then gradually make the game more complex over time until you reach the level originally stated for the game.

→ Select different equipment. It can be smaller or larger. If it is a ball, it can be replaced by a balloon or foam ball. Over time, you can gradually introduce equipment that is more difficult to use.

Adapted, by permission, from S. J. Langendorfer and L. D. Bruya, 1995, *Aquatic Readiness* (Champaign, IL: Human Kinetics), 98.

→ Give students options by offering more than one game, played in different ways, or another activity besides the game. Make up a game that uses similar movements that all students can play. Try to set it up so all students have a chance to be successful.

Third, choose an appropriate level of competition for the children involved. This will vary from group to group and individual to individual. Games should encourage practice and learning, not discourage them. Some children regress and do poorly when they have to compete. If that's the case with some of your students, adapt the game to make it less competitive, reduce the complexity of the game, ask the students to help you run the game, or drop it for a different one.

Aquatic games work best with skills that normally show definite developmental changes with time and experience. Arm and leg movements change a lot between the time when they are first attempted and the time when mastery is achieved. Games also are effective at helping children understand the concept of a movement, practice that movement, and refine it gradually.

Appendix A of this book contains descriptions of many games you can use to teach specific skills. They fall into the following categories:

→ Flotation
→ Water entry and exit
→ Buoyancy and balance
→ Body position
→ Advanced strokes
→ Breath control
→ Water orientation
→ Endurance
→ Propulsion
→ Teamwork
→ Miscellaneous

Leading Games

To make your use of them more effective, follow these tips when you lead games:

→ Know the game well enough to adapt it easily.
→ Have the needed equipment readily available.
→ Stop the game before students become bored with it or tired out. Alternate slower games with faster-paced ones.
→ Use a variety of games throughout your class, targeting specific skills you've taught.
→ Stay aware of safety concerns.
→ Make sure everyone is participating a lot. Avoid any game in which less-skilled players drop out as a penalty.
→ Help all students to be good sports, and enforce the game rules impartially.

Class Management

Using class management techniques is necessary if every child is to have the opportunity to learn. If you start each session with a discussion of what acceptable behavior is and what the consequences are for inappropriate behavior, it will be clear to students what they should do. Some additional tips on class management follow:

→ When you talk about appropriate behavior, relate it to the four values of caring, honesty, respect, and responsibility.

→ Ask children for input into class rules, and keep the number of rules to a minimum. Be very clear about limits that relate to safety.

→ Create a consistent set of consequences for children who break rules, using ideas such as the following:
  –Restate the limit to the child as a reminder.
  –Redirect the child—tell the child what *to do*, not what *not* to do.

—Put the child into time-out (see description later in this section).

These ideas are similar to the Q-1-2 method you learned in either your lifeguard or aquatic safety assistant class. Other options for consequences include these:

- —If a child does something that can be remedied, ask him or her to make restitution.
- —Take away the child's privileges.
- —Make the punishment relate directly to what was done wrong (see "natural consequences" later in this section).

Remember that children want limits and need your help in defining those limits. Be firm, consistent, and follow through with consequences.

→ If a child needs to change his or her behavior, point out to the child the consequences if the behavior continues. State them simply and clearly, and have the child repeat them. Don't say this as a threat, but as a fact, and always follow through if necessary.

→ Catch your students being good. Focus on positive behavior and praise it often.

→ When possible, ignore attention-seeking behavior.

→ Always show children respect if you want to gain their respect. Avoid judging or labeling children, and never talk about them in front of them.

→ Expect the best from children and you often get it.

→ Give each child a fresh start at the beginning of a new class. Never remind a child about poor behavior from previous classes.

→ Help children build a positive self-image. Children who feel good about themselves feel good about others, too, and want to please.

Consider the reasons a child may be acting inappropriately. Is the child angry, hungry, bored, or tired? Does he or she need more attention? Are there problems at home? Watch the child to see if you can identify a reason for or pattern to the misbehavior, such as its occurrence when a particular peer or staff member is present or at particular times during class. Try to think of what you might do to help him or her behave appropriately.

Some techniques you might use to improve the behavior of younger children are these:

→ *Distraction.* Find something more interesting to the child than what he or she shouldn't be doing.

→ *Positive redirection.* Suggest a similar but more acceptable activity.

→ *Choice.* Instead of just asking the child to do a task, give a choice: "Would you rather put away the kickboards or the safety cones?"

→ *Verbalization.* Tell children to say how they feel, rather than hurting others.

→ *Touching.* Guide the child to the area you want him or her to go; take the child's hand to calm him or her.

→ *Eye contact.* Look the child in the eye. If the child is at a lower level than you, get on the child's level. For example, kneel at the side of the pool when talking to a child in the water.

If you have to use consequences with them, try these:

→ *Natural consequences.* Make the punishment relate to the inappropriate behavior, such as making the child get out of the water if he or she is splashing others.

→ *Time-out.* Remove the child from the activity and have him or her sit alone for a set number of minutes. The number of minutes should not exceed the child's age, such as a maximum of six minutes for a six-year-old. Tell the child what the misbehavior was and suggest what he or she should have done instead. If the child returns to the group and is good, praise him or her soon after. Do not show anger toward the child.

Evaluation

In a YMCA swimming course, evaluation should go both ways. Participants, as well as parents whose young children are students, should be given the opportunity to indicate what they think about the course and would like to have change. On the other hand, you as instructor must evaluate the progress of each student and pass that information along to students and their parents.

Class Evaluation

Ask class members periodically throughout the session how they feel about the class and what they might like to add or alter. This guides you in what students want to learn and how they want to learn it. At most Ys, all participants and their parents are given a chance to comment on the course in writing at the end of the session, most often on a brief survey form. Your aquatics director usually handles getting these evaluations and sharing them with you. (Sample forms are in the *YMCA Swim Lessons Administrator's Manual.*)

Evaluation of Students

The method most used in evaluating students in YMCA swimming classes is a skill sheet. A skill sheet is a summary form that shows the skills covered at a given level (Polliwog, Guppy, and so on), the class roster and attendance, and the progress on each skill and comments for each student. A sample skill sheet appears on page 77. A complete set of skill sheets for all levels is available in the *YMCA Swim Lessons Administrator's Manual.*

You should fill out the skill sheet after every class so you have an accurate record of what each child has done. If you don't, you'll find it difficult to give a final progress report at the end of the session.

The skill sheet also is helpful if a substitute teacher has to come in to replace you. If the skill sheet has been kept up-to-date, he or she should be able to see what each student should be working on.

One effective way to chart progress toward skills is to mark one or more part(s) of an X under each skill, depending on the progress of the student:

1/4 of the X = The student attempted the skill, but has not yet accomplished it.

1/2 of the X = The student can perform the skill and has idea of the movement but still needs improvement.

3/4 of the X = The student occasionally can perform the skill, but needs to do it more consistently.

Complete X = The student can consistently perform the skill well enough to move on to the next level.

GuPPY

Personal Safety								Personal Growth			Stroke Development					Y SWIM LESSONS.

Session

Day

Time

Instructor

NAME	ATTENDANCE	Name four diving safety rules	Front and back float 1 min w/o IFD	Tread water 20-30 sec w/ or w/o IFD	Jump, paddle 15 ft, back float 10 sec, return w/o IFD	Hold HELP position 2 min	Bob 10 times w/o IFD, getting a breath each time	Get into and out of boat safely w/PFD	Sit and move in boat properly w/PFD	Danger recogn., safety advice, & emerg. procedures	Describe situation showing core values (CRRH)	Learn safety precautions	Frt alt. paddle; rud. rhy. breathing 25 yds w/ w/o IFD	Front symmetrical paddle 25 yds	Side alternating paddle 25 yds	Back alternating paddle 25 yds	Back symmetrical paddle 25 yds	NEXT LEVEL	COMMENTS
1.	1·2·3·4·5 6·7·8·9·10																		
2.	1·2·3·4·5 6·7·8·9·10																		
3.	1·2·3·4·5 6·7·8·9·10																		
4.	1·2·3·4·5 6·7·8·9·10																		
5.	1·2·3·4·5 6·7·8·9·10																		
6.	1·2·3·4·5 6·7·8·9·10																		
7.	1·2·3·4·5 6·7·8·9·10																		
8.	1·2·3·4·5 6·7·8·9·10																		
9.	1·2·3·4·5 6·7·8·9·10																		
10.	1·2·3·4·5 6·7·8·9·10																		

KEY

X = Completed
O = Needs work
✓ = Close but not ready to pass
* = Experience only
w/w/o fd = With or without Flotation device
rud. rhy. = Rudimentary rhythmic

Comments:

_____

_____

_____

Each YMCA swimming skill is either an experience or a skill that must be performed at a certain level before the student can move to the next level. Although experience activities don't have to be mastered, they are important and should be included in your classes unless you don't have the necessary facilities (such as a diving board or deep enough water).

Each student should receive a report showing his or her progress during the session. The report should be clearly written in ink and include personal notes to the student. When a student is ready to move on to another level, he or she should be given a progress report and a progress card or certificate showing all the skills that have been mastered.

Some associations track students' progress from session to session. This has proven to be helpful in keeping track of the level at which students should reenroll. The information on instructors' skill sheets can be transferred onto the association's more permanent record, and some associations allow instructors to make notes about students to advise future instructors.

Family Involvement

One of the most important points at which parents will get involved with Y swim classes is student evaluation. Parents will want to know how their children are progressing. In addition, your Y may also decide to hold a parent orientation at the beginning of the session or to provide Family Huddle and Parent handouts during the course of the session.

Discussing Students' Progress With Parents

Some Ys may have the aquatic director or head instructor talk to parents during classes about daily class activities and students' progress. However, your Y may schedule time between classes so parents have the opportunity to talk with you directly.

Make it clear to parents that children are taught and progress as individuals, not as a group. Each child will pass through the skill levels at a different rate; some may move through a level in two sessions, others in six or seven. Each level may also take the same child a different number of sessions to complete. The speed at which the child progresses can vary based on how much practice the child gets, outside stresses in the child's life, and the child's difficulty in mastering certain skills. It may even be affected by a growth spurt, which may cause the child to need to relearn some previously learned skills. A child who is having trouble passing a level needs understanding, patience, and support.

Stress that swim lessons are meant to be a positive experience, one that will stay with the child for the rest of his or her life. Getting fun and satisfaction out of class is the most important part.

Listen to parents when they express concerns. Reassure them that no child will be forced to participate in activities if he or she does not feel ready. If any unusual incidents occur in class, try to tell the parents first; children may tell them a partial or garbled version of what really happened.

Remember that talking with parents is not a one-way street; you can learn things from them about your students as well as they can learn things from you. For instance, if a child has not seemed as enthusiastic as usual about participating in class, the parent may be able to tell you that the child is being teased by other children in class. The problem may also be something outside of class, such as the death of a pet. Parents also may give you positive information about what the child is capable of doing. For example, a parent may tell you about a recent visit to a grandmother's house during which the child swam the whole length of the pool, much farther than the child has ever gone in class.

Much like the spirit, mind, and body triangle, the student, instructor, and parent also form a triangle. Without the support of the parent or the instructor,

Parent feedback can be a valuable tool in successful class instruction.

the triangle will collapse and it will be difficult to teach the child to swim. Keep an open line of communication with parents and you'll be more successful.

Parent Orientation

Many Ys have found it useful to hold a parent orientation at the beginning of each session. This meeting includes an overview of the program content, an explanation of how the program operates, and suggestions for how parents can support their children during lessons. You, as an instructor, may be asked to assist during these orientation meetings.

Family Huddles and Parent Handouts

Family Huddles are handouts sent home with swim class participants that describe activities for the whole family. These handouts serve a number of functions:
→ They reinforce what the child learned in class, improving student retention of learning.
→ They educate students and their families about the YMCA.
→ They help teach character development beyond the swim class itself.
→ They provide an opportunity for students and their families to learn about water safety and to strengthen their relationships with each other.

Each level of the second half of the Parent/Child and Preschool Aquatic Program and the YMCA Swim Lessons program has Family Huddles, which can be found in the *YMCA Swim Lessons Administrator's Manual.* Pass out a Family Huddle handout at the end of each swim class, and ask at the beginning of the following class whether the students completed the huddle activities. Have students share their experiences in doing the activities, and answer any questions they may have.

The *YMCA Swim Lessons Administrator's Manual* also includes a set of handouts for parents. These cover topic such as safety tips, ways to provide support to swim students, and orientation information.

Working with Adults

When you work with adults, expect to see a wide range of types of people. Some will come in confident and sure of themselves; others will need tender loving care and constant support.

Just as you do with children, you need to be able to change your mind-set to fit the person you are dealing with at the time. Taking the time to do this is one of the things that sets YMCA programs apart from others; we need to always demonstrate the core values of respect, responsibility, honesty, and caring when we teach. If you honor these values, you also may find that your students do, too!

Working with adults is a different type of challenge from working with children. Most adults who sign up for swimming lessons have thought about it a lot before deciding to enroll. Adults who are beginners either have had little experience in aquatics or perhaps negative experiences as children. Adults who have some experience swimming usually come to classes to improve their strokes and learn more. Both groups may have a wide range of abilities and needs. However, it can be very rewarding for you as an instructor to work with them to meet their needs.

In this chapter, we give you some ideas about the psychological aspects of working with adults and the developmental characteristics that affect learning. The skills progressions often need to be different for adults than for children, and adaptations must be

made to adjust to any physical limitations adults may have. Just as with children, adults can benefit from the proper use of equipment in teaching, and safety is as much a concern with adults as with children. Adult swim classes provide an excellent opportunity for you to provide health and fitness information to participants, and you also need to know how to motivate adults and help them set individual goals and rewards for their efforts.

Older adults have special needs and concerns when learning swimming, so the final part of this chapter describes the types of physical and mental changes you may expect to find with older adults. It also provides some ideas on how to adjust your classes to suit older adults' capabilities and interests.

Psychological Aspects

Adults often come to class feeling anxious or apprehensive. They may feel embarrassed at not having learned to swim sooner, or they may have had traumatic experiences in the water. They also may be concerned about how they look in a bathing suit, their ability to perform, or disabilities caused by aging.

Any steps you can take to reduce students' psychological stress can make learning more positive. Here are some suggestions to help you take advantage of adult students' readiness to learn and to provide them with a pleasant learning environment:

→ *Goal setting.* As students' success grows, so will their enthusiasm for swimming. Help them set appropriate goals at the beginning of the course and establish new goals as they achieve the old ones. Suggest they enroll in other swimming, water safety, or fitness classes, or perhaps even participate in masters level swimming competition.

→ *Fear of water.* Some adults will be receptive to talking about their concerns or fears about water, and holding sharing sessions in class may be helpful to them. Others may not feel comfortable talking about their fears to others, so you will have to look for nonverbal cues.

→ *Feedback.* Verbal feedback during class (individual assessment, genuine compliments, positive suggestions) along with nonverbal cues (a smile, friendly wink, pat on the back, high five, or thumbs-up) let your students know you are aware of their progress and approve. (See the later section on "Motivating Adults.")

→ *Volunteers.* As a good leader, you are always alert to new leadership talent. Remember that each adult in your class is a potential volunteer, teacher's assistant, instructor, or board member.

Volunteers provide time and enthusiasm and can make significant contributions to your YMCA's aquatic program.

Three important ways you can put your class participants at ease is to be sensitive to their concerns about being out of shape, to help them overcome any fears they may have, and to facilitate their socializing with each other.

Sensitivity to Out-of-Shape Adults

In America today, the body image usually seen in advertising is young, fit, and ultrathin. However, the adults in your swim class may reflect the characteristics of America's adult population as a whole, many of whom are overweight and out of shape. Some of your students may be in class because a doctor or other health professional recommended becoming more active.

Your role as the swimming instructor is to create an atmosphere in which all participants feel welcome and comfortable. Keep in mind that some overweight adults may feel self-conscious in bathing suits. Some adults also will have difficulty participating because they have a limited range of motion, poor cardiovascular conditioning, or lack of muscle tone. Encourage participants to feel good about themselves for engaging in a fitness activity.

Most swimming skills can be adapted to fit most individuals' needs. Find a way for every participant to experience success during each class. If necessary, use IFDs, and have large sizes and belt extensions available for students. However, it is not enough just to hand out flotation devices; students need to become successful at moving in and being supported by the water.

Overcoming Fears

Adults don't always talk about their fears. You may have to look for nonverbal signs to identify them, such as the following:

Participants in adult swim classes will likely have a wide range of physical abilities.

→ Rounding the shoulders
→ Drawing the knees to the chest
→ Wiping water off the eyes and face
→ Tensing muscles
→ Making fists
→ Pressing the lips together tightly or biting the lips
→ Being unable to float without kicking
→ Being unable to keep the face in the water for more than a few seconds
→ Shivering even in warm water
→ Keeping elbows bent
→ Gripping objects
→ Not pushing off to do the prone float
→ Stroking too short, shallowly, or quickly

The fear may be a fear of water, or it may be embarrassment or a failure to learn quickly (Torney, Jr., and Clayton, 1981). If it is a fear of the water, help students master buoyancy skills. If it is embarrassment, have them work in small groups and compare performance to their own previous achievements, rather than others' accomplishments. If learning is difficult, use progressions from easy skills to harder ones, and keep reminding students of what they have already accomplished. Use progressions in which success is highly likely.

When you sense some students might be fearful of the water, take these measures to make them more comfortable:
→ Gain students' confidence.
→ Tour the pool area and talk about pool rules and regulations and the goals of the course.
→ Orient students to the water slowly, teaching proper pool entry.
→ Motivate them before getting into the water.
→ Use games and make class fun.
→ Be patient and careful.
→ Teach students how to regain vertical standing position in the pool.

→ Teach students personal safety skills, such as turning over and changing direction.
→ Adapt strokes to each individual's abilities.
→ Stress treading water, floating, and safety in general.

Other actions you might take include the following:
→ Encourage students to practice between classes during open swims.
→ Discuss their fears.
→ Get in the water with them.
→ Get them into the deep water as soon as possible. This is usually one of their biggest fears. Use guided discovery to show them how hard it is to go to the bottom in eight feet of water. First do a feet-first bob holding on to a pole or the wall ladder as they watch you, wearing goggles. Then try it together with them. They will not be able to get down easily because the water will be pushing them up.
→ Help them make progress using fins, IFDs, snorkeling gear, or other aids. If they don't progress, they will become frustrated.
→ Teach them what they want to learn, and let them set their own goals. Succeeding at their goals will motivate them to overcome their fears.
→ Use a buddy system.
→ Use positive reinforcement.

Socializing

Participating in a swim class gives students a common interest and goal. They can watch and learn from each other and talk about how to improve their strokes. If they form a support network, it will encourage them to keep attending classes, and consistent attendance will, in turn, help them develop swimming skills. Thus, leave some time open during each class for students to talk with each other and develop a rapport. Help them to form friendships as they work toward their goals.

Be sensitive to the fact that some people may feel uncomfortable being in class with others, perhaps because of their body image. Such people might feel better taking private lessons. However, some people want to socialize, and do better with support from others. These people want and need to be in group lessons. They often bring energy to the group. It all comes down to being sensitive to people's needs and concerns.

Developmental Characteristics

Unlike children, who develop and change rapidly, adults change more slowly. It is sometimes hard for them to develop new physical skills. Think about how long you have been walking—for some adults, it will be decades. During walking, the foot is flexed. The brain has been trained to do this for years. Now, when you ask an adult to point the toes to do a flutter kick, he or she may not be able to do it. Coupling the years of practice of one foot position with the fact that adults lose mobility and flexibility over time, it makes sense that learning to point the toes might be hard. It's our job as instructors to help adults get around these problems.

You probably will find a wide range of physical abilities in your students. A young, active, and physically fit adult will have many more capabilities than an inactive older adult. The key is for you to learn about each student's capabilities during the first few lessons so you can individualize each lesson. Determine the stroke progressions based on what students can accomplish, given their physical capabilities.

Changes in Progression Between Adults and Children

Both children and adults go through the same levels in the YMCA Swim Lessons program, but adults are not likely to want to be identified as "Polliwogs" or "Guppies." Thus, many Ys have changed the terminology for adults to the following:

CHILDREN'S LEVELS	ADULT LEVELS
Polliwog and Guppy	*Beginning*
Minnow and Fish	*Intermediate*
Flying Fish and Shark	*Advanced*

These progressions can be appropriate for adults in good physical condition who have no physical limitations.

Think about what will work for the students when you first set goals with them. If you think they will achieve success more readily by learning the breaststroke or elementary backstroke first, rather than the crawl, work on that. It's much better than trying to work on the front crawl and failing.

Make the changes in the progression that are appropriate for each student. Decide on the progression early in the process, and be willing to change it as needed. Talk with your students when you decide, and let them know why you decided to change the progression. As they succeed at alternate strokes, they will become more likely to be able to do mainstream strokes like the front crawl.

Adaptations for Physical Limitations

Aquatics lends itself to adapted physical education because the pool is a great equalizer. It provides a non-weight bearing environment that allows many adults who could not exercise easily on land to do so in the water. Also, as mentioned previously, you can adjust progressions as necessary. Today a lot of innovative equipment is available to help those with disabilities participate in aquatics, so only a small minority of them are likely to be unable to participate and learn some skills.

Even adults who do not have permanent disabilities may have some physical limitations. They deal with the

Unlike children, who develop and change rapidly, adults change more slowly

results of past injuries and the aches and pains of daily life. In fact, in some cases they come to the pool because a doctor has recommended swimming for these problems. Take time at the beginning of a session to find out what physical limitations students might have. Common ones are tight tendons in the feet and ankles, limited shoulder mobility, poor eyesight, breathing problems, or a stiff neck (or back). Here are some possible solutions:

→ For tight tendons in the feet and ankles, modify strokes to minimize the problem. For example, teach a trudgen crawl and scissors kick as modifications to the front crawl. For limited shoulder mobility, teach strokes that use both arms simultaneously (such as the breaststroke) rather than strokes in which the arms alternate.

→ For poor eyesight, encourage students to wear their glasses at poolside in order to see demonstrations clearly. Also suggest they get a pair of prescription goggles so they can see while swimming. (Remember, goggles should be worn for surface swimming only. Swimming underwater or diving with goggles is dangerous because the pressure differential between the inside and outside of the goggles can cause eyes injuries.)

→ For breathing problems, have students practice bobbing rhythmically, building their lung capacity over a number of weeks.

→ For a stiff neck, have students perform strokes done on the back, eliminating the need for rotary breathing.

→ For a stiff back, suggest that students try the sidestroke, breaststroke, or any other stroke that does not use a flutter kick. The flutter kick can cause pain due to weak low back muscles.

Using Equipment

Because some adults feel silly wearing flotation devices or other aids, tell them right away why you want them to wear the devices. Assure them that the devices will help them achieve their goals. Here are some suggested uses for aquatic equipment:

→ Use float belts, water logs, or life jackets to help students bring their feet off the bottom of the pool. This also allows them to concentrate on using their arms or breathing, which might present problems without flotation.

→ Use masks, snorkels, and goggles to help students keep water out of their noses, mouths, or eyes if that poses a problem for them. Encourage them to wear bathing caps, which can help keep water from rushing onto their faces when they try to take a breath.

→ Use kick bars and boards for practice and also for learning to tread water. Have students practice getting their feet underneath themselves by putting one device under each arm, then lying in a supine position and first bringing the knees up to the chest, then lowering the feet to the floor.

→ Use fins to give students the feel of a flutter kick.

Safety

Adults need to know safety rules just as much as children do, and you need to be a good model to convince them that the rules are important. On the first day, discuss safety rules with your students and give them reasons for the rules. Take them on a tour of the pool and locker room areas to show them danger spots and the locations of the lifeguard stations. Teach them basic

Swim Facts | The YMCA introduced the idea of Learn to Swim Month nationally in 1956.

rescue techniques, and warn them of the danger of swimming out to aid someone who needs help. Also teach them how to get their feet underneath them in water, to give them confidence.

Most important, assure the class that you will be there for them. When possible, don't teach from the deck, but get in the water. Have a rescue tube nearby in case you need to assist any student. Make students feel safe.

Adult classes also provide you with an opportunity to inform students about water safety issues for backyard pools, boating, or beaches. The YMCA of the USA recommends that you talk about water safety in each class meeting. Information on aquatic safety topics is available in the *YMCA Swim Lessons Administrator's Manual*, the *YMCA Splash* program materials and the *YMCA Pool Operations Manual*. Topics you might cover include the following:

Backyard Pool Safety

→ Appropriate pool rules for home pools
→ Differences in home pool construction; hopper and spoon-shaped pool bottoms
→ Providing barriers for entrance to the pool
→ Keeping the deck area safe
→ Caring for spas, and spa safety
→ Choosing safe toys and equipment
→ Safety equipment to have on hand and how to use it
→ Safe storage and use of pool chemicals
→ Developing and practicing emergency plans for the home
→ Sun exposure

Boating Safety

→ Use of personal flotation devices
→ How to enter and exit small boats and move around safely in a boat
→ When it is safe to dive from a boat

→ What to do if a boat capsizes
→ Where to take a safe boating course
→ Sun exposure

Beach Safety

→ Wave and current action
→ Lifeguard on the beach
→ Buoys to mark deep water
→ Swimming away from piers, pilings, and diving platforms
→ Dangerous marine life
→ Swimming close to shore and what to do if caught in a current
→ Not diving into waves
→ Not jumping or diving from piers or rock jetties
→ Keeping your arms in front of you when bodysurfing
→ Sun exposure

Providing Healthy Lifestyle Information

Every day, news on the positive effects of a healthy lifestyle is seen in newspapers and magazines and aired on radio and television. Since most adults come to a swim class in order to lead a more active lifestyle, swim classes are an excellent place in which to provide health information to students.

You might want to start by giving students the Lifestyle Assessment taken from *On the Guard II* (figure 5.1, on the following page). After completing this assessment, each student can review it and decide if there are areas he or she wants to change.

Be a source of health information for your students. Often, students do not receive accurate information or really understand what they hear. Prepare handouts on various health issues and distribute them. If you do this on a regular basis, students are more likely to read them. Sources of health information for you might be your aquatic director, health and physical education director, local doctors or physical therapists, or health magazines.

Figure 5.1 **Lifestyle Assessment**

Here are some questions to help you assess your lifestyle:

1. Ⓨ Ⓝ Do you have good personal relationships?

2. Ⓨ Ⓝ Do you balance your needs with the needs of others?

3. Ⓨ Ⓝ Do you have a purpose to your life—a goal?

4. Ⓨ Ⓝ Are you in good physical condition?

5. Ⓨ Ⓝ Do you regularly spend time doing some kind of physical fitness activity?

6. Ⓨ Ⓝ Do you eat healthy foods?

7. Ⓨ Ⓝ Do you get seven or eight hours of sleep every night?

8. Ⓨ Ⓝ Are you sensitive to the feelings of others?

9. Ⓨ Ⓝ Do you control your emotions effectively?

10. Ⓨ Ⓝ Are you overweight?

11. Ⓨ Ⓝ Are you underweight?

12. Ⓨ Ⓝ Do you smoke? Drink? Take drugs?

If you answered "no" to some of items one through nine and "yes" to some of items 10, 11, and 12, you may want to consider some changes in your lifestyle. What changes would you like to make?

Integrating Character Development

Is the YMCA's character development focus just for children? No, but the approach we take with adults should be somewhat different, as we should not have to invest as much time teaching the values as with young children. We can still model the core values in our own behavior, celebrate them as being the right things to do, reinforce adult students' choices when they are consistent with the values, and encourage adult students to practice the values during our classes. (See "Teaching Character Development" in chapter one.)

Share with your students the YMCA's goals for character development. Explain that the YMCA has selected four core character development values that we want to help the people we serve accept and demonstrate in their behavior. We want to strengthen their belief in these core values as the right things to do so they use these values as guides for their behavior. We know that choices have consequences and that positive consequences usually result from doing what is right—acting on positive values.

You could ask your students to set a goal for the duration of the class of choosing to act on these four core values and monitoring the consequences. Suggest your class try the following experiment to demonstrate the consequences of acting on the Y's core values in class. First, mention that adults often come to this class feeling anxious, apprehensive, or even embarrassed at not having learned to swim sooner, or they may have had a traumatic experience in the water. Then ask students to share any positive consequences that might result for the class if each student did the following:

→ Demonstrated honesty by sharing his or her honest feelings about the water and the class

→ Demonstrated respect for each other's feelings about the water or the class

→ Demonstrated responsibility by taking complete responsibility for his or her own feelings and behavior

→ Demonstrated caring by being sensitive to each other's feelings and by encouraging and supporting each other

Summarize by reminding your students that positive consequences come from striving to do what is right and to do our best. Encourage them to take on the Y's character development challenge, to accept and demonstrate the core values during this class. As your students discuss how choosing to demonstrate these values can have a positive impact on your class, note any changes in attitude, behavior, or level of anxiety.

Finally, throughout your class, affirm sincerely and appropriately the choices that students make that support the core values.

Motivating Adults

Starting with your first few classes, you can do some things that will be motivating to your adult students:

→ Demonstrate your desire to help them learn, and take time to understand their language, perspectives, and attitudes. Give clear instructions and present a rationale for why you want students to do something.

→ Show your enthusiasm when you teach.

→ Give adults who are beginning to swim the same physical support as you would children. However, before you physically assist students, ask their permission to do so and explain why you are doing it.

→ Help students experience success quickly and often. Make the first lesson as successful as possible, and use positive reinforcement throughout the course.

→ During class, check to see if you are holding students' interest and if they are getting tired. If you can keep them interested and involved, they will work harder toward their goals and will be less likely to drop out. Encourage students to ask questions, and use a variety of teaching methods.

→ Give students choices of activities so they can choose the ones that best fit them.

→ Recognize students' personal goals and help them to attain them.

→ Help students socialize, and spend time with them yourself.

To keep them motivated, try to do the following:

→ Gain a realistic understanding of students' needs and expectations for class.

→ Adapt your instruction to the students' level of experience and skill development.

→ Always consider your students' perspective.

Make every lesson worthwhile, and provide reinforcement and encouragement at the end of each session.

Goal Setting and Rewards

Students will get more out of swim classes if they set their own goals. They also will be more motivated if they set rewards for themselves for reaching both the final goal and intermediate steps toward the goal.

Setting Student Goals

Each student should set an overall goal for the class and a personal goal based on the previous Lifestyle Assessment. Once these goals are set, your job as an instructor is to individualize the lessons so participants have an opportunity to work toward their goals in each class.

Students should set class goals even before they get into the pool. Help them make sure that the goals they choose are achievable. For example, an adult might tell you, "I want to swim 500 yards, and if we can achieve that by tomorrow, that'd be great!" Some people might be able to achieve it, and for others, doing that by next year would be pushing it. Ask the student questions and then set goals jointly. Some good questions might be these:

→ Why do you want to swim?

→ When was the last time you swam?

→ Do you mind getting your face wet?

→ When you get your face wet, do you get water in your nose?

From these and similar questions, decide whether this person can reach this goal. If not, suggest more reasonable goals. Adults usually will listen to your suggestions. For example, you might say "Swimming 500 yards is a great goal, and we can work toward that, but for now, why don't we set our sights at swimming to the other side of the pool and refining your strokes?"

For personal goals, ask students to share their goals with the class. If the goals involve physical activity, relate them to the swim class. If they don't, encourage students to discuss their progress on their personal goals periodically.

You may want to create a progress form for adults listing skills taught in your course. You then can hand out this form to students so they can keep track of what they have achieved and see what skills might be future goals.

Setting Student Rewards

Students should choose rewards they will give themselves when they achieve their goals. Some participants already have an idea of what that reward will be, such as taking a trip or participating in a triathlon; others will need some prodding. Make sure that whatever they choose, it is a reward they can actually obtain.

Once students choose an end reward, help them also select smaller rewards for attaining steps toward their course goal. Such rewards might be a new swimming suit, a special cup of coffee, or a new book.

When your participants reach their goals, encourage them to give themselves their rewards. Once they reach that first step and reward themselves, they will feel more motivated.

Be encouraging and point out to students the progress they are making; remind them of where they started from and where they are now. Written progress reports also can be meaningful rewards.

Working With Older Adults

You may not have any experience working with older adults, and if not, you may feel a bit apprehensive about doing so. However, you will find that older adults are usually eager to learn and respect your knowledge. If you keep their needs in mind, both their physical limitations and their personal motivations for learning to swim, you can have a successful class.

With age come physical changes that can affect how older adults learn and how you teach them to swim. We will describe general changes that occur, and follow with some tips on working with older adults.

Physical Changes in Older Adults

The changes that commonly occur over time in older adults can be divided into seven categories: sensory, mental, body size and appearance, mobility and response time, cardiorespiratory system, musculoskeletal system, and lower digestive and urinary systems (Åstrand and Rodahl, 1986; Birrer, 1989; Shepard, 1978). These may differ from individual to individual, so consider the changes listed here as possibilities but ask your students about specific limitations they have and observe their performance. Be prepared to change the skills you teach or how you teach them based on what you learn.

Sensory

Peoples' sensory perceptions change with age, although at differing individual rates:

→ Vision changes may include decreases in sharpness of perception or size of visual field, an increase in sensitivity to bright light, a slowing of dark adaptation, and more difficulty in judging the speed of moving objects. Many older adults are not aware of changes in their vision, and as many as a quarter of those who wear glasses may have the wrong lens prescription.

→ Hearing changes can involve decreased acuity, decreased ability to hear significant sounds apart from background noise, and sensitivity to loud sounds. Problems with hearing increase with age, with one in three individuals having problems between the ages of 75 and 84 and one in two for people 85 and over.

→ Taste and smell acuity may decline, although certain types of tastes or smells may lessen before others.

→ Touch sensitivity to pain, pressure, or temperature may decline.

Mental

Most older adults stay mentally alert until they reach an advanced age. Staying active helps them to stay sharp. Memory loss does occur, but it is mainly for intermediate memory (minutes to months after an event), not long- or short-term memory. The amount of memory loss may be affected by the person's physical and emotional health.

Older adults can learn new and complex information, but they need extra time to do it. This may be because older adults have to relate the information to a large store of previous knowledge. They may have to unlearn old habits before they can learn new ones.

If they can set the pace, older adults enjoy learning. They tend to react negatively to competition or stress. A safe, accepting environment is the best for learning. Keep in mind that their rate of learning may also be affected by fluctuations in their sensory abilities and energy levels.

The information you teach older adults should be relevant and meaningful to them. Hands-on experiences work well, and they like to be involved in planning and evaluating training objectives.

Body Size and Appearance

Some of the visible signs of aging are these:

→ Body height decreases, mainly because of loss of height in the spine.

→ Body weight may increase starting in mid-life, then gradually decrease starting in the 60s.

→ The relative ratios of body fat and lean body mass change as muscle mass decreases.

→ Abdominal and chest girth increase and limb girth decreases.

→ Hair thins and may change color.

→ Skin becomes less elastic, drier, and wrinkled.

Mobility and Response Time

Response time is slower for older adults. If the sensory information coming in is complicated or requires a highly coordinated response, the reaction may be visibly slower. Thus, it's best not to rush older adults, who need more time to react.

Some older adults do also experience poor balance and coordination as they age, but these functions can be improved with use. Spatial awareness also declines, as the sensors in our bodies that help us avoid bumping into things or tripping become fewer and less acute.

Cardiorespiratory System

The components of the cardiorespiratory system are the heart, lungs, blood, and blood vessels. While the condition of this system is strongly affected by genetics, lifestyle, and disease, some changes will occur with age:

→ The maximal attainable heart rate declines with age, although resting heart rate normally stays the same. This means that less heart rate reserve is available for vigorous activity.

→ The volume of blood pumped by the heart each minute decreases, reducing older adults' work load capacity.

→ Both systolic and diastolic blood pressure increase with age.

With age come physical changes that can affect how older adults learn and how you teach them to swim.

→ Blood vessels rupture more easily, causing bruising.

→ Blood vessel valves in the veins become less efficient, causing fluid retention and swelling. Sitting for long periods of time can cause swelling in the feet and legs.

→ Regulatory systems that control blood flow redistribution, breathing depth and rate, and blood pressure adjustments become less efficient. This means it takes an older person longer to switch from one level of activity to another or to adjust to changes in body position, such as sitting to standing.

→ Regulatory systems that control responses to cold and heat are less efficient. This means that the ability to shiver or sweat has been reduced as well.

→ Immune responses are less efficient, so illnesses occur more often and recovery takes longer.

→ The vital capacity of the lungs (total volume of air that can be forcibly expired following a maximal inspiration) and respiratory efficiency decrease.

Musculoskeletal System

This system includes the bones, muscles and tendons, ligaments, and cartilage. It responds well to exercise. However, many of the following changes may occur:

→ Bone density decreases, making older adults more likely to have bone fractures.

→ Muscle strength decreases because of a decrease in the number and volume of muscle fibers. However, this can be slowed by regular exercise. Some muscle groups, such as the back, decline at a faster pace than others.

→ Muscle cramping seems to occur more often. The cause is not known, but contributing factors seem to be inactivity, poor flexibility, and inadequate potassium in the diet.

→ Muscle flexibility is less, and muscle tearing is more common. Muscle soreness or injury may result.

→ Tendons are more prone to strains, tears, and ruptures, especially during unusual bursts of activity.

→ Ligaments are less strong and also may tear.

→ Cartilage (like discs in the spine) becomes less elastic and is less able to cushion compressive forces. Sharp, jarring movements are more likely to cause pain or injury.

→ Joint mobility decreases for several reasons. The body's production of synovial fluid that lubricates the joints slows down, making joints stiffer. Blood circulation around the joints is lessened. Calcification deposits may grow and impede movement. Joint surfaces become furrowed or irregular.

Lower Digestive and Urinary Systems

Several changes in the digestive and urinary systems may cause embarrassment to older adults. Kidney efficiency declines, and this may cause fluid retention. As the thirst sensation also decreases with age, older adults may not drink enough water unless encouraged to, but the added water intake will help ease the kidney problems. However, an added water intake may also mean a need to go to the bathroom more frequently. Bowel problems are also more common in older adults than in younger ones. Diet, exercise, and lifestyle changes can improve these problems.

Tips for Working With Older Adults

Here are some ideas for you on how to make older adults comfortable in your classes, help them learn better, and make classes fun!

Be Sensitive to Older Adults' Needs

→ Allow extra time for older adults to move or complete tasks.

→ Set goals that allow older adults to experience success early; too much of a challenge can be frustrating and discouraging.

→ Because it is harder for older adults to adjust to changes, minimize changing the class schedule on short notice.

→ Treat older adults with respect and dignity and don't think of them as stereotypes.

→ Don't walk ahead of an older person while you are talking, as he or she may not be able to hear you. Also, don't sit or stand with your back to a window or a bright light, as an older person then may not be able to see your face.

→ Use nonverbal cues and a total communication approach in your class, including amplification, gesturing, audiovisual aids, and signing (when appropriate).

→ When you speak to older people, hold your head still and face them. Speak clearly in a normal tone of voice, and build breaks into your conversation.

→ Give older adults written versions (in large type) of instructions and announcements you give them verbally. Printed materials set in small type can be enlarged on a copying machine.

→ Regularly check the swimming area and locker rooms for safety hazards, and report or correct problems as soon as possible.

Make It Easy for Participants to Socialize

→ Ask program participants if it is OK to hand out a list of their telephone numbers and addresses. If they approve, the list can help them make contact outside the Y.

→ Introduce new participants to everyone, and plan get-acquainted activities in your class or program schedule. For example, ask participants to find someone else who graduated in the same year or decade, has ancestors from the same country, or has the same number of grandchildren.

→ During class, encourage mixing by pairing or grouping participants for certain activities.

Emphasize the Personal Touch

→ Celebrate birthdays, recovery from an illness, a return from travel, and other special events. Take every opportunity to make individuals feel special. For example, if someone in the group is ill, have participants sign a get-well card and help arrange visits.

→ Talk with participants one-on-one.

→ Set up a phone call system for unexplained absences, so you or a volunteer can call the absent party. This accomplishes several things:
  – It tells the person that he or she is missed and that the Y cares.
  – It alerts staff to an illness, family problem, or other problem situation.
  – It reassures the person that someone will check on his or her condition.

→ Address participants by name, but first ask them how they would like to be addressed. Some older adults will not want to be called by their first names.

→ Provide recognition for good attendance and progress toward personal goals.

Add Special Touches to Your Program

→ Celebrate holidays by playing appropriate music or wearing costumes.

→ Have a lunch social, maybe a barbecue, to which each student can bring a guest.

→ Begin each class or session with a "thought for the day" contributed by either you or participants.

→ Educate participants about the YMCA, its history and international scope, its program offerings, and the benefits of being a member.

→ Be receptive to criticism, and consider it to be a suggestion for improving the program. Recognize those whose suggestions are incorporated into the program.

Chapter six

Working with Different Populations

The Y welcomes all people, regardless of their differences. Because of this, you may find the student population is very diverse in your program.

It may include people with disabilities, individuals who are from other cultures or who speak languages other than English, groups of children of various ages or of families, or day camp or day-care groups. We are offering some suggestions on how to accommodate these students' differences and make them comfortable at the Y.

Working With People With Disabilities

In recent history, a number of laws have been passed that make discrimination against individuals with disabilities illegal; however, Ys have always welcomed people with disabilities and continue to do so today. In the past, people with disabilities were given separate instruction and special classes, but today they are more likely to be included in regular classes.

A wide number of possible disabilities exist, and some of the more common types are briefly described here, along with tips for teaching people with those disabilities. This section also includes some general ideas on working with individuals with disabilities, including how to refer to people with disabilities appropriately (Behrman, 1987; Horvat, 1990; Miller and Bachrach, 1995; Stevens, 1985).

History of Legislation

In 1973, the U.S. government enacted the Rehabilitation Act (Public Law 93-112). This law states that "no otherwise qualified handicapped individual shall solely by reason of his handicap be excluded from participation or denied benefits of or be subjected to discrimination under any program receiving federal assistance." This generally applies to public education, but it also extends to athletics and includes a provision for barrier-free access to programs. This concept was further strengthened in 1975 by the passage of the Education for All Handicapped Children Act (Public Law 42-142), which provided for children to receive a free public education and be educated in the least restrictive environment, allowed parents the right to be part of the decision-making process, and mandated that students receive services from age three through 21.

Individuals with spinal cord injuries need to have a method of managing their bowel and bladder functions in the pool. A catheter bag for urine is acceptable as long as it is secure. Someone who normally wears diapers for bowel incontinence should wear a tight-fitting suit and rubber pants or a swim diaper.

Modifications of the arm stroke usually are not necessary for those with spinal cord injuries. However, they may be necessary for the kick. Those with spinal cord injuries may also find that their center of buoyancy shifts, affecting their ability to lift the head for a breath. Performance of safety skills may be affected as well if the individual is not able to climb in and out of the water without help.

Spina bifida

This is a neurological problem that occurs during the development of the fetus. The central nervous system does not close properly and results in brain or spinal cord damage. In its least obvious form, it is a defect in the bones of the back that does not create paralysis. In its most severe form, extensive brain damage and mental retardation are present. Those who are seen in community-based programs often have a moderate form, which acts like a spinal cord injury in the low back.

Individuals with spina bifida may use a catheter for bladder management or may wear diapers. They may walk with braces and crutches or use a wheelchair. Many also have *hydrocephalus,* or excessive fluid pressure in the brain. If they do, they are likely to have a surgically implanted drainage tube called a *shunt,* which allows the excess fluid to drain into the chest cavity. The tube is completely under the skin and is safe for swimming.

Those who have spina bifida may have some degree of mental retardation as well as their physical disability. In such cases, you may need to use teaching strategies similar to those both for individuals with mental retardation and those with spinal cord injuries.

Amputations

Amputations may be the result of accident or cancer treatment, or may be present at birth (congenital). Congenital amputations more often affect the arms, while certain bone tumors requiring amputation are more common in the legs. When amputations are a result of cancer, chemotherapy or radiation therapy may also have been part of the treatment.

Many of those with amputations wear a *prosthesis,* or artificial limb. A prosthesis cannot be worn in the pool unless it is a special swimming type. A person with a leg prosthesis probably will wear it to the edge of the pool; if this occurs, make sure the prosthesis is protected from the water while the person is swimming.

Those with amputations often do not require any stroke adaptations. The loss of a limb may have changed their center of buoyancy, but they usually can adjust to that. If desired, you can try placing a fin on the remaining limb (arm or leg).

Help individuals who wear a prosthesis to prevent chafing of the skin. Such chafing might interfere with use of the prosthesis on land.

Medical Conditions

Children who have chronic medical conditions may require some special care from you. Three types of conditions you may encounter are asthma, HIV/AIDS, and epilepsy.

Asthma

Asthma is a chronic obstructive lung disease in which children are highly reactive to stimuli such as allergens, dust, chemicals in the air, or animal dander. When they react, they cough, wheeze, and have difficulty getting a full breath of air. Children with asthma may have frequent colds and respiratory infections, missing many days of school. Asthma has a strong psychological component, so attacks may be triggered or made worse by emotional situations.

Most children who have asthma benefit from regular exercise, and the warm, humid air of an indoor pool helps them breathe. Sometimes exposure to the smell of pool chemicals can be an irritant, so watch initial reactions of these children to the pool environment.

Many children with asthma take medications orally on a regular basis and use an inhaler when their symptoms become acute. Allow them to keep an inhaler in the pool area so it is available in case it is needed. Discuss this with the parent prior to the first class, and determine whether it will be the child or the parent who decides when the inhaler should be used.

No special equipment or teaching techniques are required for children who have asthma.

HIV and AIDS

AIDS (acquired immunodeficiency syndrome) is an infectious disease caused by a virus. HIV (human immunodeficiency virus) is generally thought to cause AIDS. AIDS is spread by intimate body contact, such as sexual intercourse, sharing of contaminated hypodermic needles, or other exposure to blood. Children born to mothers who have HIV or AIDS usually develop the disease themselves.

AIDS causes the body to have lowered resistance to infections from viruses and bacteria, and many people get other types of infections as well. Children who are HIV-positive or who have AIDS may be on a number of medications to slow the progress of the disease and to treat infections that occur, but at the present time, AIDS is an irreversible disease.

Otherwise, students with HIV should be allowed to participate in an aquatics program. Parents should consider whether they should expose their HIV-positive children, who have compromised immune systems, to the infection risks inherent in an aquatic setting, such as fungal infections. If an accident should occur in which children's blood or body fluids are present, staff should take the usual universal precautions to prevent exposing people to HIV.

Epilepsy

Epilepsy is a general term referring to a central nervous system disorder in which the child has seizures. Other terms applied to epilepsy are *seizure disorder* or *convulsions*. Seizures are caused by excessive abnormal electrical activity in the brain, and there are many causes and many types. An isolated seizure may be associated with a high fever, or a seizure disorder may develop following a head injury, brain tumor, or central nervous system infection. For most people with epilepsy, the cause is unknown.

Most children with epilepsy are able to control the seizures with medication and have no activity restrictions

Most children who have asthma benefit from regular exercise, and the warm, humid air of an indoor pool helps them breathe.

or special needs. It is up to the parent or care giver to notify you if special accommodations are needed for a child with epilepsy, and those can be handled on an individual basis.

If a child should have a seizure while in the pool area, normal first aid guidelines would apply. The primary concern is to maintain the child's face out of the water with an open airway and to prevent injury to the child. It is not possible for someone having a seizure to swallow the tongue, so do not place anything in the child's mouth or airway as part of the first aid treatment.

Not every seizure requires hospital treatment afterward, but the child likely will be very tired and need to rest. The parent or care giver should be involved in the decision of whether to seek follow-up care, and you should document the seizure just as you would any other incident.

Tips for Working With People With Disabilities

Here are some general ideas on how to work with people with disabilities:

- → Before the class begins, discuss issues of bowel and bladder management with those whose disabilities may affect it.
- → Approach each child as an individual, and involve the child—and the care giver—in your planning.
- → Keep a cautious watch on students with disabilities for possible dangers or physical difficulties.
- → Make sure that students have adequate breath control.
- → Eliminate noise and distractions when possible.
- → When you explain or demonstrate, talk slowly and distinctly. Teach one thing at a time, and keep progressions simple.
- → Don't keep students in one position for too long.
- → Expect students with disabilities to work at skills to their capacities. Try to accomplish something each lesson.

- → Focus on what a person with a disability can do, not what he or she can't. Adapt strokes, use aquatic equipment, and try different methods as necessary to accommodate students.
- → Have an aide or parent in the water to assist if it will help students participate more fully.
- → If any problems develop, seek help.
- → Be accepting and caring.
- → Stay patient and firm.
- → Provide plenty of praise and enthusiasm. Make class fun!

Part of treating people with disabilities respectfully is addressing them appropriately. The following suggestions from *People With Disabilities Terminology Guide* (Goodwill Industries, 1992) are good guidelines.

When you talk about people with disabilities, use the phrase *people with disabilities* rather than *disabled people* or *the disabled*. This stresses that they are people first, and that the disability is secondary. Use the word *handicap* to mean something in the environment that causes a problem for someone with a disability; a set of stairs would be a handicap to someone using a wheelchair. Avoid using euphemisms that may be in fashion, such as *physically challenged* or *special*. Most people with disabilities think these terms are not correct and are demeaning.

Some terms appropriate for describing specific types of disabilities are the following:

→ Someone with extensive hearing loss is *deaf,* but someone with any type of hearing loss can be described as being *hearing impaired.*

→ The word *blind* usually means extensive loss of vision, but either *blind* or *visually impaired* are acceptable words for all levels of loss of vision.

→ Any severe mental or physical disorder that began before the person was 22 and will continue is called a *developmental disability.* Examples of such disorders would be cerebral palsy or mental retardation.

→ To describe someone who has any form of mental illness, use the phrase *person with a mental disability.*

→ People who do not have disabilities should be called *nondisabled,* rather than *normal* or *healthy.*

Finally, don't look at or portray people with disabilities as being either superhuman or tragic. They just want to be regarded as others are.

For more information on specific disabilities, refer to the resources listed next. You also can sign up for one of the YMCA's related courses. Working With People With Disabilities is a basic course that provides an overview of different disabilities. The YMCA Aquatics for Special Populations Instructor course goes into more depth on how to work in aquatics classes with people who have disabilities.

Working With People From Other Cultures

At the Y, we expect to see diversity in our members and class participants. With the Y's history, philosophy, and mission, people of different races, ethnicities, religions, and nationalities are likely to be attracted to and comfortable at the YMCA.

> **R**emember that diversity in your class gives you a good opportunity to use differences to teach character development and to express appreciation of diversity.

Your job as a swimming instructor is to get to know the demographic makeup of your community. If you will be working with students from cultures other than your own, you need to learn about those cultures in order to accommodate any differences that might affect your teaching. For example, a child from another culture who nods his head may be expressing embarrassment at not understanding what you are saying, rather than indicating he understands.

Bilingual and multilingual classes can pose a difficult problem for you. You first need to determine if some class members do not speak and understand a common language. If not, try to recruit someone who knows the language to interpret and to assist with the class. Possibly a class participant who is fluent in both your language and that of the other participants can perform this task. If you can't find someone who can interpret, concentrate on showing what you teach visually, much as you would if you were working with students who have hearing impairments. Provide slow, careful demonstrations and use simple sign language.

Working With Classes of Varied Ages or With Families

Your facility may, from time to time, sponsor special classes that include children from a wide range of ages, or classes for families. For example, a Boy or Girl Scout troop may want to learn about snorkeling, or boat and beach safety. Your Y may want to provide family or sibling swim classes for those who want to learn to swim together.

Start by finding out what specific skills the students wish to learn or what type of lessons the group wants, then plan your lessons around those interests. Assess the swimming ability of each participant and adjust your teaching accordingly.

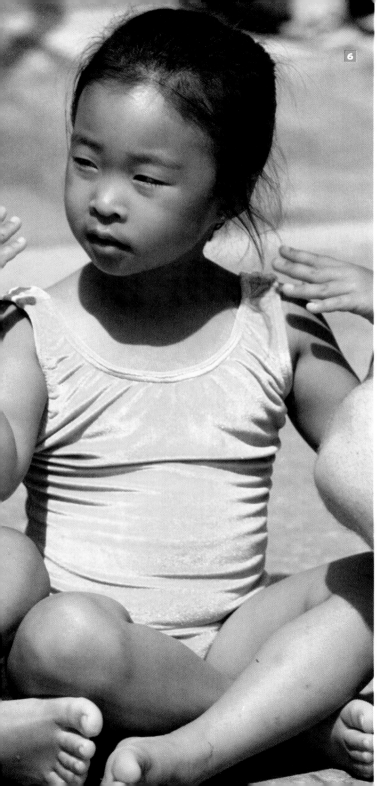

Working With Day Camp and Day-Care Groups

Although most children like day camp and day-care, keep in mind that some may not have chosen to be there—and some may be there for the whole season. To keep classes from becoming repetitive both for you and the children, follow these tips:

→ Have a daily or weekly theme each session, with corresponding activities.
→ Be creative—but keep safety in mind.
→ Use games and educational activities to raise children's awareness of international/world service needs.
→ Teach character values through examples and games (see appendix A).
→ Keep in mind that not all children enjoy the water and not all will like the activities or want to follow the rules.
→ Be sensitive to children's needs and concerns.

Day camp or day-care programs may schedule lessons daily, a few times a week, or once a week. Make sure you understand the aquatic program for camp or day-care: Are they regular swim lessons, part lessons and part free swim, or part lessons and part water games?

To motivate students, post an enlarged skill chart on the wall, then mark each child's progress on the chart. Include spaces for checking off positive behaviors such as helping to clean up or taking a shower, so that children who master skills more slowly than the rest of the group can still see some progress.

Send home daily checklists of the skills worked on, so parents can see what their children have been doing in class. In this way, parents can feel more involved and know what their children are learning.

helpful Resources

ADA Technical Assistance Information
(800) 466-4232 (V/TDD)

American Association on
Mental Retardation
(800) 424-3688

American Foundation for the Blind
(800) 232-5463

Asthma and Allergy Foundation
of America
(800) 727-8463

Attention Deficit Disorder Association
(800) 487-2282

Disability Rights Education and
Defense Fund, Inc.
(800) 466-4232

Epilepsy Foundation of America
(800) 332-1000

Hearing Information Center
(800) 622-3277

National AIDS Information Clearinghouse
(800) 458-5231

National Easter Seal Society
(800) 221-6827

National Head Injury Foundation
(800) 444-6443

National Rehabilitation Information
Clearinghouse/ABLEDATA
(800) 346-2742 (V/TDD)

National Spinal Cord Injury Association
(800) 962-9629

Spina Bifida Association of America
(800) 621-3141

United Cerebral Palsy Association
(800) 872-5827 (V/TDD)

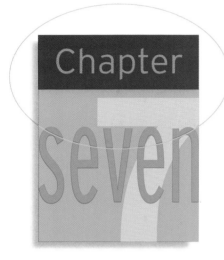

Chapter seven

Teaching Strokes

The YMCA Swim Lessons Program always has built incrementally from one skill level to the next. It now has been adjusted to build on a set stroke progression and on children's natural developmental progression through various sequences of change.

In addition, we have included some activities you can use to discuss the principles of physics with your students as they apply to stroke movements. Although your expectations for student performance should be based on students' current level of performance, we do provide in this chapter a full, formal description of each of six major strokes so you can see what the ultimate goal is for your students. We also describe some commonly used starts and turns.

Stroke Progression

All the swimming strokes you teach should be approached from a similar developmental perspective. Common elements of these strokes are listed in the column at the right. As you teach each stroke, you will begin at the lowest levels with the conditions shown in the first row of table 7.1. As students move through the levels, the stroke will become more refined and students will require less support, will be able to swim farther, and will improve their speed and coordination.

Task/complexity	How hard is the movement?
Flotation or support provided	Does the instructor provide support or is the student using an IFD?
Distance to swim	How far can the student swim the stroke?
Speed/tempo required	Can the student perform the stroke either faster or slower?
Degree of refinement	How much does the movement being performed by the student resemble the advanced stroke?

Table 7.1 Skill Progression

Task/complexity	Flotation or support provided	Distance to swim	Speed/tempo	Degree of required stroke refinement
Simpler/easier	Instructor support	Less than 1 body length	Speed/tempo not required	No pattern requirements
	IFD used	1–5 body lengths	Faster tempo	Body position
	Less-buoyant IFD used	6–20 body lengths	Slower tempo	Limb movements
More complex/ difficult	No IFD	More than 20 body lengths	Variable tempo	Interlimb timing

Developmental Sequences of Swimming

Students will move through a series of steps as they work toward skills mastery. The order of the steps has been identified through studies in which children's and adult's swimming patterns were observed, primarily for the crawlstroke. A natural progression, called developmental sequences, is listed for each of the following skills: water adjustment and orientation, water entry, breath control, buoyancy, body positions, arm actions, leg actions, and combined movement (Langendorfer and Bruya, 1995).

Water Adjustment and Orientation

Water adjustment and orientation change in a sequence from strong, debilitating fear to no reluctance or fear.

1. **No voluntary entry.** The student expresses fear, including crying or refusing to enter the water.

2. **Voluntary entry.** The student expresses reluctance to enter the water, but can be coaxed. This attitude interferes with movement, entry, and submersion activities.

3. **Voluntary entry with no fear of the water.** The student displays no fear or reluctance to participate in water activities.

Water Entry

Water entry patterns change in a sequence from no entry without assistance to diving .

1. No voluntary entry. The student re-fuses to enter the water or cannot enter the water without assistance.

2. Assisted feet-first entry. The student enters using the support of an adult to climb, slide, or jump into the water, with feet entering the water first.

3. Unassisted feet-first entry. The stu-dent enters the water feet-first with no visible support from an adult.

4. Assisted head-first entry. The stu-dent enters the water touching hands, arms, head, or chest to water first, while an adult maintains physical sup-port or contact.

All head-first entries should be done in water that is at least nine feet deep. Head first entries from an elevated height or board should have at least 11.5 feet of depth.

Breath Control

Breath control patterns change in a sequence from reflexive breath holding to repeated rhythmic breaths during stroking.

1. Reflexive breath holding. The student holds the breath "automatically" when the face is covered by water.

2. Spitting or shipping. The student vol-untarily takes water into the mouth and can expel it.

3. Voluntary face submersion. The stu-dent permits part of the face to get wet by either splashing or partial submer-sion and holds the breath briefly (one to four seconds).

4. Repeated breath holding. The student can repeat submersion and breath holding while in the water.

Buoyancy

Buoyancy patterns change in a sequence from supported buoyancy to sustained relaxed floating, with no movement, on the front or back.

5. Unassisted head-first entry. The student enters the water without support from an adult and makes initial water contact with the hands or arms.

1. No flotation. The student does not permit the water to buoy the body up and shows fear.

2. Flotation with assistance. The student will maneuver in the water with the direct support of an adult.

3. Flotation with support. The student floats in the water while supported by a flotation device or minimal adult assistance.

4. Unsupported flotation. The student floats using water support only.

5. Extended breath holding and/or rhythmic breathing with stroke. The child combines breathing with stroking in a rhythmical manner for five or more breaths or holds the breath longer than five seconds while submerged.

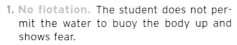

Body Positions

Body positions change through sequences from vertical to horizontal in both front and back positions.

1. Vertical. The trunk is 90 degrees to 45 degrees from a horizontal surface.

2. Inclined. The trunk is 44 degrees to 20 degrees from a horizontal surface.

3. Level. The trunk is 19 degrees to 10 degrees from a horizontal surface.

4. Horizontal. The trunk is maintained less than 10 degrees from horizontal.

Arm Actions

Arm action patterns change in two regular sequences. The first focuses on propulsion, changing from no action to using the arms like paddles to using the arms to produce "lift" like a propeller. The second sequence focuses on the shift in recovery patterns from no action to underwater recovery to straight and bent-elbow overwater recovery patterns.

Arm Propulsion:

1. No arm action. The arms are not used to propel or move. They either hang at the sides or extend forward.

2. Short downward push. The arm pushes downward rapidly with virtually no backward pulling action; the action is short and rapid, producing little forward movement.

3. Long push-pull paddle. The arm action is a downward push, followed by a backward pull with arm extension.

4. Lift propulsion. The arm enters the water by driving forward, catching (beginning to push the water outward), and pulling backward, with an "S" pull action, high elbow, and rapid backward acceleration. The main propulsion is lifting (lift force) rather than paddling action (drag force).

Arm Recovery:

1. No arm action. The arms show no recovery motion during swimming.

2. No overwater recovery. The arms make all their recovery under the surface of the water. Arms may be moving opposite to each other (alternating) or moving in the same pattern (symmetrical).

3. Rudimentary overwater recovery. The arms come above the water's surface either only briefly or part way through the recovery.

4. Straight overwater recovery. Arms are fully or mostly extended throughout the recovery. The palms of the hands are put into the water first.

5. Bent-elbow overwater recovery. The elbow recovers out of water first and is the highest arm point throughout much of recovery. The thumb side of the hand and fingers enter the water first.

Leg Actions

Leg action changes in a sequence from no leg action to bicycling to rudimentary and then advanced forms of the flutter kick.

1. No leg action. No leg propulsive motion is apparent.

2. Bicycling. Alternating pushing downward and up, like riding a bike. The sole of the foot is pushing the water.

3. Rudimentary flutter kick. This is an alternating bending and straightening at the knee with toes partially pointed.

4. Bent-knee flutter. The knee is bent while kicking.

Combined Movement

Combined swimming movement changes on the front in a sequence from a rudimentary dog paddle to advanced formal strokes. The combined movement includes the body position, arm actions, leg actions, and breath control.

1. No locomotor behavior. The student is unable to move forward independently in the water.

2. Dog paddle. This front stroke is characterized by the rudimentary flutter kick, a circling downward of the arms, and a vertical or inclined body position.

3. Human stroke. This front stroke is characterized by a bent-knee flutter kick, pull-push arms, and inclined body position. Some rhythmic breathing may occur, but probably not rotary breathing.

4. Rudimentary crawl. This front stroke is characterized by rudimentary alternating arms with flutter kicking. Rhythmic breathing is used.

The beginning skills of the YMCA Swim Lessons Program are designed to match the natural early developmental levels of a child as closely as possible. Thus, as the student performs, you should be able to predict what skill he or she will be ready to learn next. You can plan new activities ahead of time that will help the student reach the next developmental levels.

By following the natural order of a child's aquatic skills acquisition as closely as possible, we hope to enhance children's ability to perform successfully and to build upon that success. Stroke refinement naturally will occur as the child progresses.

The Physics of Swimming

During the program, your students and parents may often ask you about the reasons behind what they are learning. *Why* may be as important to them as *how.* If you can either respond knowledgeably or readily admit you don't know the answer but will find out more for the next class, you will be respected much more than if you pretend to know the answer or simply not answer them.

Because the YMCA emphasizes developing the mind as well as the body and spirit, we encourage you to go beyond answering questions. Help guide your students toward appropriate answers and direct them to additional sources of information. You may want to incorporate an "understanding why" discussion into your classes on a regular basis.

The teaching instructions in this chapter should help you when you talk about the principles of physics behind swimming instruction. Each of the following lessons covers one of eleven principles:

→ Flotation (Archimedes' principle)
→ Action and reaction (Newton's third law of motion)
→ Volume (Archimedes' principle)
→ Center of buoyancy
→ Symmetrical movement
→ Water resistance
→ Law of levers
→ Inertia (Newton's first law of motion)
→ Acceleration (Newton's second law of motion)
→ Individual physical differences
→ Bernoulli's Theorem (lift force)

5. Straight-leg flutter. The advanced flutter kick is being performed when knees bend less than 30° and ankles are pointed and relaxed.

5. Crawlstroke. This front stroke is characterized by defined arm, leg, and breathing patterns in a horizontal body position.

By knowing the stages the beginning student will go through, you can assign developmentally appropriate tasks as you teach skills.

These lessons are geared toward young students; you can either simplify them or make them more complex, depending on the level of your students. You may need a few special items for experimentation or demonstration; these will be listed at the beginning of the section under "Items Needed." Feel free to include additional principles or reasons for specific stroke styles as appropriate.

Flotation (Archimedes' Principle)

A floating body displaces exactly its own weight in water. A body will sink if it isn't big enough to displace water that weighs as much as it does, even when submerged.

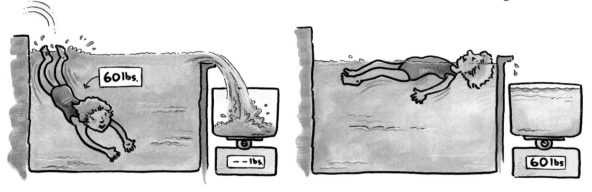

Show your students the illustration above.

Girl is floating in water tank with face above water (girl is labeled "60 pounds"). Tank has spout in side that pours water into a container suspended by a spring scale. The spring scale shows 60 pounds.

"What happens to some of the water in this tank?" [It spills out (is displaced) and flows down into the container below the spout.]

"Notice that the weight of the water displaced is 60 pounds. She floats! Let's say that she can float with parts of her body sticking out of the water. If you were that person, which parts would you like out of the water?" (It would be your face—particularly your nose and mouth.)

"Let's see what happens to us with only our face sticking out of the water." (Encourage students to try this. Beginners should do this in the shallow water, wearing float belts if they wish.)

"What is the difference between a person who weighs 100 pounds and floats and a stone that weighs 100 pounds and sinks?" [A stone is more compact—dense—whereas a person has air space (lungs) and soft body parts, like fat.]

"Which person is more dense or compact like a stone—a fat person or a lean person?"

(The lean person is more dense. Therefore, a lean person might not be able to float because his or her body is too compact, like a stone.)

"But some lean people do float. Why do you think this happens?" (The air in their lungs is lighter than the water it displaces.)

Action and Reaction (Newton's Third Law of Motion)

For every action there is an opposite and equal reaction.

"What causes a space ship to leave the launching pad and travel to the moon?" (Help students find the answer that the thrust from the engine pushes down, which forces the ship up).

"How does this law apply in swimming?" Have students get into the water and experiment. (If you push back on the water, you will go forward, and if you push down, you will go up.)

Volume (Archimedes' Principle)

The bigger something is, the greater its volume.

"Which would be bigger—a 100-pound person or a 100-pound stone?" [The person is bigger (has more volume) and can push aside (displace) more water.]

"Who takes up more space, a fat person or a lean person?" [A fat person takes up more space (volume) and can displace a larger amount of water. The person

floats because he or she gets bigger faster than he or she gets heavier. Fat is less dense than water; that is, fat displaces more than its own weight in water when submerged, so fat doesn't stay submerged. It rises to the surface and floats.]

Center of Buoyancy

When the lungs are filled with air, the chest is the most buoyant part of the body.

"Have you ever tried to balance a pencil or stick lengthwise (horizontally) on your finger? The place on the pencil or stick where it balances is its center of gravity."

"Where is a person's center of gravity on land— is it the head, the feet, or someplace in between?" [The center of gravity is approximately in the hip area.]

"In the water, the body does not rotate around its center of gravity. Instead, it rotates around its center of flotation, or buoyancy—the lightest part of the body for its size. Where is the center of buoyancy?" [The chest area is the center of buoyancy because that is where the lungs are located. When the lungs are filled with air, they are quite light for their size and are the most buoyant part of the body.]

"What are some other buoyant things you use around the swimming pool or bathtub?" [Buoyant objects would include items used in throwing assists, kickboards, water logs, and bathtub toys such as rubber ducks, toy boats, and sponges.]

Center of Buoyancy

Center of Mass

Symmetrical Movement

The most efficient way to do certain strokes is to move both arms and legs at the same rate, in the same way.

"How do you move your arms and legs when you do the elementary backstroke? During this stroke, you move both your hands and arms at the same time in the same way. Your hands start out at your side. You then bring them up to your shoulders, keeping the elbows bent. Next you put your hands outward, slightly above the shoulders. Finally, you pull your hands downward to your sides. While your hands and arms do this, your legs and feet are also busy. Your feet are pulled up so that your big toes point at your ankles."

"How easily does this stroke move you in the water?" [Quickly and smoothly]

"Why is it important to move both arms and legs in the same way at the same time?" [When both move at the same rate in the same way, the stroke is more efficient and balanced. The action forces will be in the same direction, causing movement in a straight line.]

"If you move the two sides of your body at different times and in different ways, what happens when you swim?" Have students get in the water and experiment with uneven movements. [The stroke is jerky and uneven, and the swimmer may not move at all, may move in a circle, or may move diagonally.]

Water Resistance

Water is denser and has more resistance than air. It slows forward motion but also allows the swimmer to move.

"What is a good body position for swimming?" Let students experiment in the water. Have students try doing strokes with the body streamlined, then with the body held loosely in the water, then with the legs held low and arms spread wide. Other experiments might include running across the pool or swimming first with head up and feet down, then with face in water and feet up. [Keeping the body streamlined and all on the same level cuts water resistance.]

"How else can you minimize water resistance?" [Keep the body moving in one direction, not from side to side; when the smallest possible body surface is available for water resistance, the swimmer moves most efficiently.]

"Recovery strokes also can be made more efficient. Is it easier to move through air or water?" Have the students walk in the pool, then walk on deck. [It is easier to move through air; water has more resistance.] "If it's easier to move through air than water, where should the arm recover?" [Recovery strokes should be done as much in the air as possible to minimize resistance. The arms in the crawl stroke should be recovered as much out of the water as possible. Legs should be recovered in line with the body.]

In advanced levels, have students demonstrate the different ways to do the strokes. Then let them have fun showing how inefficient poorly executed strokes and bad recoveries can be.

Law of Levers

A shorter lever arm can apply more force than a long one.

"Watch a good swimmer doing the front and back crawl. See how the swimmer's elbow is bent? Why is it important to bend your elbow during these strokes?" [A bent arm can apply more force than an extended arm.]

Have students pick up a stool with the arm straight, then with the arm bent.

"Why is it easier to pick up a stool with your arm bent?" (A bent arm can apply more force than an extended arm.)

Inertia (Newton's First Law of Motion)

A body in motion wants to stay in motion; a body at rest wants to stay at rest.

"When pulling a wagon, when must you exert the greatest force: to get it started, or to keep it going?" (To get it started) "When does a body at rest start moving?" (A body at rest starts moving when it is acted upon by a large enough external force.)

"What determines how fast a body moves in water?" [The faster a body moves in water, the more the water resistance pushes back. A body moves at the speed at which the force pushing the body through the water (the effort of the stroke) is exactly the same as the force of water resistance pushing back. To go faster, which makes water resistance push back harder, you have to put out more effort. As water resistance usually pushes harder against large objects than smaller ones, given the same force, a smaller body will move faster through the water than a larger one.]

"When would a body in motion stop?" [A body in motion will stop when it is acted upon by a large enough force.]

"Why is it important to perform a flip turn in competitive swimming?" [The flip turn permits you to maintain your forward movement with a minimum loss of motion, rather than stopping to turn. As you flip, you use your forward swimming motion to speed your dive and turnaround with little or no loss of speed. What you are doing in an effective flip turn is keeping your body in motion.]

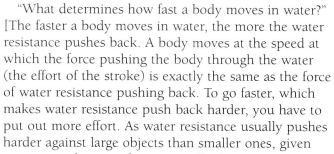

Acceleration
(Newton's Second Law of Motion)

The rate at which a body changes speed is directly related to the force applied.

Items Needed: several toy trucks or cars, small boxes, or other moveable objects

"When you push something hard, will it move faster or slower than if you push gently?"

Have students try pushing toy trucks, small boxes, or similar objects on deck. [The harder you push (the more force applied), the faster the object will move.]

"When you push something directly, does it move in the same direction as the force you are applying?" Again, let the students experiment with objects on deck. [The object moves in the same direction as the applied force.]

"How can this law help you swim better?" [Force should be applied in the direction you want to move. The arm action in the crawl is an example. When it is parallel to the midline of the body and as close to the body as possible, the stroke is more effective and less effort is wasted.]

Individual Physical Differences

No single style of swimming is best for everyone.

"Have you ever seen a professional or Olympic swimmer do the front crawl? The breaststroke? The backstroke? Do they do these strokes exactly as you or I do them?" [No, they do not. Every outstanding swimmer has a particular style.]

"Is it a good idea to imitate the style of an Olympic swimmer?" [Not necessarily, once you know the mechanics of the strokes, you should adapt them to your own physical abilities and body type. Swimmers are not all built alike and cannot all do each stroke in precisely the same way.]

Choose some swimmers who do several strokes very well and have them demonstrate those strokes. Ask students who are observing to point out the differences in the way each swimmer performs the same stroke.

Bernoulli's Theorem

If water molecules have to go around an object, the molecules will move apart from each other and reach the other side of the object at the same time. If the molecules on one side have to travel a longer distance than those on the other side, they speed up, creating less pressure, which in turn creates lift force.

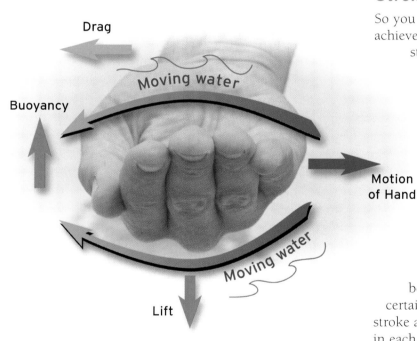

Drag

Moving water

Buoyancy

Motion of Hand

Moving water

Lift

Item Needed: kickboards

Have students stand in shallow water and give each student a kickboard.

"Place your arm and hand on the kickboard. Move the board back and forth on the surface of the water. Pitch your hand out when you move the board out-

ward. Pitch your hand in when you move the board inward. See how fast you can move the board back and forth without losing the kickboard." [The board should stay in place.]

"Why does the board stay in place? Can you feel the pressure of the board against your hand?" [The board stays in place because the water molecules on the top of the board are moving faster, creating less pressure, and so the water on the bottom of the board is lifting up.]

Stroke Overview

So you know what your students are striving to achieve, an advanced efficient form for each of six strokes is described in this section: the front crawl, the back crawl, the breaststroke, the butterfly stroke, the sidestroke, and the elementary backstroke. Each is accompanied by a stroke observation checksheet. We also have included starts and turns for the front crawl, back crawl, breaststroke, and butterfly. (Additional strokes and skills are taught within each level and are described in The Parent/Child and Preschool Aquatic Program Manual and The Youth and Adult Aquatic Program Manual.) Keep in mind that your students will adapt the stroke movements to their own bodies and may only be capable of reaching a certain level in their progression on a particular stroke at this time. Those steps will be described within each level in the manuals for the Youth and Adult Aquatic Program and the Parent/Child and Preschool Aquatic Aquatic Program.

Front Crawl

The front crawl is shown in figure 7.1 A–F.

In the front crawl, the arms provide most of the propulsive force. The hand goes into the water thumb down, fingertips first, with the palm facing down and out diagonally. The elbow is higher than the hand. The hand enters at a spot directly in front of the shoulder, not crossing the center of the body, thumb aligned with the shoulder. The arm is not quite fully extended as it enters the water.

The arm then accelerates, pulling outward, downward, and back, with the elbow bending until it reaches about a 90-degree to 110-degree angle. At this maximum bend, the arm crosses the middle of the body down to the thigh. The arm then pushes back, out, and up toward the hips. The pull forms an inverted "S" pattern, and throughout the pull the elbow should be higher than the hand.

Figure 7.1 Front Crawl Sequence

Recovery of the opposite arm begins before the pull ends, as the elbow emerges from the water while the hand is still submerged. The hand recovers out of the water pinkie finger first. Recovery is done in a rounded, relaxed, and controlled movement.

The opposite arm starts to pull as the other one starts to recover. This keeps the body moving forward as one arm recovers through the air and reenters the water.

The continuous leg action during the front crawl is not so much a kick but a flexible, alternating movement that starts in the hip. The heels move up and down as the legs move with the rest of the body. Knees are bent less than 30° only by the reaction to the force of the leg movement and do not add much to the movement of the body. The legs should be vertically separated by 10 to 16 inches (depending on body size), and the ankles should be relaxed, with the ankles held loosely. The toes may be pointed in slightly but do not require a conscious effort, and the toenails should just reach the surface. The downbeat is emphasized.

Usually this leg movement is done once to three times for each arm stroke, although competitive swimmers usually kick three times when sprinting.

Rotary breathing is performed during every stroke cycle of the front crawl in synchronization with the body roll and arm recovery. The swimmer breathes in through the mouth as the body moves sideways, taking in air from the trough created by the front of the face. The cheek rests on the water and the lips curl out to keep water out of the mouth, with the head turned as little as possible.

As soon as the mouth goes underwater, the swimmer begins gently exhaling through the nose and pursed lips. He or she continues exhaling and moves the head slowly and smoothly to a centered position with eyes forward (head is at about a 45-degree angle to the surface), then to slightly past center. The swimmer finally turns the head back to the side, forcefully exhaling the remaining air in the water before inhaling again.

When performing the front crawl, the swimmer should keep the body near the surface as streamlined and flat as possible. The head should stay within the long axis of the body, and the waterline should cross the forehead. The body will roll naturally with the arm stroke, and the head turn for breathing should occur right after one arm enters the water. The entire movement should be continuous and smooth.

See the observation checksheets on pages 171–172 in Appendix F for the front crawl.

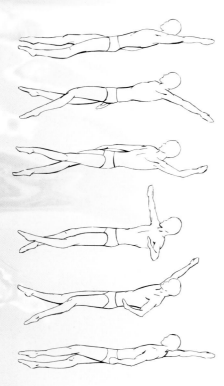

Back Crawl

Figure 7.2 A–F demonstrates the back crawl.

The arm enters the water little finger first, at 1 or 11 o'clock from the shoulder.

Fingers are together and point to the side of the pool. The body rolls toward the entering arm, and recovery momentum moves the arm down 12 to 18 inches. When the pull starts, the elbow bends, pointing toward the bottom of the pool, and the upper arm rotates. Fingers point to the side of the pool. At the point at which the hand is adjacent to the shoulder, the elbow is at about a 90-degree angle. Then the hand pushes back and down past the thigh in a rounded motion, palm facing the bottom of the pool at the end of the pull briefly, but does not pause there. The entire pull is a down, up, down motion or flattened "S" or question-mark motion, with the hand accelerating throughout.

Figure 7.2 **Back Crawl Sequence**

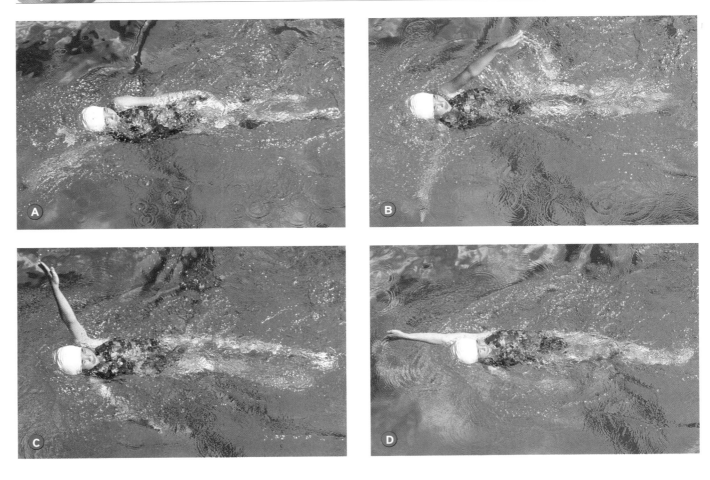

When the hand presses downward, the body starts to roll to the other side. This makes the shoulder of the arm that finished the stroke rise, leading into recovery.

The arm recovers out of water in a straight, vertical line, with the hand thumb-first. The arm should be relaxed and the elbow straight. As the recovering arm passes the head, the palm should be facing out and sideways, ready for entry.

During the back crawl, the legs alternate in a shallow, continuous wave. The kick starts in the hips, legs rolling with the body. The legs are extended and relaxed at the hips. Most of the force of this kick is generated on the upbeat. Knees are bent (30-45°) on the upbeat but straighten for most of the downbeat, and they stay underwater. Usually this leg movement is done six times per arm cycle of both arms.

Feet and ankles should be relaxed, and the feet should stay within the body line. Feet move up and down 12 to 15 inches. Toes are pointed on the upbeat. The toes come near the surface and create a small wave.

Inhalation is through the mouth. Breathing is rhythmical, inhaling during recovery of one arm and exhaling during recovery of the other arm.

During the back crawlstroke, the body is elongated and horizontal in the water near the surface. The chest breaks the surface, and the hips are high in the water but just below the surface. The push down at the end of the pull may make the shoulders and hips roll a bit, as the body rolls on its long axis. The head remains stationary at a constant water level; the waterline crosses the back of the head. Ears skim along the surface. The arm recovering moves to enter slightly faster than the arm that is finishing the stroke.

The observation checksheets for the back crawl are on pages 173–174.

Back Crawl arm recovery

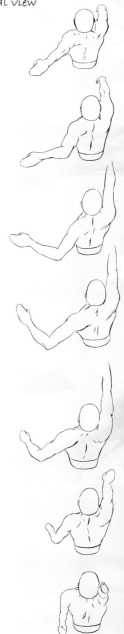

Back Crawl arm movement, frontal view

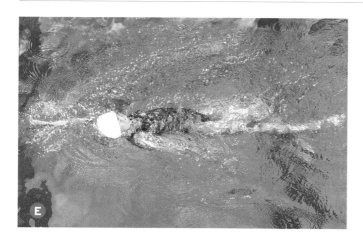

E

F

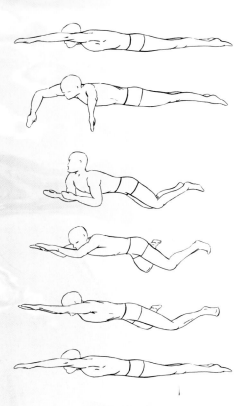

Breaststroke

In figure 7.3 A–H you can see the components of the breaststroke.

The arm pull begins with a catch of the water six inches to eight inches deep, with the elbows extended and palms facing diagonally to the sides. Wrists are flexed as the hands separate, while elbows remain high and then start to bend when the hands are about a foot apart.

The hands then pull outward and downward in a

begins with flexion of the knees and hips, with feet close together. As the heels approach the buttocks, the feet flex up toward the shins and the heels and knees separate. Knees and feet are maximally flexed, with ankles flexed up toward the shins, as the toes turn out. The kick begins with the knees being extended and driving the feet outward and backward, engaging the water with the insteps of the feet. (Knees do not lead.) This part of the kick is performed at a steady, moderate speed, but when the legs kick backward, the speed of the feet gradually increases. Maximum speed is reached during the last quarter of the kick. The feet come

Figure 7.3 **Breaststroke Sequence**

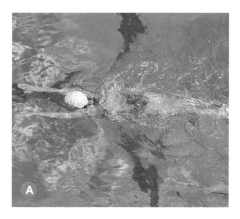
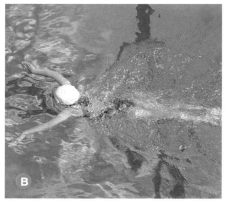
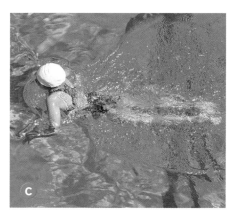

narrow heart-shaped pattern underwater, approaching the shoulder line. The angle of the hands then changes from outward to inward (with palms facing each other). The upper arms drop as the hands get closer. Arms move right from the pull to the recovery with no pause, moving forward strongly to complete extension.

The kick is performed by both legs simultaneously, and the feet are just below the water's surface throughout the kick. When the feet are not kicking, they are pointed, fully extended, and streamlined. Recovery

together in a semicircular pattern as the legs straighten, and the kick ends with the knees extended, the feet pointed, and the toes together.

During the glide phase, the body should be horizontal and streamlined, near the water's surface. During the arm pull, the upper body rises above the surface of the water with the head up just high enough (after the start of the pull) to allow the swimmer to inhale (which happens as the pull ends) through the mouth. Shoulders rise above the surface during recovery, then the body submerges slightly and streamlines as the arms are fully extended. Exhalation, through the mouth or the nose and mouth, starts as the hands begin to pull. It starts slowly, gradually increasing in intensity until a final forceful pull just prior to inhalation.

The action is coordinated in the following order:
→ Glide
→ Pull and breathe
→ Kick
→ Glide

The pull and kick alternate. Arms pull while legs are extended, then the head is raised for inhalation at the end of the pull. Legs start their recovery as the pull finishes. The face submerges right after inhalation and before arms are completely extended; the kick starts just before complete arm extension. The arms remain extended until the kick is finished, then the body is held in full extension, horizontal, for a short glide. The body is submerged but near the surface.

The observation checksheets for the breaststroke are on pages 175–176.

Breaststroke kick

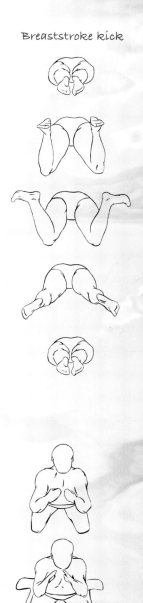

Breaststroke arm movement, frontal view

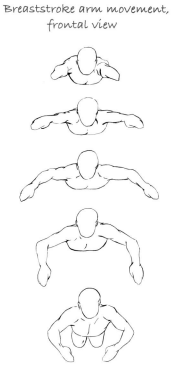

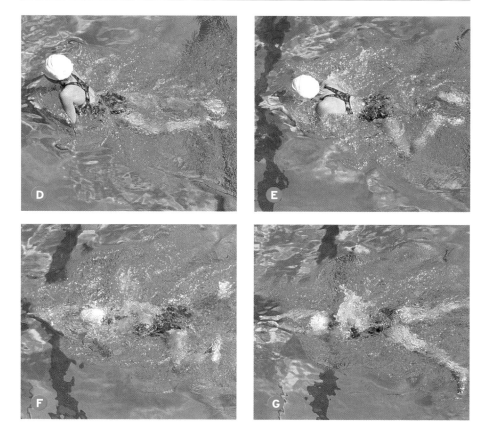

Butterfly Stroke

The butterfly stroke is shown in figure 7.4 A–H.

Both arms pull together symmetrically, creating the pattern of an "S" or hourglass. The hands enter the water with the thumb leading, just wide of the shoulder line, and press downward and to the side. Elbows are flexed and held high while the hands lead.

As the arms become almost vertical (90 degrees to the trunk) the hands move closer together under the trunk. Then the push phase begins. Hand movement

the larger of the two. The knees lead the legs on the downbeat of the kick, which is emphasized. The speed on the downbeat should be twice that of the uplift.

The legs are raised first from the hip (straight up) and then from the knee (a bent position). As knee flexion comes to a 30-degree to 45-degree angle, the knees spread slightly and the feet are pointed. Toes are just beneath the surface. Sudden, strong extension of the knees drives the feet back and down, and the hips lift slightly in reaction to this movement. The heels are almost two feet down on the bottom of the downbeat. Leg recovery is gradual and relaxed.

Figure 7.4 Butterfly Stroke Sequence

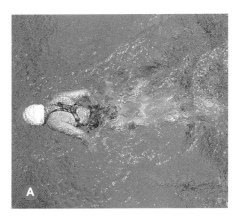 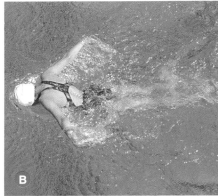 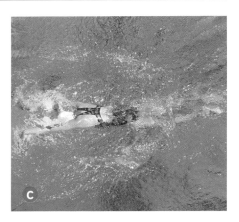

accelerates as the elbows extend vigorously, wrists extended far back to direct pressure backward. In tracing this pattern, the hands perform a sculling motion, pitching outward, inward, and then outward again. Thumbs finish near the thighs.

Wrists and elbows are relaxed as the arms "round off" into recovery. The little finger leads as the arms move out and up. Arms swing forward in a low, flat, bowl-shaped curve back to the point of entry.

The dolphin kick is used. It begins in the hips. Two kicks are used per arm cycle, with the first kick being

The body continuously moves up and down, moving more than in any other stroke. Throughout the stroke, the hips remain near the surface. The back arches as the head surfaces to breathe. As the arms plunge forward at entry, the head usually submerges, although this action is offset by the simultaneous first kick. The second kick occurs during the finish of the pull.

The timing of head movements is crucial to the rhythm of the whole stroke. Following inhalation, the face returns to the water a moment before the hands enter. The face rises above the water for inhalation a moment before the hands leave the water. Inhalation is through the mouth only; exhalation can be through either the mouth alone or both mouth and nose simultaneously.

The swimmer eases the chin forward at the beginning of the stroke. The face lifts gradually forward in synchronization with the arm stroke. As the hands move closer together, the shoulders and head rise in the water. From this position, the swimmer can easily raise the face above the water in time to inhale. At the push of the arms, the neck is extended and the chin

moves slowly forward, raising the mouth above the water (as the inhalation is made, the chin stays in the water). Lips are curled outward to keep water out of the mouth. Inhalation is finished as the arms pass the head in recovery, and the face submerges a moment before the hands do. The forehead is at the waterline during exhalation.

The observation checksheets for the butterfly stroke are on pages 177–178.

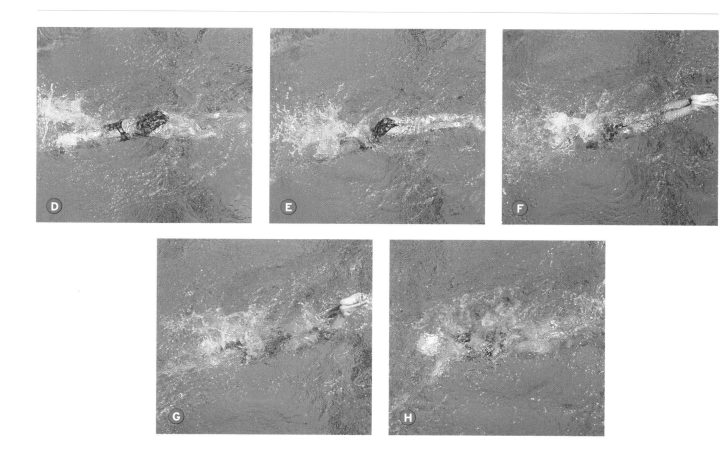

Butterfly arm movement, underside view

Sidestroke

Figure 7.5 A–D illustrates the sidestroke.

When the leading (bottom) arm pulls, the hand leads. The wrist and elbow flex so the palm presses backward to shoulder height, opposite to the direction of movement. The elbow bends and, as the leading arm reaches a 90-degree angle to the torso (hand is at or near the chin), the wrist is hyperextended beyond the head. The trailing (top) arm is simultaneously recovering from its position at the thigh, with the hand drawn, fingers leading, across the hip and chest to just below the chin (where it meets the hand of the leading arm). The flexed elbow is close to the trunk to reduce resistance. With the wrist slightly flexed, the hand pulls directly back toward the feet, close to the body, pressing through to the thigh. The elbow extends strongly as the hand moves from flexion to hyperextension, keeping the palm facing backward. The glide phase follows recovery.

In the glide phase of the sidestroke, the leading arm is fully extended underwater (beyond the head) in line with the body. The trailing arm is extended at the surface beside the torso, with the hand at the thigh.

Figure 7.5   **Sidestroke Sequence**

During the glide, the swimmer rests on the leading arm. Both legs are extended together, aligned with the body, ankles relaxed.

On the drive, the top leg moves forward when the upper leg extends at the knee, then at the hip. The lower leg extends from the hip. Heels are pulled up toward the buttocks. The legs are then moved apart, so the swimmer looks as if he or she is taking a giant step, and pulled together simultaneously, feet pointed, to a streamlined position for the glide. One kick is made per stroke cycle.

Breathing should be through the mouth, in an easy, rhythmical manner. Inhalation occurs as the legs recover, and exhalation occurs during the kick.

The trunk is horizontal and on its side. The head rests on the water. The body should stay streamlined, with no bending during leg recovery. The leading arm finishes pulling at the same time the trailing arm is recovering and the legs finish; the trailing arm should pull at the same time the leading arm recovers and the legs kick. During the glide, the leading arm is extended almost directly in line with the long axis of the body, parallel to the surface. The trailing arm is extended along the side of the body.

The observation checksheets for the sidestroke are on pages 179–180.

Elementary Backstroke

The elementary backstroke is shown in figure 7.6 A–F.

The arms move in a symmetrical pull-push movement. Because both arms pull simultaneously, the body does not roll, and the arms move in a shallow, flat "S" pattern. The arms fully extend from the shoulder at a 30-degree angle (11 o'clock and 1 o'clock), with palms flexed and facing out. Elbows are held at or just beyond shoulder level and remain high as they rotate forward. This rotation provides a muscular/mechanical advantage at the beginning of the push phase of the bent-arm pull. The wrist is flexed, extended, then extended even farther until the palms are pressing directly downward as the arm extends to the thigh.

In recovery, the elbows are bent as the hands move up the length of the trunk to return to the shoulder. Arms move slowly and close to the body to minimize resistance. Arm recovery starts slightly before kick recovery.

The kick is similar to a breaststroke kick, only done on the back and little hip flexion. Legs start in a fully extended, streamlined position close to the water's surface. With the hips at the surface, the feet are drawn toward the trunk and the thighs rotate slightly. The knees bend more but don't lift, then spread a bit,

Figure 7.6 Elementary Backstroke Sequence

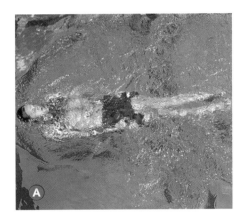
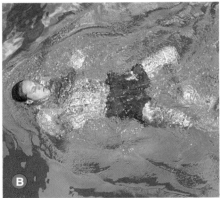

and the feet are extremely flexed toward the shins. The lower leg rotates through a short arc, then the hip and knee strongly and abruptly extend, carrying the lower leg through an arc to return to full extension. The instep and inside of the calf press back against the water.

The diameter of the arc depends largely on knee and hip rotation. The greater the rotation, the wider the legs sweep. The feet will appear to move in mirror image through opposing arcs (a two-phase symmetrical kick).

Breathing is rhythmic, through the mouth. Inhalation occurs during arm recovery and exhalation occurs during arm propulsion.

Keeping a streamlined and horizontal position near the surface is important for performing the elementary backstroke efficiently. (Head tilts down toward feet only slightly during the stroke.) Hips are held high and the head is back with chin up and ears below the surface. The simultaneous recovery of both arms and legs (as the arms pass the shoulder, the legs begin) increases the resistant surface area, which can impede forward movement. This problem is accentuated if the swimmer pikes at the waist (sitting in the water) or allows the elbows to wander during recovery.

The observation checksheets for the elementary backstroke are on pages 181–182.

Elementary Backstroke kick

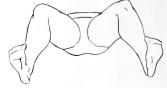

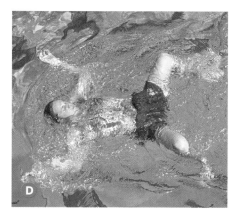
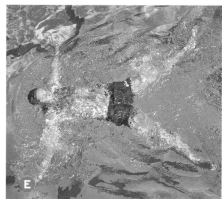

Figure 7.7   Forward Start Sequence

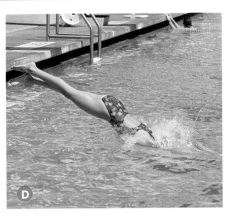

Starts

The starts described here are the forward start and back crawl start.

Forward Start

A good start allows the student to gain momentum and speed through proper pullouts and streamlining during the glide. The same start is used for the front crawl-stroke, breaststroke, and butterfly stroke, although the movements differ once the swimmer enters the water. This is also referred to as the grab start. Remind students that arms must remain extended to help protect their heads.

Figure 7.7 A–D shows the forward start.

Teach this skill in water that is at least nine feet deep. Begin teaching by having swimmers start from the deck. Once they have demonstrated that they can control the dive, you can have them start from the starting blocks.

For the start, the swimmer stands at the front of the starting block or on the edge of the deck, relaxed. Knees are slightly flexed, with the feet a hip-width apart and toes curled over the front edge of the block or deck. Arms and face are forward with the palms facing back, and the head is down. Stress to all swimmers that they cannot make any movement until the gun sounds or the "go" command is given.

At the starting signal, forward motion begins with the head dropping. The swimmer pulls down on the block with the hands, the head pops forward and up, and the eyes seek the entry spot. As the arms move up and around the body like a windmill, the swimmer raises the heels off the blocks; the momentum from this will move the swimmer forward. After the arms have circled 360 degrees, they continue out in front of the body, leading it off the block or deck. The head is raised slightly as the legs thrust back (the swimmer straightens both the knees and ankles). The legs begin the drive to leap, while the hands and arms stretch out and aim at the entry spot. During the flight of the dive, the swimmer tucks the head down between the arms, which remain extended. The swimmer imagines entering the

wide pullout and push-through motion, with the hands ending by the hips. The swimmer then counts one, two before beginning the recovery with the hands under the body, palms up and elbows tucked in. As the hands pass the face on the way back to the front, the swimmer kicks once to the surface. Once the head breaks the surface, the swimmer begins the regular breaststroke and breathes for the first stroke.

For the butterfly stroke, the swimmer enters the water streamlined and takes two or three quick kicks and

Figure 7.8 **Back Crawl Start Sequence**

water through a single "hole." During flight, the swimmer keeps the back straight to streamline the body, and he or she lowers the head as the body begins to fall. The body enters the water in sequence, beginning with the hands. As soon as they enter the water, the swimmer adjusts them to provide a shallow dive angle and swims back up to the surface, arms extended and hands grabbed. The start should be performed to gain speed and distance, not depth.

For the front crawl, the swimmer enters the water streamlined and begins to kick first, then takes two pulls before the first breath.

For the breaststroke, the swimmer enters the water streamlined, keeping the head tucked between the arms. He or she counts one, two, three, and then does a

times the first arm stroke to break smoothly through to the surface. The swimmer should complete one or more strokes before breathing.

Back Crawl

The back crawl start is illustrated in figure 7.8 A–E.

Teach this skill in water that is at least nine feet deep. The back crawl start is like a back dive starting in the water, in which the swimmer arches the back out over the water. The swimmer is curled loosely at the starting block or at the edge of the pool. His or her knees are flexed, with the feet against the wall about one foot underwater, either side by side or one foot slightly in front of the other. The hands grip the starting block with an overhand grip, a shoulder-width apart. At the

signal "Take your mark" the swimmer draws into the wall in a tight position, pulling the body out of the water. The head is lowered toward the knees and the feet remain underwater.

At the start signal, the head snaps back and the hands push the body away from the wall in a back dive. The legs drive the body up, out, and away from the wall in a back dive. The extended arms sweep over the top and reach for the entry spot. The swimmer looks back over the shoulders as he or she visualizes entering the water through a "hole."

The body enters about 19 to 20 inches below the water's surface, and excessive arching can force it even deeper. The head is held well back, and the swimmer exhales forcefully through the nose. Once in the water, the swimmer streamlines and glides until he or she starts to slow down, then kicks using the dolphin or flutter kick and takes the first pull, which breaks the body through the surface. The first kick and arm pull are taken on the same side, and the free arm is momentarily extended above the head.

Turns

The turns described here are the crawlstroke open turn, crawlstroke flip turn, back crawl open turn, spin turn, back crawl turnover turn, breaststroke turn, and butterfly turn.

Crawlstroke Open Turn

Figure 7.9 A–E illustrates the crawlstroke open turn.

In this turn, the swimmer kicks into the turn as he or she approaches the wall, with the leading arm extended.

After the touch, the one arm recovers under the water and the other arm over, near the swimmer's ear, as the swimmer positions on the side to push off the wall. The lower body (hips) drops, and the legs tuck underneath to swing toward the wall. As the feet come together on the wall, the swimmer pushes against the wall and brings the arms together in front of the body, over the head. He or she then pushes off with the body streamlined and extended, holding the "one, two, three" count just before the pullout as described in the forward start done for the breaststroke. The head must break the water's surface before the second arm stroke starts.

Crawlstroke Flip Turn

The crawlstroke flip turn is illustrated in figure 7.10 A–C.

This turn sometimes is referred to as a flip turn, but it really is more like a shoulder roll with a twist. The swimmer should know how many strokes away from the wall it takes before he or she starts the "flip." On the last stroke before he or she approaches the

Figure 7.9   Crawlstroke Open Turn Sequence

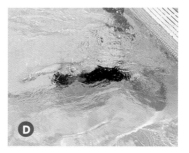
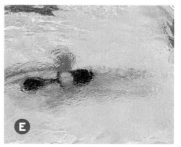

Figure 7.10 Crawlstroke Flip Turn Sequence

wall, the swimmer should lower one shoulder and roll on it, throwing the feet to the wall. The legs should bend as if they were jumping on land. The swimmer's arms extend over the head into a streamlined position, with the back of the head tightly against the upper arms, as the swimmer pushes hard with the legs off the wall. As the body decelerates, the legs begin to kick, then the arms start, with two strokes before the first breath.

Back Crawl Open Turn

This turn is similar to the crawlstroke open turn, except that the swimmer needs to count the number of strokes from the stroke flags to the wall in order to know when to expect the hands to hit the wall.

In figure 7.11 A–E you can see the components of the back crawl open turn.

In the open turn, the swimmer approaches the wall with his or her dominant arm in full extension. With fingertips down, he or she touches the wall almost five inches below the surface. Once the swimmer contacts, he or she tucks the legs as the body flexes slightly. The swimmer starts the spin (turn) toward the touch arm, and as the body moves, the lower legs break the water's surface. The legs drop with knees flexed and the feet hit the wall underwater. The touch hand leaves the wall and joins the free hand above the head. Hands are together as the arms extend and the upper body straightens, completing the turn. The legs push against the wall. The swimmer, who is in a streamlined position, takes the first kick and arm pull on the same side.

Figure 7.11 Back Crawl Open Turn Sequence

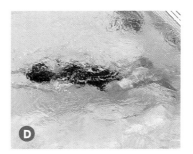

Back Crawl Flip Turn

The back crawl flip turn is illustrated in figure
7.12 A–E.

The swimmer should maintain a continuous kick
while approaching the turn at the wall. He or she is
allowed to turn over to the stomach after the last
stroke and execute a somersault, throwing the feet
to the wall and pushing off on the back into a streamlined position. Again, the swimmer should kick first,
then pull.

Breaststroke Turn

The breaststroke turn is illustrated in figure 7.13 A–D.

The breaststroke turn is similar to the crawlstroke
open turn, except that two hands must touch the end
wall before beginning the turn.

Figure 7.12 **Back Crawl Flip Turn Sequence**

Figure 7.13 **Breaststroke Turn Sequence**

Butterfly Turn

The butterfly turn is illustrated in figure 7.14 A–E.

The swimmer's hands must touch the wall at the same time. The mechanics of the turn are the same as the breaststroke turn, with the swimmer leaving the wall on the side, then executing two quick kicks and initiating the first pull. The swimmer should take one complete pull before the first breath to avoid coming up and breathing into the bow wave or turn wave of the other swimmers.

Figure 7.14 **Butterfly Turn Sequence**

    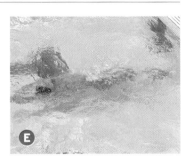

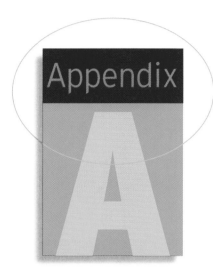

Appendix A

Aquatic Skill Games

This appendix includes aquatic skill games you can use to help your students improve specific abilities. The games are grouped by the following skills:

→ Water orientation
→ Water entry and exit
→ Buoyancy and balance
→ Flotation
→ Breath control
→ Body position
→ Propulsion
→ Endurance
→ Advanced strokes
→ Teamwork
→ Miscellaneous

Games that also include character development are indicated by an asterisk.

Within each category the games are arranged from those for the lowest to the highest levels. A suggested skill level for each game is indicated next to the game's title, but you should take into account the abilities of your own class as well as their assigned level and choose games accordingly. Feel free to adapt the games to make them easier or harder so they are appropriate for the skill level of your class. To help you locate specific games by title, a games index appears at the end of this appendix. The games are listed alphabetically, with the category, skill level, and page number given for each one.

Water Orientation

Canoe, Train, Bus

Equipment Needed: water logs, one for each pair of students

Have students pair up with each other and give each pair a water log. Then teach them three sounds and motions to make, depending upon whether you say the word *canoe, train,* or *bus.*

→ On *canoe,* both players straddle a water log, paddle their arms like oars, and say "Stroke, stroke, down the river we go."
→ On *train,* both players hold one water log under the same arm (right or left), moving their arms to chug like a train and saying "Choo, choo, choo."
→ On *bus,* the first player holds the ends of the water log to form a steering wheel and the partner stands behind him or her. They sing the song "The Wheels on the Bus Go Up and Down."

Hokey Pokey (Parent/Child and Preschool and Polliwog)

Equipment Needed: recording of the "Hokey Pokey" and a record, CD, or tape player (optional)

Have the class form a circle in waist- to chest-deep water (parents also, if they are with young children). Then, either play the song or sing it as a group:

"You put your right hand in,
You put your right hand out,
You put your right hand in,
and you shake it all about.
You do the hokey pokey,
and you turn yourself around.
That's what it's all about."

Sing various verses, putting different parts of the body into and out of the circle.

Simon Says (Parent/Child and Preschool and Polliwog)

Have students line up in the water along one side. You stand some distance away from them and give them commands, such as, "Put your hands on your heads," "Bob up and down in the water," or "Duck under the water." However, they should follow the commands only when those commands are preceded by the words, "Simon says." If a student responds to a command that was not preceded by "Simon says" or responds too slowly to a "Simon says" command, that student is eliminated. Those students who are not eliminated are the winners, and one of them can be the next leader.

Name Game (Parent/Child and Preschool and Polliwog)

Have students form a line in knee- to chest-deep water, depending on their skill level (with young children, parents may also be included). Tell students to chant the following rhyme together:

"Names, names, what's in a name?
I've got a name, and you've got a name.
What's your name?"

You then choose a student, who calls out his or her name and simultaneously performs a skill. The group then repeats the name three times and tries to repeat the skill the student performed. Each student gets a turn. You and parents can give students suggestions for skills and can provide assistance in flotation. At the end, have the class form a circle and review the names and skills performed. A variation on this game is having the named student perform a new skill plus skills previously performed.

Pop Goes the Weasel (Parent/Child and Preschool and Polliwog)

Equipment Needed: recording of "Pop Goes the Weasel" and a record, CD, or tape player (optional)

Have students form a circle in waist- to chest-deep water and sing the song "Pop Goes the Weasel":

"'Round and round the mulberry bush,
The monkey chased the weasel;
The monkey thought it was all in fun;
Pop goes the weasel!"

On "Pop," the students jump up or duck under. You also can change this so they perform a swimming action on "Pop."

For very young children whose parents are present, the parents can form the circle while holding the children. The parents then move side to side during the song (like a washing machine agitator) and lift the children up into the air on "Pop."

Ring-Around-the-Rosy (Parent/Child and Preschool and Polliwog)

See this game in the Breath Control section.

Head, Shoulders, Knees, and Toes (Preschool and Polliwog)

See this game in the Body Position section.

Cork Scramble (Preschool, Polliwog and up)

See this game in the Advanced Strokes section.

Red Light, Green Light (Parent/Child and Preschool and Polliwog to Minnow)

Have students line up in the water along one side. Choose one student to be the "traffic light" and have him or her stand 20 to 30 feet away from the other students with his or her back to them and with eyes closed. Explain to students that when the "traffic light" student calls out, "One, two, three green light!" they should run or swim toward the "traffic light." However, when the "traffic light" student calls out, "One, two, three, red light!" and turns around, everyone must be motionless. Anyone caught moving must return to the starting line and begin again. This continues until someone reaches the "traffic light" student. That person is the winner.

Choo-Choo Train (Parent/Child and Preschool and Polliwog to Minnow)

Equipment Needed: a large plastic hoop (optional)

Move students to shallow water. Ask them to travel in a circle, lines, or zigzag while they move their arms like the pistons of a steam loco-motive. They can also add whistling, chugging, or other train sounds. Variations on this activity include using a large plastic hoop for the students to hold on to as they walk in a circle, letting each child be his or her favorite train car, or moving in various directions and at various speeds.

Did You Ever See a Swimmer? (Polliwog to Minnow)

Sing the following rhyme to the tune of "Did You Ever See a Lassie?" and perform a skill as you sing:

"Did you ever see a swimmer, a swimmer, a swimmer,
Did you ever see a swimmer go this way and that?
Go this way and that way, go that way and this way,
Did you ever see a swimmer go this way and that?"

The students should follow you, doing the same things. You then can choose students to lead, doing other skills.

Over and Under Passing (Polliwog to Fish)

See this game in the Buoyancy and Balance section.

Water Entry and Exit

Easter Egg Coloring Time (Parent/Child and Preschool and Polliwog)

Have children line up on the deck by the shallow water. Tell them to pretend they are Easter eggs and the pool is coloring dye. Ask each to choose which color they want to be. Tell them that, when you call out their color, they should jump or slide into the water. After they enter the water, they should right themselves, turn, and paddle back to the side and get out. This activity also can be done with all children jumping in at each color.

Instructor Note: Children in the Preschool and Polliwog levels should perform this only with instructor or parental assistance.

Humpty Dumpty (Parent/Child and Preschool and Polliwog)

Have students sit along the pool edge by waist-to chest-deep water. Their parents stand next to them in the water. You and the parents chant the following rhyme while the parents rock their children:

"Humpty Dumpty sat on a wall;
Humpty Dumpty had a great fall;
Humpty Dumpty swam back to the wall."

At "great fall," the parents pull the children into the water, then help them back to the wall during the last line. As the children's skills improve, parents can assist them less, and the water depth and length of submersion can be increased. The activity can be varied by having the parents jump into the water with the children.

Instructor Note: Observe children under three so that they do not ingest water. Children of this age who ingest too much water can develop water intoxication, a rare condition in which a large amount of water disturbs the body's electrolytes.

Children in the Preschool and Polliwog levels should perform this only with instructor or parental assistance.

Jump Into My Circle (Parent/Child and Preschool and Polliwog)

Equipment Needed: plastic hoops (one for each parent)

Perform this in water that is waist- to chest-deep. Have the students stand or sit on the side of the pool while their parents hold plastic hoops on the water's surface and count, "One, two, three." On three, the students should jump into the hoop, submerging briefly. If the children grab the side of the hoop, the parents can help them back to the side.

Parents can hold the children's hands throughout the jump, if desired. This activity can be varied by having the children jump from different heights, such as from sitting or from standing on a diving block.

Instructor Note: Children in the Preschool and Polliwog levels should perform this only with instructor or parental assistance.

Parachute Jump (Parent/Child and Preschool and Polliwog)

Perform this in shallow to moderate water. Have students line up along the edge of the pool. Tell them that they are in a plane and are parachute jumpers. Say that when they hear you call out their name they should yell their own name (or they jump in order, calling their own names), jump into the water, go down to the bottom, turn around, push off, then return to the side and climb out. You can give individual support to beginners, if desired. Students also can pretend to be frogmen jumping from a speedboat.

I Make My Arms Go Up and Down (Parent/Child and Preschool and Polliwog)

Have students bob, bubbling in the water, as you sing the following to the tune of "Mulberry Bush":

"I make my arms go up and down,
I make my arms go up and down,
I make my arms go up and down,
JUST LIKE THIS!"

Students bob on the words "up and down." Other verses are "I make my arms go round and round" and "I make my legs go up and down."

I'm a Little Teapot (Parent/Child and Preschool and Polliwog)

Have students sing this song and perform the accompanying motions while in the water:

"I'm a little teapot, short and stout.
This is my handle, [Put one hand on hip.]
This is my spout. [Extend opposite arm sideways, hand out.]
When I get all steamed up, then I shout,
'Just tip me over and pour me out.' [Bend body toward extended arm.]
S-S-S-S-S"

"I'm a clever teapot, it is true.
Here is something I can do.
I can change my handle and my spout,
[Change position of hands.]
Just tip me over and pour me out. [Bend body toward extended arm.]
S-S-S-S-S"

Rocket Booster (Guppy and up)

For this activity, the water depth should be at least nine feet. Have students sit (or kneel, squat, or stand) along the side of the deep end of the pool. Tell them that, on your signal, they should blast off into the water by diving. They are to see who can glide the farthest underwater without surfacing or kicking and pulling. They can use any stroke to return to the side. Vary this activity by using more and more advanced dives (sitting to kneeling to squatting to standing) and by changing the type of stroke used to return.

Buoyancy and Balance

Can't Touch Me (Preschool and Polliwog)

Equipment Needed: a water log

Have students form a circle in the shallow end of the pool. One student, the leader, stands in the center holding a water log on the surface of the water in front of him or her. The leader slowly swings the log in a circle, and the players duck under the log as it comes near them. If the student is touched by the log, he or she must perform a stunt. Students who don't like to get their faces wet can be the leader or help in some other way.

Tidal Wave (Preschool and Polliwog)

Equipment Needed: Water polo ball or small playground ball

Have students stand in the water in a circle. Tell them to try to move the ball around the circle by making waves with their arms, not touching the ball. When the ball goes all around the circle, move it back the other way.

Flip Flops (Polliwog to Minnow)

See this game in the Flotation section.

Over and Under Passing (Polliwog to Fish)

Equipment Needed: Water polo balls, small playground balls, or beachballs (one for each line)

In knee- to chest-deep water, have students form lines from the pool wall out into the pool. Give a ball to each of the students at the head of the lines. Tell students to alternate between passing the ball above the head or through the legs, passing it until it reaches the end. The person at the end should then walk or run to the front and start passing again. They should repeat this until they cross the pool or until everyone has had a turn.

In chest-deep water, students can submerge as they pass the ball. This activity also can be performed as a relay race between two or more lines.

Hoops (Minnow and up)

Equipment Needed: two large plastic hoops

Move your class to chest-deep water and divide the students into two equal teams. Tell each team to form a circle by holding hands, then place a hoop over the linked hands of two players on each team. Tell them that, when you give a signal, the student next to the hoop should move his or her body through the hoop without letting go of the other students' hands. The other students will have to help that student move through the hoop. The team on which all members pass through the hoop successfully first wins. If a student lets go of another player, the hoop is returned to the starting position and the team must begin again.

Kickboard Stunts (Minnow and up)

See this game in the Flotation section.

Squid Swim (Minnow and up)

See this game in the Flotation section.

Treasure Hunt (Fish and up)

Equipment Needed: a diving brick, an inner tube or plastic hoop, and a stopwatch or a watch that will time to the second

Place a diving brick on the pool bottom and float an inner tube or plastic hoop near it. Then have students line up along the pool wall in the water. Tell students to take turns diving down to the bottom to get the brick, swimming up, and putting the brick through the tube or hoop. You can time each student to see who can do this fastest or to compare trials.

Each student should replace the brick in its original position for the next student to use.

Synchro Chain*
(Flying Fish to Shark)

This activity stresses the value of respect. Have students work together to form a synchro chain in the deep end of the pool. (See instructions for forming a chain in the shark level of YMCA Progressive Swimming Instructor's Guide.) Explain to them before they begin that, in order to complete the chain, they will need to help each other out and to respect those students who may have trouble forming the chain.

Honesty Pass* (All levels)

Equipment Needed: Water polo balls or small playground balls (one for each team)

This activity focuses on the value of honesty. Divide the class into teams, then have students pass the ball and spell out h-o-n-e-s-t-y by earning one letter each time a team member catches the ball without dropping it. If someone drops

the ball, the team has to start over. The first team to spell "honesty" wins.

After the game, discuss with the class why it's important to be honest. Ask "Were you all being honest when you were playing the game?"

Flotation

Gingerbread Cookie
(Preschool and Polliwog to Guppy)

Move to water that is waist- to neck-deep. Ask students to pretend to be gingerbread cookies that cannot move while floating without breaking off an arm or leg. With your help, have them try one at a time to float front or back as motionless as possible. The class should clap for each person's attempt.

A variation on this is a tag game in which a "fox" (who is "It") eats up any gingerbread person who is not floating. Students can use flotation devices or a partner to assist flotation.

Glide and Slide (Polliwog to Guppy)

Move into water that is waist- to chest-deep and have students line up along the pool wall. Have them push off from the side or shallow bottom and glide as far as they can, staying streamlined. Once the glide slows, they should pull their knees up and stand. Compare how far they glide among class members or between trials.

Variations include adding a leg kick and arm motions to the glide, pushing off only from the bottom, or performing glide or kick-glide skills on the back.

Instructor Note: *Watch students and don't let them go too far.*

Flip Flops (Polliwog to Minnow)

Equipment Needed: kickboards or balls the same size as a soccer ball (one for each student)

Move your students to shallow- to chest-deep water (depending on their skill level). Hand out a kickboard or ball to each student, then ask them to kick across the pool on either the front or back while holding it. Tell them to listen for an audible signal from you. At that signal, they should turn over and keep kicking.

Vary this activity by either having swimmers front kick with their faces in the water (with signals no more than five seconds apart) or having them wear life jackets.

Superman (Polliwog to Fish)

In waist- to chest-deep water, have students lie face down in the water with body extended, then push off and glide as far as possible. They can try gliding on the back (an upside-down Superman) or go in groups, waves, two-by-two, or individually.

"Timber!" (Polliwog to Fish)

In waist-deep water, have swimmers stand at least an arm's length apart. Tell them that when you shout "Timber!" they should fall like a tree into the water. At different times, ask them to fall with hands at sides or over the head and to fall into a front or back float. After floating for various periods of time, have swimmers get up and start over. Intermediate students can do this from the side of the pool into deeper water.

Honest Abes* (Minnow to Fish)

Equipment Needed: pennies (four or five per student)

This game reinforces not only treading water, but also the value of honesty. Divide the class into two groups, then hand out four or five pennies to each student. Ask the students to place half of the pennies turned face down on the deck and half with Honest Abe turned up.

Have the students tread water about four feet from the side. Tell them that you will call out a statement. If they think it is true, they should rush out of the water and turn over all their pennies so Honest Abe is showing; if they think it is not, they should turn over all their pennies so Abe is face down. The first team to turn all the pennies over correctly is the winner.

As it is a quick game, you can play it several times; just remember to turn half the pennies over before you begin again.

Kickboard Stunts (Minnow and up)

Equipment Needed: kickboards (one for each student)

Move students into deep water. Hand out a kickboard to each, then ask them to try to balance on it in a sitting position. Once they have achieved this, ask them to try variations such as these:

- Spinning in a circle
- Pretending to row while sitting on the board, using the breaststroke or crawl stroke pulls or variations of sculling
- Performing a front or back flip while squeezing the board behind the knees, with the arms pulling opposite the direction of the flip

- Placing the board underneath the body to practice front crawl, butterfly, and breaststroke arm strokes (with no kick)
- Performing a handstand on the board
- Balancing on the board in a kneeling position
- Floating on the back with the board under the feet or behind the legs at the knees

Instructor Note: *Make sure that students control the boards if they slip off. Otherwise, the boards may pop up and hit other students. Make sure students are in the middle of the pool away from the sides. Then, if they fall off, they won't hit the edges of the pool.*

Squid Swim (Minnow and up)

Move students to chest-deep water. Tell them to try to move feet first and face down on the bottom of the pool. Explain that they should first lie on the bottom, then bend their elbows and bring their hands to their shoulders. With the hands kept close to the body, they should slowly move the arms back to the sides. Then, with palms facing away from the body, they should forcefully pull their arms overhead as if to clap their hands above the head. (This is the same action used in a feet-first surface dive.) Legs should be held together and straight. Students should repeat this series of actions to continue moving backwards.

Instructor Note: *Make sure no one hyperventilates during this activity.*

Breath Control

London Bridge (Parent/Child and Preschool)

Equipment Needed: a large plastic hoop (optional)

You and another instructor or two parents make a bridge by holding hands (or a hoop may be used instead). Have the students go through the bridge until the end of the song, when the bridge is dropped down and a child is caught inside. Sing the following song:

"London Bridge is falling down,
Falling down, falling down,
London Bridge is falling down,
My fair lady/gentleman."

Other verses include "London Bridge is all washed out," "Here's a fish that we have caught," and "In the water it must go."

Teeter-Totter (Preschool and Polliwog)

In water no more than chest deep, have students choose partners and face each other holding hands or grasping each other's wrists. One partner bobs underwater and exhales through the mouth and nose. As that partner returns to the surface for another breath, the other partner goes underwater and exhales. The action looks like that of a teeter-totter. Variations include these two:

- Both buddies jump up at the same time and move a quarter or a half turn in the same direction. When they land, they go underwater and blow bubbles.
- One partner tows the other in a front float position. The partner being towed practices rhythmic breathing.

Jack-in-the-Box (Preschool and Polliwog)

Move the students to waist- to chest-deep water. Then move to each one and have that student place his or her hand on your head. Go under the water, then pop back up as a jack-in-the-box would. Next place your hand on the student's head and have him or her go under, then pop up. (Don't force the child under; just apply a little pressure, and the student usually will go under.) You also can try having the student hold a body part (foot, hand, ear) as he or she goes under and pop up still holding that part.

Ring-Around-the-Rosy*
(Preschool and Polliwog)

Equipment Needed: recording of "Ring-Around-the-Rosy" and a record, CD, or tape player (optional)

Have students form a circle in waist- to chest-deep water. In the circle, which may include parents for young children, sing "Ring-Around-the-Rosy":

   "Ring-around-the-rosy,
   Pocket full of posies,
   Ashes, ashes [or water, water],
   We all fall down [or substitute other skill name]."

At the last line, everyone submerges together. Besides submerging, you also can end the rhyme with skills such as blowing bubbles or floating on the front or back. For very young children who should not be submerged, their parents can hold them as they stand in a circle and put the children into the water on the last line, but not submerge them.

To make this an activity that emphasizes the value of honesty, ask students to keep their eyes open when they go underwater. Tell them that

they can wave while underwater if they want. Afterwards, ask them if they kept their eyes open, then ask whether they are being honest and whether they saw anyone wave.

Obstacle Course
(Preschool, Polliwog and up)

Equipment Needed: diving bricks, kickboards, buoyed lines, rope, large plastic hoops, mats, poker chips, buckets, balls, or other pool equipment as desired, and a stopwatch or a clock that times to the second

Create an obstacle course in water that is waist-deep to over the head (depending on students' skill level) using some of the equipment listed above. Specify which skills you want students to use in different parts of the course in order to provide skill-specific practice. Swimmers first try to swim through the course without stopping, then swim through for time. This also can be done as a relay race. For beginners, you can create a shallow-water course that emphasizes above-water skills. Add variety by having students perform different skills or strokes to get to each obstacle.

Instructor Note: *Caution students not to hyperventilate before going underwater.*

Chin Ball Relay (Polliwog and up)

Equipment Needed: small balls (tennis, table tennis, racquetball), one for each team

Move students to thigh- to chest-deep water and divide the class into teams, with half of each team on opposite sides. Hand out a ball to the first person on each team. Then ask them to push the ball with the chin, mouth, or face while walking across the pool holding the hands behind the back. They are to push the ball until

it touches the far edge of the pool, then have another team member standing on the opposite side of the pool take over. The relay continues back and forth until all students have participated at least once. Variations on this activity are having students carry and pass the ball by tucking it between the chin and chest, or playing the game as an exploration without teams. Intermediate swimmers can swim in deeper water to perform this activity.

Dive Sticks* (Guppy and up)

Equipment Needed: dive sticks or discs with numbers on them

This activity focuses on honesty. Put at least five dive sticks (or discs with numbers) on the bottom of the pool. Then give the students 30 seconds to pull up as many different sticks as they can. When they see the number, they drop the stick back into the pool. After 30 seconds, the students come to the side and tell you how many points they got. Talk about being honest when adding up points, even though there is no way anyone would know how many they got.

Water Scramble (Guppy and up)

Equipment Needed: 100 or more of any of the following—blocks, rubber rings, pennies, poker chips

Scatter 100 or more sinkable objects randomly over the area of the pool you want to use. Then tell the students to dive to the bottom to collect as many objects as they can. The student with the most objects wins. This can be played with teams or individually.

Frogmen (Minnow and up)

Equipment Needed: bright objects that are heavy enough to sink (one for each team)

Divide the class into teams and have each team line up single file in chest-deep water facing the other side of the pool. Place a bright object that sinks at the feet of the first student on each team. Tell them that, on the signal, "Go!" the first student must go underwater and, without coming up, move the object toward the opposite side of the pool as far as possible. Then the next student must go underwater and move the object as far as he or she is able without coming up. One by one, each student takes a turn. The first team to get the object across the pool wins.

Instructor Note: *Caution students not to hyperventilate before going underwater.*

Hot and Cold (Minnow and up)

Equipment Needed: a small object the same color as the pool bottom, a stopwatch or clock that times to the second

Have all students stand on the deck at the side of the pool. Choose one student to close his or her eyes and face away from the water as you place the object on the bottom of the pool. The other students see where you place it. Then tell the chosen student to open his or her eyes, enter the water, and search for the "hidden" object. The students on the deck yell "hot" if the student who is searching is getting closer to the object and "cold" if the student who is searching moves farther away from it. Each student gets a chance to search and is timed. The student who finds the object the quickest wins.

Scrabble* (Minnow and up)

Equipment Needed: scrabble letters

This activity emphasizes the core values. Drop Scrabble letters that spell one of the four core values into the pool. Then have students swim out and try to bring one of the letters back. Have them place the letters on the deck, try to figure out what the word is, and spell it with the letters. Give them hints as necessary. Do this for each value.

Submarine Relay (Minnow and up)

Move students to shallow water and divide them into groups of four or five. Have each group line up single file starting at the pool wall and going out into the pool. Students should stand with their legs spread wide. The student nearest the wall goes underwater, pushes off the side or bottom, and swims through the other students' legs to come up in front. The person next closest to the wall then does the same thing, and students continue doing this until their group is across the pool.

Over and Under (Minnow and up)

Divide the class into two teams. Have them face each other from opposite sides of the swimming area. On your command, one team swims across the pool under water and the other one swims it on the surface. The teams then switch swimming under or on top of the water.

Instructor Note: *Warn students not to hyperventilate before swimming underwater and explain the dangers of doing this.*

Buddy Swim Relay (Fish and up)

Divide the class into teams with an even number of players. Move all teams to water at least chest-deep at the same end of the pool, then have each student pair off with a teammate as a buddy. Each buddy pair must complete two legs of the race. One leg is done with one buddy leading, then they trade places and the second buddy leads. When all buddy pairs have completed their part of the race, the team has finished. The winning team is the one that completes all legs of the race the fastest.

Variations could include either having one buddy do the arm stroke and the other do the legs or having them swim a different stroke for each leg of the race.

Ring/Letter Dive (Fish and up)

Equipment Needed: weighted rings or plastic letters

Either form teams or have students play individually. Scatter the rings or letters on the bottom of the pool, then have students dive for them. Weighted rings that stand upright on the bottom of the pool can be brought up by color or number. Another option is plastic letters, which can be gathered in order to form a word. Then the team or individual who brings up the most rings in the right order or who forms the most words wins.

Charlie, Over the Water (Flying Fish)

Equipment Needed: a big plastic ring or similar object

Have students form a circle in waist-deep water and tread water. One student should be in the middle; this is "Charlie." "Charlie" says the following rhyme:

"Charlie on the water,
  Charlie on the sea,
  Charlie catch a big fish,
  But can't catch me."

On the first line of the rhyme, all students drop a big plastic ring in front of them. On the last line, everyone dives underwater, finds the ring, and comes up and swims to the shallow end. Charlie tries to tag someone before he or she comes up. The tagged person becomes Charlie and the game continues.

Brick Recovery Race (Minnow to Shark)

Equipment Needed: a diving brick

Place a diving brick in about six and a half feet of water, two-thirds of the pool's length from the starting position. Have students start from a mark about 15 yards from the water, run through the water, swim to the point above the brick, surface dive, recover the brick, and return it to the starting point. The brick must be carried in one hand and cannot be placed inside the person's bathing suit. Students may form pairs to carry the brick, or one person may recover the brick and give it to a buddy to carry.

Variations include using a smaller object such as a hockey puck or, for beginners, playing in waist- to chest-deep water, recovering objects with the feet.

Instructor Note: Warn students not to hyperventilate before swimming underwater and explain the dangers of doing this.

Body Position

Head, Shoulders, Knees, and Toes (Preschool and Polliwog)

Equipment Needed: kickboards (optional)

Have the children form a line in waist- to chest-deep water facing you or another leader. The leader gives rapid-fire directions for which body parts to touch. Students try to touch those parts with both hands as fast as the parts are called out. They may have to submerse themselves to touch the knees and toes. Make the game splashy so everyone gets wet. A variation on this game would be to touch the called-out body parts to the water's surface or to a kickboard floating in front of each student.

Superman II (Preschool and Polliwog)

Move the students to waist- to chest-deep water, depending upon their skill level. Tell them to pretend to be Superman or Superwoman flying and to assume an extended flying position (front float) with arms extended and legs straight. This can also be done with the back float, with some modification. Students can be asked to float for a certain period of time and can float holding hands with a partner, if desired.

Zig Zag (Preschool, Polliwog, and up)

Have students stand single file in a line from the pool wall out into the pool. One at a time, each student should swim around the other students in a figure-eight pattern, then return to his or her place in line. They can use any stroke. Try relay races between lines or timed trials for individual swimmers.

Fox and Rabbit (Ray, Starfish, Polliwog, and up)

Equipment Needed: two water polo balls (or balls of similar size)

Move students to water waist- to chest-deep and ask them to form a circle. Give the student who is designated the "fox" one ball. Give the student opposite the "fox" in the circle, who is designated the "rabbit," the other ball. Tell students that, on your signal, they should quickly pass the ball in a clockwise direction, seeing if the "fox" ball can catch the "rabbit" ball. The game ends when the "fox" ball catches up with the "rabbit" ball.

Up and Over (Minnow and up)

Equipment Needed: two plastic hoops big enough for students to dive through

Have students line up in the water along the pool wall. You should stand a distance away from them in the pool, holding one hoop in one hand and one in the other. One at a time, have students dive from the water through one hoop, go to the bottom, push up, and then dive through the second hoop. Encourage students to try to go through both hoops without stopping, with arms extended and hands grabbed.

Porpoise Dives (Flying Porpoise) (Guppy and up)

Move students to chest-deep water. Tell them to pretend to be porpoises. Explain that they should begin in a standing position, with the arms above the head and hands grabbed, then bend their knees and push off the bottom, dive over the surface of the water, and reach for the bottom of the pool. They should tuck the head between the arms during the dive, keeping the arms in front of the head until the hands touch the bottom. They then should push off the bottom with their hands and return to a standing position.

Instructor Note: Watch to make sure all students keep their arms over their heads throughout the dive to keep from hitting the head on the bottom. Tell students to keep their eyes open and to travel in the same direction so they don't collide.

Propulsion

Canoe, Train, Bus

(see this game in the Water Orientation section)

Kickboard Push
(Preschool, Polliwog, and up)

Equipment Needed: kickboards (one for each pair of students)

Have students pair up, and give each pair a kickboard. Each student should hold one end of the board. When you give the signal, both students should begin to flutter kick vigorously. The object is to push the opponent backward three out of five times. When the first round is over, students should pair up with new partners.

Twenty Ways (Preschool, Polliwog, and up)

Ask students to show as many ways of moving through the water as possible. Beginners can use skills they can do standing on the bottom, while intermediate and advanced students should use swimming skills. You can demonstrate movements for entering, leaving, going through, or moving under the water. Variations on this activity include working as a group or as competing teams to come up with skills, or limiting skills to one type (entering, propulsion on front or on back).

Wave to the "Fishies"
(Ray, Starfish, and Polliwog to Minnow)

Have students stand in a line in the shallow end of the pool. Tell them "We are going to lie on our backs and kick to the other end. We are going to pretend that there are 'fishies' at the bottom of the pool." Tell the students to move their hands in a sculling movement as they wave to the "fishies." You can also have students vary the speed, distance, and direction of movement (feet first or head first).

Forty Ways to Get There
(Polliwog and up)

Have students line up at one end (or side) of the pool. Have the first student in line swim across the pool using a stroke of his or her own choice. The second student should then swim across using a different stroke. Each student should swim across using a stroke different from those that came before, and any innovative way to move through the water is acceptable. If you play for more than one round, change the order of the students for each round.

Paddle-Push (Polliwog and up)

Equipment Needed: soft balls (one for each team)

Divide the class into teams and have them line up on deck at the side of the pool. Give the first person in each line a ball, and tell them that they should paddle across the pool pushing the ball with the chin. When they get to the other side, they should turn and throw the ball back to the next person in line, who will then jump into the water and push the ball across again. They should do this for each person on the team until all team members are on the other side of the pool. The first ones to do this win.

Plastic Jug Races (Polliwog and up)

Equipment Needed: empty plastic jugs or other IFDs, rinsed (two for each student)

Hand out two plastic jugs to each student. Tell them to place one jug under each arm and to hold the handles. They should practice balancing (with the body aligned vertically) and moving forward. You can end the activity with races in which students move forward while holding the jugs.

Variations on this activity include treading water, rotating in a circular motion, changing directions, and racing a shorter distance.

Log Push (Polliwog and up)

See this game in the Endurance section.

Chin Ball Relay (Polliwog and up)

See this game in the Breath Control section.

Newspaper Race (Fish and up)

Equipment Needed: full pages of newspaper (one for each student)

Have students line up along one side of the pool, either on deck or in the pool, and give each student a newspaper page. Tell them that they must swim across the pool holding the page out of the water. The object is to keep the page as dry as possible, and splashing another student's page is not allowed.

The winner of the race is determined by adding together two scores, one for order of arrival and one for how dry the paper is, to find the highest score. The first swimmer to arrive receives a number equal to the number of students in the race, with each subsequent finisher getting a score one less than the previous finisher. The swimmer with the driest paper gets a score equal to the number of students in the race, also, and the student with the next-driest paper gets one less than that, and so on. If there is a tie, the two students should have a race-off.

Variations on this activity include doing it as a team relay race or using umbrellas or flags instead of newspaper (no scoring for wetness).

Newspaper Relay (Fish and up)

Equipment Needed: full pages of newspaper (one for each student)

Have students line up along one side of the pool in waist-deep to over-the-head water, and give each student a newspaper page. Tell students to swim a set distance on their backs while reading the page aloud and without getting the page wet. Variations on this include forming teams and doing it as a relay race, having them swim with an adapted sidestroke, or holding an endurance contest to see who can swim the farthest without soaking the newspaper.

Endurance

Marco Polo* (Polliwog and up)

Equipment Needed: a blindfold

Move students to water at a depth that is comfortable for them. Choose one student to be "It" and blindfold him or her. He or she must try to locate and tag the other students by calling "Marco" and listen as the other students say "Polo" in return. When "It" tags someone, that person becomes "It."

To make this activity one that emphasizes the value of honesty, talk about being honest before playing. Ask "Is the game any fun if you cheat? Who thinks he or she can be honest when we play?" After the game, ask students what they learned about being honest.

Log Push (Polliwog and up)

Equipment Needed: an eight-foot water log or a reaching pole

Divide the class into two equal teams. Then place the log or reaching pole in the center of the pool. Have each team move to the center and tread water on opposite sides, with each student facing inward with both hands placed on the log or pole. Tell students that, on your signal, they all should start kicking in order to force the opposing team to the opposite side of the pool.

Battleship (Polliwog and up)

Have students imagine that the pool is a battleship. The deep end is the *bow* of the ship, the shallow end the *stern, port* is the left side as you face the bow, and *starboard* is the right side as you face the bow. Tell students that you will say one of these directions and that they should respond by swimming to that side and sitting on or touching the pool edge. For instance, if you said "port," the students should swim to the left side of the pool.

Balloon Relay (Guppy and up)

Equipment Needed: blown-up balloons (one for each student)

Have students line up in the water along a pool wall and give each one a blown-up balloon. Tell them that, on your signal, they should push the balloon with the nose, cheeks, or forehead while swimming across the pool. This also can be played as a relay team game: One person pushes the balloon across the pool to a teammate on the other side of the pool, who swims it back. The relay continues until all members of each team finish.

Baton Relay (Guppy and up)

Equipment Needed: two batons

Move your class to the deck and divide the students into two teams. Have each team line up. Give the first player on each team a baton, and tell students that on the signal, that player should jump into the water and paddle stroke to the end of the pool, where you will be standing. The player must tap you with the baton, turn over on his or her back, swim back to the start, and hand the baton to the next person in line. If someone loses the baton, he or she must retrieve it before continuing. The race continues until both teams have finished.

Tube Relay (Guppy and up)

Equipment Needed: inner tubes (one for each team)

Divide the class into teams, with half of each team at opposite sides of the pool. Each person on the team will end up crossing the pool three times, switching off to a teammate on the other side of the pool between lengths. In the first heat, everyone sits in the tube. In the second heat, everyone lays on his or her stomach on the tube. In the last heat, everyone pulls the tube across.

Water Baseball (Guppy and up)

Equipment Needed: a soft playground or foam ball

Divide the class into two teams. The batter starts on deck, and the pitcher throws the ball to him or her. The batter hits the ball with his or her arm, then jumps or dives into the pool (depending on water depth) and swims bases. The basic baseball rules apply to this game, and you should establish where foul territory is when you begin. As a variation, the batter can start in the water.

Instructor Note: Make sure no one dives in water that is too shallow. Set up play to avoid collisions. Younger children may want to try kickball.

Water Scramble (Guppy and up)

See this game in the Breath Control section.

Hang on Harvey (Minnow and up)

Divide the class into teams. Half of each team should be standing at either end of the pool. The first student in line should swim one length. At the end of the length, he or she picks up the next team member, who hangs on to the first student's feet throughout the return lap. When the first student touches the end, he or she gets out of the pool and the second team member becomes the lead swimmer. The third team member then holds on to the second member's feet as he or she swims back, and so on. The race continues until all team members except the first have had a turn at hanging on.

T-Shirt Relay (Minnow and up)

See this game in the Advanced Strokes section.

Over and Under (Minnow and up)

See this game in the Breath Control section.

Blockade Runner (Fish and up)

Equipment Needed: kickboards

Mark off a large, rectangular playing area in the pool. Then divide the class up into two equal teams and hand out a kickboard to each student. Have each team line up at its end of the playing area. Once you give the signal, the students should kick toward the opposite side, trying to reach it without being blocked by the other team. Students must hold both hands on their kickboards at all times. The boards can be used for either flotation or blocking, but they must remain flat at all times. The first team to have three students make it to the other side wins.

Three-Legged Swim Relay (Fish and up)

Equipment Needed: rubber leg bands made from inner tube strips (one for each pair of swimmers)

Divide the class into teams of even numbers. Have each teammate choose a partner. Then have each pair put on a rubber leg band over the inside legs and swim with their legs together. The race is done as a relay, with the team that finishes first winning. Supervise the game closely.

Buddy Swim Relay (Fish and up)

See this game in the Breath Control section.

Advanced Strokes

Cork Scramble (Preschool, Polliwog, and up)

Equipment Needed: corks, table tennis balls, tennis balls, small rubber balls, life jackets, or other small items that float

Ask the class to turn their backs as you spread various floating objects in a designated area of the pool. Then tell them to turn around on your signal, enter the water (in whatever way you tell them), and gather as many floating objects as they can. When all the objects have been collected, each student should count his or hers. The student with the most objects wins.

A fun variation on this activity is a mystery scramble. In this version each floating object has a number value assigned to it, but the value is not told to the students until after the objects have been collected. For example, in the first round, rubber balls might be worth 10 points; tennis balls, 15 points; and life jackets, 20 points. The points assigned would then change in the subsequent rounds. The winner in these games is the student whose objects have the highest number of points.

Either of these games can be played by teams rather than individuals.

Zig Zag (Preschool, Polliwog, and up)

See this game in the Body Position section.

Carps and Cranes (Polliwog and up)

Mark off a square or rectangular playing area in which a lane line divides the center. Mark end lines clearly, as they will serve as home bases for the teams. Then divide your class into two equal teams and have them line up along the lane line facing each other, with the end lines behind them. One team is called "carps," and the other team is called "cranes." Tell students that you will call out either "carps" or "cranes," and that when you do, the team that is called out should try to catch members of the opposing team before they can reach the safety of their end line. The captured members join the other team. The team that has the most players at the end of play wins.

Hunter (Guppy to Fish)

Equipment Needed: kickboards or other floating objects (one for each student)

Assign each student to a special spot, which is marked by a kickboard or other floating object. Then designate one student as the "hunter" and ask him or her to lead the other students out into the pool using a specific stroke or movement. The students should follow the hunter in follow-the-leader fashion. Warn them that you will give a signal, and that when you do, they all must race back to their special spots. The first player back to his or her spot wins. To keep students alert, you can shout out words other than the designated signal.

Pennies for Respect* (Minnow to Fish)

Equipment Needed: pennies (three for each student)

Place two or three pennies per student on each side of the pool. Then name one side *respectful* and the other side *disrespectful*. Tell them that you will make a statement, such as "Just because someone has an opinion different from mine doesn't mean I don't like him or her," or "Johnny is only five years old, so I don't have to listen to anything he says," and they must decide whether that statement is respectful or disrespectful. When the statement is respectful, they have to swim a penny from the disrespectful side to the other side and vice versa, until all the pennies are on the respectful side. Tell them which stroke to swim.

T-Shirt Relay (Minnow and up)

Equipment Needed: big T-shirts (one for each team)

Divide the class into relay teams, with half of each team at opposite sides of the pool. (Weaker swimmers can swim in the shallow end. This exercise is done across the pool widthwise.) In moderate to deep water, have the first member of each team swim a prescribed stroke and distance wearing a big T-shirt. At the end of the lap, he or she pulls the T-shirt off and passes it to the next swimmer, who puts it on and crosses

back, then hands the shirt to the next teammate. The team that finishes first wins. (The game also can be played using socks, caps, goggles, pajamas, and so on.)

Repeat with students performing other strokes or having swimmers do a medley, where each performs a different stroke. Another variation is having two swimmers wear one T-shirt and swim together.

Hurray for Hollywood (Fish)

Have one student sit on the diving board opposite the others, who are lined up on the other side of the pool. The student on the diving board thinks of a movie or television show and gives the other players clues, one at a time. When someone thinks he or she knows the answer, that player asks to swim across. The student on the diving board names the stroke that must be used, and the player swims across to the student using that stroke in order to whisper to him or her what the answer is. If the answer is right, the two exchange places. If more than one person claims to know the answer, they all swim over, with the one who gets there first giving the answer first.

Corkscrew Swim (Fish and up)

In water at least three feet deep (deeper for better swimmers), have students swim the front crawl (face in or out). Ask them to perform one stroke of the front crawl using the right arm, roll over, then perform one stroke of the back crawl with the left arm. They should continue alternating as they swim across the pool, always rolling in the same direction. This looks like a corkscrew.

This activity also can be varied by combining different strokes. For example, the first stroke cycle can be the front crawl, then a roll to the side and two sidestrokes, and then a roll to the back for one stroke cycle of the backstroke. Another example is performing two breaststrokes, rolling to the side for two sidestrokes, then rolling to the back for the elementary backstroke or back crawl.

Instructor Note: Watch that students don't become dizzy or disoriented. To help students avoid dizziness, tell them to keep their faces out of the water, spot something at the end of the pool, and swim toward it.

Cat and Mouse (Fish and up)

Divide the class into two teams. The students on Team 1 can swim any stroke they want in order to tag a member of the second team, but they may not climb out of the pool. The students on Team 2 may swim only the breaststroke, but they have the advantage of being able to get in and out of the pool to avoid being tagged. As soon as a student is tagged, he or she gets out of the pool. The goal is to be the last one tagged.

Stroke Switch (Fish and up)

Have students dive into deep water (at least nine feet deep) and swim across the pool on your command. Switch the type of stroke they do at the end of each lap. The number of consecutive laps can be varied. Variations include increasing the number of laps; assigning different strokes to different students; or running it as a switching medley relay, with each swimmer doing a different stroke in each round.

Teamwork

Baton Relay (Guppy and up)

See this game in the Endurance section.

Fan Race (Minnow and up)

Equipment Needed: fans (one for each student)
Divide the class into teams, and have each team line up at a starting line. Give each student a fan. Tell students that, on your signal, the first team members should swim to the finish line on their backs, holding the fans out of the water. You may assign a particular kick or allow them to choose one. The next team members start when the first ones reach the finish line.

T-Shirt Relay (Minnow and up)

See this game in the Advanced Strokes section.

Frogmen (Minnow and up)

See this game in the Breath Control section.

Cat and Mouse (Fish and up)

See this game in the Advanced Strokes section.

Buddy Swim Relay (Fish and up)

See this game in the Breath Control section.

Miscellaneous

Hug Our Baby* (Parent/Child or Parent/Child and Preschool)

This highlights the value of caring. Sing these verses to the tune of "Mulberry Bush":
"This is the way we splash our hands, etc." [Splash with hands.]
"This is the way we kick our feet, etc." [Kick with feet.]
"This is the way we hug our baby, etc." [Hug pretend baby.]

Values Review* (Guppy)

This activity is a review of the four core values previously discussed in class. Tell students that you are assigning a skill to each of the four values, as in this example.
→ Caring: bobbing
→ Honesty: kicking while holding on to the wall
→ Respect: blowing bubbles
→ Responsibility: floating on the back

Then call out a value and have the students perform the skill that corresponds to it.

Honest Ball* (Shark)

Equipment Needed: two beach balls or small playground balls
This activity highlights the value of honesty. Divide the class into two groups. Give the groups a few minutes to come up with a water game using the ball and decide on rules. Then have each group share the game that will be played and the rules to follow, and have the class as a whole play the game for a few minutes.

After playing the games, discuss the rules of the games. Were they followed? Did the rules change during the game? Why? Talk about the importance of being honest and playing by the rules. Even if the rules need to be changed, the changes need to be discussed and agreed upon. Talk about a time during the games when one of the rules had to be changed and how it was changed.

Games Index

An asterisk (*) after the name indicates the game also addresses one or more of the core values. If more than one category is listed for a game, the description of the game appears in the first category named.

Game	Category	Skill Level	Page Number
Balloon Relay	Endurance	Guppy and up	144
Baton Relay	Endurance Teamwork	Guppy and up	144
Battleship	Endurance	Polliwog and up	144
Blockade Runner	Endurance	Fish and up	145
Brick Recovery Race	Breath control	Minnow to Shark	142
Buddy Swim Relay	Breath control Endurance Teamwork	Fish and up	141
Canoe, Train, Bus	Water orientation Propulsion		134
Can't Touch Me	Buoyancy Balance	Preschool and Polliwog	137
Carps and Cranes	Advanced strokes	Polliwog and up	145
Cat and Mouse	Advanced strokes	Fish and up	146
Charlie, Over the Water	Breath control	Flying Fish	141
Chin Ball Relay	Breath control	Polliwog and up	140
Choo-Choo Train	Water orientation	Parent/Child and Preschool, Polliwog to Minnow	135
Cork Scramble	Advanced strokes Water orientation	Preschool, Polliwog and up	145
Corkscrew Swim	Advanced strokes	Fish and up	146
Did You Ever See a Swimmer?	Water orientation	Polliwog to Minnow	136
Dive Sticks*	Breath control	Guppy and up	140
Easter Egg Coloring Time	Water entry and exit	Parent/Child and Preschool and Polliwog	136
Fan Race	Teamwork	Minnow and up	147
Flip Flops	Flotation Buoyancy Balance	Polliwog to Minnow	138
Forty Ways to Get There	Propulsion	Polliwog and up	143
Fox and Rabbit	Body position	Ray, Starfish, Polliwog and up	142
Frogmen	Breath control Teamwork	Minnow and up	141
Gingerbread Cookie	Flotation	Preschool and Polliwog to Guppy	138
Glide and Slide	Flotation	Polliwog to Guppy	138
Hang on Harvey	Endurance	Minnow and up	145
Head, Shoulders, Knees, and Toes	Body position	Preschool and Polliwog	142
Hokey Pokey	Water orientation	Parent/Child and Preschool and Polliwog	135
Honest Abes*	Flotation	Minnow to Fish	139
Honest Ball*	Misc.	Shark	147
Honesty Pass*	Buoyancy Balance	All levels	138
Hoops	Buoyancy Balance	Minnow and up	137
Hot and Cold	Breath control	Minnow and up	141
Hug Our Baby*	Misc.	Parent/Child	147
Humpty Dumpty	Water entry and exit	Parent/Child and Preschool and Polliwog	136
Hunter	Advanced strokes	Guppy to Fish	145
Hurray for Hollywood	Advanced strokes	Fish	146
I Make My Arms Go Up and Down	Water entry and exit	Parent/Child and Preschool and Polliwog	137
I'm a Little Teapot	Water entry and exit	Parent/Child and Preschool and Polliwog	137
Jack-in-the-Box	Breath control	Parent/Child and Preschool and Polliwog	140

Game	Skill	Level	Page
Jump Into My Circle	Water entry and exit	Parent/Child and Preschool and Polliwog	136
Kickboard Push	Propulsion	Preschool, Polliwog and up	143
Kickboard Stunts	Flotation Buoyancy Balance	Minnow and up	139
Log Push	Endurance Propulsion	Polliwog and up	144
London Bridge	Breath control	Parent/Child and Preschool	139
Marco Polo*	Endurance	Polliwog and up	144
Name Game	Water orientation	SKIPPERS and Polliwog	135
Newspaper Race	Propulsion	Fish and up	143
Newspaper Relay	Propulsion	Fish and up	144
Obstacle Course	Breath control	Preschool, Polliwog and up	140
Over and Under	Breath control Endurance	Minnow and up	141
Over and Under Passing	Buoyancy Balance Water orientation	Polliwog to Fish	137
Paddle-Push	Propulsion	Polliwog and up	143
Parachute Jump	Water entry and exit	Parent/Child and Preschool and Polliwog	136
Pennies for Respect*	Advanced strokes	Minnow to Fish	146
Plastic Jug Races	Propulsion	Polliwog and up	143
Pop Goes the Weasel	Water orientation	Parent/Child and Preschool and Polliwog	135
Porpoise Dives	Body position	Guppy and up	142
Red Light, Green Light	Water orientation	Parent/Child and Preschool and Polliwog to Minnow	135
Ring-Around-the-Rosy*	Breath control Water orientation	Preschool and Polliwog	140
Ring/Letter Dive	Breath control	Fish and up	141
Rocket Booster	Water entry and exit	Guppy and up	137
Scrabble*	Breath control	Minnow and up	141
Simon Says	Water orientation	Parent/Child and Preschool and Polliwog	135
Squid Swim	Flotation Buoyancy Balance	Minnow and up	139
Stroke Switch	Advanced strokes	Fish and up	146
Submarine Relay	Breath control	Minnow and up	141
Superman	Flotation	Polliwog to Fish	138
Superman II	Body position	Preschool and Polliwog	142
Synchro Chain*	Buoyancy and balance	Flying Fish to Shark	138
Teeter-Totter	Breath control	Preschool and Polliwog	139
Three-Legged Swim Relay	Endurance	Fish and up	145
Tidal Wave	Buoyancy and balance	Preschool and Polliwog	137
"Timber!"	Flotation	Polliwog to Fish	138
Treasure Hunt	Buoyancy and balance	Fish and up	138
T-Shirt Relay	Advanced strokes Endurance Teamwork	Minnow and up	146
Tube Relay	Endurance	Guppy and up	144
Twenty Ways	Propulsion	Preschool, Polliwog and up	143
Up and Over	Body position	Minnow and up	142
Values Review*	Misc.	Guppy	147
Water Baseball	Endurance	Guppy and up	144
Water Scramble	Breath control Endurance	Guppy and up	140
Wave to the "Fishies"	Propulsion	Ray, Starfish, and Polliwog to Minnow	143
Zig Zag	Body position Advanced strokes	Preschool, Polliwog and up	142

Appendix B

Medical Advisory Committee Statements
Related to Aquatics

This appendix contains statements made by the YMCA of the USA Medical Advisory Committee on the following topics:

→ AIDS: Operating Guidelines for YMCAs
→ Child Abuse Identification and Prevention: Recommended Guidelines for YMCAs
→ Diving Board Guidelines for YMCAs
→ Exposure to Natural Sunlight in YMCA Programs for Children and Adults

AIDS: Operating Guidelines for YMCAs

Statement of the YMCA of the USA Medical Advisory Committee:

All YMCAs are obligated to act in compliance with the Occupational Safety and Health Administration (OSHA) training and documentation requirements regarding AIDS. They are also required to have an exposure control plan relative to AIDS and other infectious diseases that meets OSHA requirements, and to comply with local and state standards regarding infectious materials.

These approved operating guidelines for YMCAs are based on scientific information that says people with AIDS and those who test HIV positive do not pose a significant health risk to others in a YMCA setting. It is well known that AIDS is transmitted by intimate sexual contact or by exposure to contaminated blood.

The United States Public Health Service states that there is no risk created by living in the same house where an infected person lives, eating food handled by an infected person, being coughed or sneezed upon by an infected person, casual kissing, or swimming in a pool with an infected person. There is no medical evidence to exclude members from gymnasiums, pools, locker rooms, showers, snack bars, or any other recreational areas.

These guidelines are consistent with YMCA values that encourage youth and adults not to use drugs and encourage people not to have sexual relations unless they are in mature, caring, monogamous relationships.

YMCA values further compel us to help and show compassion to those who have the disease and to those who don't share the same values.

Finally, *the guidelines should not be seen as a blanket policy, but rather should be applied on a case-by-case basis* by local YMCAs as new medical information becomes available. To help in this effort, YMCAs should seek the best medical advice available in the operation of programs and facilities by appointing a medical advisory committee. Members should know about the evolving body of information related to AIDS and YMCA support actions that are consistent with the best information available.

1. Implement an AIDS education program for staff, volunteers, members, and the public.

Member associations should take a proactive stance regarding the education of staff, volunteers, members, and the public as to the nature of the AIDS disease, how it is contracted, and how it can be avoided.

Educational efforts should emphasize that current medical knowledge indicates that YMCA staff, volunteers, and members infected with the AIDS virus do not pose a significant health risk to others involved in YMCA programs, activities, or facilities.

Generally, AIDS education should include four key elements: a) the facts on the AIDS virus and how it is transmitted; b) how to protect oneself from the AIDS virus; c) communicating information about AIDS to others; and d) the local YMCA policies and procedures related to AIDS.

Resources for AIDS education are available from many local and national health organizations.

2. Accept AIDS-infected individuals in YMCA programs, evaluating participation on a case-by-case basis.

Most children and adults diagnosed as having the AIDS virus should be admitted to full participation in YMCA programs without fear of infecting others through casual contact. Decisions on participation should be made on a case-by-case basis by the YMCA.

Exceptions to this practice should be made in accordance with the guidelines established by the Federal Centers for Disease Control.

Refusal to permit any person with AIDS to join the YMCA or to participate in YMCA programs may violate laws protecting the handicapped and should only be undertaken with advice of legal counsel.

3. Consider employees with AIDS as handicapped or disabled, without risk of infecting others through casual contact in the workplace.

The YMCA recognizes its obligation as an employer to provide an objectively safe environment for all employees and the public at large, and an environment where there are no concerns by employees for their personal health and safety.

The YMCA considers AIDS to be a handicapping or disabling condition. An individual who has been diagnosed with AIDS should be treated similarly to any other individual who is handicapped or disabled.

Supervisors should make a concerted effort to educate themselves about AIDS infection and assist in making this information available to all YMCA leadership, both staff and volunteer.

YMCA employees with life-threatening illnesses, including AIDS, may wish to continue to work. As long as they are able to meet acceptable performance standards, and medical evidence indicates that their condition is not a threat to themselves or others, employees should be assured of continued employment.

Federal and state laws may also mandate, pursuant to the laws protecting handicapped or disabled individuals, that those individuals not be discriminated against on that basis, and that if it becomes necessary, some reasonable accommodations be made to enable qualified individuals to continue to work.

Given current technology, and the recommendations of the Federal Centers for Disease Control, testing applicants or current employees for AIDS is not recommended. However, information on voluntary testing should be available to all employees.

The YMCA may deny employment to any individual who cannot meet the bona fide qualifications of the job due to any physical or mental condition or who presents an immediate and real risk to the health or safety of others.

The YMCA recognizes that an employee's health condition is normally personal and confidential. Personnel and medical files or information about employees are generally protected from public disclosure.

4. Encourage practices that protect staff, volunteers, and members.

Because other infections in addition to AIDS can be present in blood or body fluids, YMCAs should adopt routine handling procedures for them, such as these:

Hands should be washed well with soap and water after exposure to blood and body fluids.

Razors and other implements that may become contaminated with blood should not be shared in locker, bath, shower, or steam/sauna rooms.

Rubber gloves should be worn if available when first aid is given to anyone who is bleeding.

Surfaces soiled by blood or body fluids should be promptly cleaned with disinfectants, such as diluted household bleach. Disposable towels or tissues should be used whenever possible.

There is no evidence that in the absence of bleeding the AIDS virus is transmitted through rescue breathing or through "buddy breathing" in scuba training. For protection against blood-borne diseases in rescue breathing situations, it is recommended that a barrier protection device such as a face mask with a one-way valve be used to shield the rescuer from contact with the victim's bodily fluids.

January 1988
Revised May 1991
Revised November 1997

Child Abuse Identification and Prevention: Recommended Guidelines for YMCAs
Statement of the YMCA of the USA Medical Advisory Committee:

Child abuse is damage to a child for which there is no "reasonable" explanation. Child abuse includes nonaccidental physical injury, neglect, sexual molestation, and emotional abuse. The increasing incidence of reported child abuse has become a critical national concern. The reported incidence of physical abuse, sexual abuse, and neglect has tripled since 1980. It is a special concern of the YMCA because of the organization's role as an advocate for children and its responsibility for enhancing the personal growth and development of both children and adults in all YMCA programs.

Each YMCA is encouraged to develop a written policy that clearly defines management practices related to the prevention of child abuse. This policy should include approved practices for recruiting, training, and supervising staff; a code of conduct for staff relationships with children; reporting procedures for incidents when they do occur; and the responsibility to parents on this issue.

To assist YMCAs, the YMCA of the USA has developed a *Child Abuse Prevention Training* manual. This manual includes two three-hour training designs, one for staff who hire and supervise and a second for front-line program staff. Sample policies and procedures are included in both designs. Each YMCA received a copy of the manual in 1994. Additional copies are available from the YMCA Program Store (Item no. 5268). YMCAs are encouraged to offer training on a regular basis for all staff.

The following guidelines have been developed to stimulate thinking about the potential for child abuse in YMCA programs and the need to develop a YMCA policy related to this important issue. Common sense and good judgment should guide the development of required procedures. Good management policies and practices will vary based on local situations. Laws differ from state to state. YMCA administrators need to be aware of changing state and local requirements and monitor YMCA programs to ensure that they are in compliance.

Guidelines for Local YMCAs for Staff Recruitment, Training, and Supervision

1. Reference checks on all prospective employees and program volunteers will be conducted, documented, and filed prior to employment.

2. Fingerprinting and criminal record checks of adults who work in programs such as child care and camping, where authorized or required by state law, are included in the employment process.

3. Photographs will be taken of all staff and attached to personnel records for identification at a later time if needed.

4. All new staff and volunteers must participate in an orientation program that includes written materials explaining YMCA policies, procedures, and regulations. They should be aware of legal requirements and by their signature acknowledge having received and read appropriate policies, standards, and codes of conduct. Documentation of attendance in the Child Abuse Prevention training should be added to the employee's personnel file.

5. Staff and volunteers working directly with children will be provided information regularly about the signs of possible child abuse. They should be educated about "high-risk parents" and "high-risk families" (for example, drug-addicted, alcohol-addicted, mentally ill, unemployed, or teenage parents, and parents who were abused themselves as children). Staff training will include approved procedures for responding to the suspicion of abuse.

6. Administrative staff supervising programs involving the care of children will make unannounced visits to each program site to assure that standards, policies, program quality, and performance of staff are being maintained. Written reports on these visits will be completed.

Guidelines for Staff Relationships with Children

7. In order to protect YMCA staff, volunteers, and program participants, at no time during a YMCA program may a program leader be alone with a single child unobserved by other staff.

8. Young children will never be unsupervised in bathrooms, locker rooms, or showers.

9. Staff members and volunteers are not encouraged to relate to children in YMCA programs in non-YMCA activities, such as babysitting or weekend trips, without the knowledge of the responsible YMCA executive.

10. Adult YMCA staff and volunteers are not encouraged to socialize with program participants under the age of 18 outside of YMCA program activities.

11. YMCA staff and volunteers will not discipline children by use of physical punishment or by failing to provide the necessities of care, such as food and shelter.

12. YMCA staff or volunteers will not verbally or emotionally abuse or punish children.

13. Staff and volunteers providing direct care for very young children will be identified by a badge/name tag or uniform that is familiar to the children with whom they work. Children will be instructed to avoid any person not so identified.

14. Staff and volunteers should be alert to the physical and emotional state of all children each time they report for a program and indicate, in writing, any signs of injury or suspected child abuse.

Guidelines for the YMCA's Responsibilities to Parents

15. Invite parents to serve on interview committees to screen and select staff and volunteers. Caution should be taken in the selection of parents for this function. They should have a thorough understanding of, and be in agreement with, the YMCA's philosophy and operating procedures.

16. Ask parents to sign a Parent Statement of Understanding, which includes a statement limiting staff and program volunteers in their conduct with children and families outside of the YMCA program and which informs parents of the YMCA's mandate to report suspected cases of child abuse or neglect.

17. Conduct an intake/orientation session with all parents to share the program's policies and procedures. Be sure to include the preemployment screening, supervision, code of conduct, training, and other child abuse prevention policies established to protect children.

18. Daily communication should inform parents of their child's health, behavior, positive anecdotes from their day, and so forth.

19. The YMCA should maintain an open-door policy that encourages parents to drop by and observe or share in the program with their child at any time.

20. The YMCA should offer information and assistance to parents through workshops, counseling, book and video lending libraries, and other resources.

21. The YMCA should try to identify families in distress and offer referral information to agencies that can assist them.

22. Through newsletters, conferences, and modeling appropriate interaction skills, the YMCA should inform and educate parents about age-appropriate expectations and discipline.

23. The YMCA curriculum should emphasize children making choices, developing positive self-esteem, sharing feelings, and practicing their assertiveness skills. The YMCA should encourage parents to reinforce these skills at home, as they leave children less vulnerable to maltreatment.

24. The YMCA should sponsor guest speakers who address the issues of child abuse and child-abuse prevention, teach personal safety to children, and cover other related topics. Administrators should screen all individuals and their material before allowing them to present.

Reporting Procedures

25. At the first report or probable cause to believe that child abuse has occurred, the employed staff person it has been reported to will notify the program director, who will then review the incident with the YMCA executive director or his/her designate. However, if the program director is not immediately available, this review by the supervisor cannot in any way deter the reporting of child abuse by the mandated reporters. Most states mandate each teacher or child care provider to report information they have learned in their professional role regarding suspected child abuse. In most states, mandated reporters are granted immunity from prosecution.

26. The YMCA will make a report in accordance with relevant state or local child abuse reporting requirements and will cooperate to the extent of the law with any legal authority involved.

27. In the event the reported incidents involve an employed program volunteer or employed staff, the executive director will, without exception, suspend the volunteer or staff person from the YMCA.

28. The parents or legal guardian of the child(ren) involved in the alleged incident will be promptly notified in accordance with the directions of the relevant state or local agency.

29. Whether the incident or alleged offense takes place on or off YMCA premises, it will be considered job related (because of the youth-involved nature of the YMCA).

30. Reinstatement of the program volunteer or employed staff person will occur only after all allegations have been cleared to the satisfaction of the persons named in (25).

31. All YMCA staff and volunteers must be sensitive to the need for confidentiality in the handling of this information, and, therefore, should only discuss the incident with the persons named in (25).

Possible Indicators of Abuse

Sexual Abuse—Behavioral Indicators

Employees and volunteers may suspect sexual abuse if a child

1. is reluctant to change clothes in front of others,
2. is withdrawn,
3. exhibits unusual sexual behavior and/or knowledge beyond that which is common for his/her developmental stage,
4. has poor peer relationships,
5. either avoids or seeks out adults,
6. is pseudo-mature,
7. is manipulative,
8. is self-conscious,
9. has problems with authority and rules,
10. exhibits eating disorders,
11. is self-mutilating,
12. is obsessively clean,
13. uses or abuses alcohol and/or other drugs,
14. exhibits delinquent behavior, such as running away from home;
15. exhibits extreme compliance or defiance,
16. is fearful or anxious,
17. exhibits suicidal gestures and/or attempts suicide,
18. is promiscuous,
19. engages in fantasy or infantile behavior,
20. is unwilling to participate in sports activities,
21. or has school difficulties.

Sexual Abuse—Physical Indicators

Employees and volunteers should suspect sexual abuse if a child

1. has pain and/or itching in the genital area,
2. has bruises or bleeding in the genital area,
3. has venereal disease,
4. has swollen private parts,
5. has difficulty walking or sitting,
6. has torn, bloody, and/or stained underclothing;
7. experiences pain when urinating,
8. is pregnant,
9. has vaginal or penile discharge, or
10. wets the bed.

Emotional Abuse—Behavioral Indicators

Employees and volunteers may suspect emotional abuse if a child

1. is overly eager to please,
2. seeks out adult contact,
3. views abuse as being warranted,
4. exhibits changes in behavior,
5. is excessively anxious,
6. is depressed,
7. is unwilling to discuss problems,
8. exhibits aggressive or bizarre behavior,
9. is withdrawn,
10. is apathetic,
11. is passive,
12. has unprovoked fits of yelling or screaming,
13. exhibits inconsistent behaviors,
14. feels responsible for the abuser,
15. runs away from home,
16. attempts suicide,
17. exhibits low self-esteem,
18. exhibits a gradual impairment of health and/or personality,
19. has difficulty sustaining relationships,
20. is unrealistic about goal setting,
21. is impatient,
22. is unable to communicate or express his/her feelings, needs, or desires;
23. sabotages his/her chances of success,
24. lacks self-confidence,
25. or is self-deprecating and has a negative self-image,

Emotional Abuse—Physical Indicators

Employees and volunteers may suspect emotional abuse if a child

1. has a sleep disorder (nightmares or restlessness),
2. wets the bed,
3. exhibits developmental lags (stunting of his/her physical, emotional, and/or mental growth),
4. is hyperactive,
5. exhibits eating disorders,

Physical Abuse—Behavioral Indicators

Employees and volunteers may suspect physical abuse if a child

1. is wary of adults,
2. is either extremely aggressive or withdrawn,
3. is dependent and indiscriminate in his/her attachments,
4. is uncomfortable when other children cry,
5. generally controls his/her own crying,
6. exhibits a drastic behavior change when not with parents or care giver,
7. is manipulative,
8. has poor self-concept,
9. exhibits delinquent behavior, such as running away from home;
10. uses or abuses alcohol and/or other drugs,
11. is self-mutilating,
12. is frightened of parents or going home,
13. is overprotective of or responsible for parents,
14. exhibits suicidal gestures and/or attempts suicide,
15. or has behavioral problems at school,

Physical Abuse—Physical Indicators

Employees and volunteers should suspect physical abuse if a child

1. has unexplained* bruises or welts, often clustered or in a pattern;
2. has unexplained* and/or unusual burn (cigarettes, doughnut-shaped, immersion-lines, object-patterned),
3. has unexplained* bite marks,
4. has unexplained* fractures or dislocations,
5. has unexplained* abrasions or lacerations,
6. or wets the bed.

(*Or explanation is inconsistent or improbable.)

Neglect—Behavior Indicators

Employees and volunteers may suspect neglect if a child

1. is truant or tardy often or arrives early and stays late,
2. begs or steals food,
3. attempts suicide,
4. uses or abuses alcohol and/or other drugs,
5. is extremely dependent or detached,
6. engages in delinquent behavior, such as prostitution or stealing;
7. appears to be exhausted,
8. or states frequent or continual absence of parent or guardian.

Neglect—Physical Indicators

Employees and volunteers should suspect neglect if a child

1. frequently is dirty, unwashed, hungry, or inappropriately dressed;
2. engages in dangerous activities (possibly because he/she generally is unsupervised),
3. is tired and listless,
4. has unattended physical problems,
5. or may appear to be overworked and/or exploited.

Family Indicators

Family behavior and background may be a clue to possible child abuse or neglect. Employees and volunteers should be alert for

1. extreme paternal dominance, restrictiveness, and/or overprotectiveness;
2. family isolation from community and support systems;
3. marked role reversal between mother and child,
4. history of sexual abuse by either parent or by children,
5. substance abuse by either parent or by children,
6. other types of violence in the home,
7. absent spouse (through chronic illness, depression, divorce, or separation),
8. severe overcrowding,
9. complaints about a "seductive" child, or
10. extreme objection to implementation of child sexual abuse curriculum.

Source: Becca Cowan Johnson. 1992. *For Their Sake: Recognizing, Responding to, and Reporting Child Abuse.* Martinsville, IN: American Camping Association. Reprinted by permission of the publisher. For permission to reprint please contact the publisher at (756) 342-8456.

Family Indicators section from Committee for Children.

Note: These indicators can also be indicative of emotional dysfunctions that merit investigation for emotional problems and/or being the victims of abuse.

YMCAs are urged to share copies of their management policies related to child abuse with other YMCAs and the YMCA of the USA. A bibliography of printed and audiovisual educational resources for use with parents and children is included in the Child Abuse Prevention Manual, or available from the Program Development Division, YMCA of the USA, 101 North Wacker Drive, Chicago, Illinois 60606.

June 1989
Revised April 1996

Diving Board Guidelines for YMCAs
Statement of the YMCA of the USA Medical Advisory Committee:

Diving has been part of the progressive aquatic program used by YMCAs for years, and springboard diving is an important feature of competitive swimming. These programs are a portion of the developmental component in many swimming programs. They present an exciting and fun part of swimming. However, many YMCAs, because of·liability insurance and other pressures, are reevaluating diving and diving boards to determine whether they will continue to include diving boards in YMCA pools.

The relationship of diving boards to water depth and serious, irreversible injury is being studied by many YMCAs throughout the country Although quality instruction and excellent supervision are of paramount importance in conducting any program safely, certain construction features should be considered.

Many YMCA pools were built to accommodate diving boards unlike the modern springboard being used today. Modern springboards and moveable fulcrums permit the diver to go higher and, therefore, deeper into the swimming pool or diving well. Modern springboards are designed for skilled diving competition and, if properly supervised, can be used safely. If, however, the use of these boards is not properly supervised, a potentially dangerous situation may exist.

The YMCA of the USA follows the National Collegiate Athletic Association (NCAA) rules for diving competition. The preferred water depth for a one-meter board is eleven feet, six inches at the plummet and eleven feet, two inches at sixteen feet, five inches out from the plummet. For a three-meter board, the preferred water depth is twelve feet, six inches at the plummet and twelve feet, two inches at nineteen feet, nine inches out from the plummet. The plummet is measured vertically from the tip of the board to the bottom of the pool. Several organizations (e.g., high schools) and state codes permit ten feet as a minimum depth for one-meter springboard diving or qualify the depth for pools constructed prior to a certain date—a grandfather clause—with deeper water required after that date.

The evaluation and review process usually starts as a recommendation from staff. A standing committee may be assigned the task of studying springboard diving, or a special committee could be organized for that purpose. In any case, program goals and objectives, safety and liability, and equipment replacement and construction or renovation should all be part of the study. Members of the committee should have knowledge or expertise in the areas just mentioned.

The following guidelines are offered to YMCAs examining the safety of their diving programs and facility construction:

1. Supervise the diving board when in use by various groups, teams, or classes. Prohibit diving when the board is not supervised.

2. Train supervisors, instructors, and lifeguards in the proper way to use a diving board, with emphasis on detecting potentially unsafe practices such as the following:

    a. The diver with more courage than common sense

    b. Divers who are fatigued, sometimes indicated by signs of balking, knees buckling at takeoff, or erratic body control in the air

    c. Poor approaches toward the end of the board

    d. Diving headfirst without the arms being used in an extended position

    e. Diving deep toward the bottom of the pool

    f. People attempting dives beyond their level of training

    g. Divers doing multiple bounces

    h. Two or more divers on the board at the same time

    i. Diving either out too far or diving toward the sides of the pool

    j. Clown diving or "splash" dives such as "can-openers" or "cannonball dives"

    k. Shotgun takeoffs

3. Replace a modern springboard with a wood-core fiberglass board.

4. Replace a 14-16-18-foot diving board with a shorter board that still meets the NCAA requirement of extending five feet, eleven inches (1.80 meters or 5 feet, 10 and 8 tenths inches) from the plummet (tip of the board) back to the pool wall.

5. Secure a moveable fulcrum so greater bounce cannot be obtained. This is usually done by locking the fulcrum in the most forward position to minimize bounce.

6. Lower the diving standard to twenty inches (20 inches) above the surface of the water. This will eliminate official competitive springboard diving but permit basic instruction and recreational diving to continue.

7. Post warning signs and/or diving board regulations prominently near the diving board.

If YMCAs are unable to meet these guidelines, removal of the diving board is recommended.

Association projects or studies resulting in decisions must, out of necessity, be based on local factors and leadership. However, several resources might be utilized in gathering information:

Nearby YMCAs, for information regarding their diving programs

The YMCA of the USA BFS/Property Management Department

The YMCA of the USA Program Development Department

November 1988

Revised May 1991

Revised April 1996

Exposure to Natural Sunlight In YMCA Programs for Children and Adults

Statement of the YMCA of the USA Medical Advisory Committee:

According to the American Academy of Dermatology, severe sunburns may be related to the development many years later of the most dangerous kind of skin cancer, called melanoma. Overexposure to the sun's light rays may also cause cumulative, invisible damage to epidermal and dermal skin cells through the years. In addition, too much exposure can damage the lens of the eye, and recent medical research shows that the immune system may be damaged.

The YMCA of the USA Medical Advisory Committee endorses the sun protection guidelines of the American Academy of Dermatology and urges YMCAs to educate staff, members, and program participants on the risks associated with overexposure to natural sunlight. In particular, staff in a supervisory role with children should take proper steps to limit the exposure of children to sunlight in all outdoor programs and activities, such as aquatics, child care, youth sports, and camping.

Attachment: "Sun Protection for Children: A Parents' Guide," distributed by the American Academy of Dermatology, 1993.

November 1988

Revised April 1996

The ABCs for Fun in the Sun

WHY protect against the sun?

Sun exposure has long been thought to be a healthy benefit of outdoor activity. Recent information, however, has shown some unhealthy effects of sun exposure, including early aging of the skin and skin cancer.

WHAT kinds of damage does sun exposure cause?

Part of the sun's energy that reaches us on earth is composed of rays of invisible ultraviolet (UV) light. When ultraviolet light rays enter the skin they damage the skin cells, causing visible and invisible types of injury.

Sunburn, a visible type of damage, appears just a few hours after sun exposure. In some people this type of damage also causes tanning. Ultraviolet light rays also cause invisible damage to skin cells. Some of the injury is repaired by the cells, but some of the cell damage adds up year after year. In 20 or 30 years or more the built-up damage appears as wrinkles, age spots, and skin cancer.

WHICH types of skin damage lead to skin cancer?

Severe sunburns, the early visible type of damage, may be related to the development many years later of the most dangerous kind of skin cancer called melanoma, which is potentially fatal. Melanomas can develop in all age groups, including teenagers and young adults. Melanomas can spread to other parts of the body.

The built-up invisible type of sun damage can lead to skin cancers on the face, ears, and neck. Basal cell cancers usually develop in middle life and later life, but can appear in one's 20s. These cancers rarely spread to other parts of the body. Their continuous growth, however, makes their removal a necessity. Squamous cell cancers can spread to other parts of the body if they are not treated early.

WHEN should sun protection begin?

Sun protection should begin in infancy and continue throughout life. It is estimated that we get about 80 percent of our total lifetime sun exposure in the first 18 years of life. Therefore sun prevention in childhood is very important to prevent skin cancer later in life.

HOW can I protect my children from the sun?

Begin NOW to teach your children to follow the "ABCs for Fun in the Sun."

A AWAY. Stay away from the sun in the middle of the day.

B BLOCK. Use SPF 15 or higher sunblock.

C COVER UP. Wear a T-shirt and a hat.

S SPEAK OUT. Talk to your family and friends about sun protection.

WHAT should be avoided?

Stay AWAY from midday sun and its intense rays. Schedule play times and outdoor activities before 11:00 a.m. and after 3:00 p.m. daylight saving time (10:00 a.m. to 2:00 p.m. standard time). The sun's energy is greatest when it travels through less atmosphere at midday. It is also more intense closer to the equator, in the mountains, and in the summer. The sun's damaging effects are increased by reflection from water, white sand, and snow.

Avoid long periods of direct sun exposure. Sit or play in the shade.

Avoid sunburn. Be aware of the length of time you are in the sun. It may take only 15 minutes of midday summer sun to burn a fair-skinned person.

HOW can sun damage be blocked?

BLOCK sun damage by applying a sunblock lotion or sunstick of at least SPF 15. The protective ability of sunblock is rated by Sun Protection Factor (SPF)—the higher the SPF, the stronger the protection. SPF numbers indicate the length of time one can spend in the sun without risk of burning. When using a 15 SPF sunblock, a fair-skinned person who normally sunburns after 20 minutes of midday sun exposure may tolerate 15 times 20 minutes (= 300 minutes) without sunburning.

Choose a sunblock with a 13 SPF or higher. Apply as much sunscreen as you would a lotion for dry skin. Spread it evenly over all uncovered skin, including ears and lips, but avoiding eyelids, about 30 minutes before sun exposure. Reapply after swimming or excessive sweating.

Invisible sunblocks work by trapping the ultraviolet energy and preventing that energy from damaging the skin.

Visible opaque white or colored sunblock creams prevent all light from entering the skin. They usually contain zinc oxide or titanium dioxide. They are useful for high risk areas such as the nose, lips, and shoulders and may also be used on babies.

Infants under six months of age are best kept out of direct sun and covered by protective clothing.

HOW can clothing be used for sun protection?

COVER UP with a hat and light clothing when outdoors. Don't play or work outdoors without a shirt. Put on your shirt and hat after swimming or wear a T-shirt while swimming. In addition to filtering out the sun, tightly-woven clothing reflects heat and helps to keep you feeling cool. Sunglasses that block ultraviolet rays protect the eyes and eyelids.

WHAT else can be done?

SPEAK OUT for sun protection now. Do your part to protect others from sun damage. Show your family how to apply a sunblock by spreading it evenly and invisibly over your skin. Remember to keep babies out of the sun and use an umbrella over the stroller. Talk to the coach, camp counselor, Scout leader, gym teacher, and other leaders about the "ABCs for FUN in the SUN." Ask them to help you with the simple changes that can prevent sun damage. Start preventing sun damage in childhood now.

Reprinted, by permission, from the American Academy of Dermatology, 1989 (rev. February 1993), *Sun Protection for Children: A Parents' Guide* (Schaumburg, IL: American Academy of Dermatology).

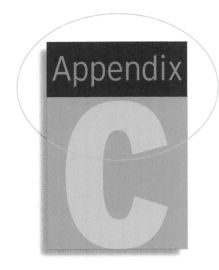

Appendix C

Values

Worksheets

The four worksheets in this appendix are meant to help you develop appropriate character development activities for your YMCA Swim Lessons classes.

Each worksheet addresses one of the four core values: caring, honesty, respect, and responsibility. Supplement your program with these character development activities, integrating the activities when they fit.

As you develop your activities, see if they meet the following criteria:

→ Are age-appropriate and developmentally appropriate.
→ Account for varied personal backgrounds and differing views on values.
→ Attempt to change people's attitudes as well as actions.
→ Focus on long-term results.
→ Are planned and intentional.
→ Fit logically with what you are doing.

→ Are positive and constructive, not putting participants down.
→ Are inclusive and reflect diversity.
→ Are significant, not trivial or corny.
→ Are fun!

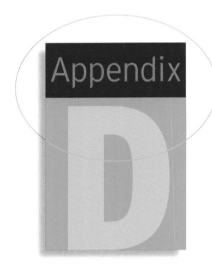

Appendix
D

Child Abuse Prevention
YMCA Checklist

1. The YMCA accepts that child abuse *can* happen at the YMCA and pledges to do everything within its power to prevent it.
    → Make sure staff and volunteers in supervisory positions are as rigorous as possible in screening out potential offenders.
    → Communicate to all staff and volunteers through tone and action that the YMCA is serious about doing everything it can to prevent abuse or accusations of abuse.

2. The YMCA trains *all* staff and volunteers on child-abuse prevention.
    → Select an experienced staff person in a leadership position with proven group facilitating skills to lead training.
    → Schedule training on a regular, ongoing basis, especially when new staff or volunteers begin their employment.

3. The YMCA has a rigorous preemployment screening process that includes the following:
    → Applications that seek information that could indicate a potential for child abuse

    → Background and reference checks on all those working directly with or in proximity to children (including criminal history and fingerprinting where available)
    → Interviews in which candidates are asked open-ended, leading questions designed to uncover possible indications of a potential for child abuse
    → Observation of candidates interacting with children
    → A statement of the YMCA's policies and stance on child abuse

4. The YMCA checks all applicant resumes and applications, references, and criminal histories and keeps complete records on file of the entire checking process.

5. The YMCA educates staff and volunteers on the characteristics of child abusers and the patterns abusers often follow. Reporting of suspicious behavior is everybody's responsibility.

6. The YMCA communicates with and educates parents about the YMCA's policies, procedures, and commitment to the safety of their children. Assure them that they may visit and observe any program at any time and express any concerns they may have to the staff in charge.

7. All programs operate with the safety of participants foremost in mind (supervision, age-appropriate activities and groupings, pick-up and release systems, staff or volunteer never alone with a single child, segregation of children by age, and so on). Administrators and supervisors regularly make unannounced visits.

8. YMCA facilities are secure and provide administrators and supervisors with an unobtrusive means of supervision. There are no private areas or unsupervised corners, including nap rooms, bathrooms, and locker rooms.

9. All staff and program volunteers sign a code of conduct, read and sign all policies related to identifying, documenting, and reporting child abuse, and attend training sessions on the subject.

10. The YMCA has established a process and forms for documenting incidents, unusual observations, and suspicions of child abuse. All staff and volunteers are aware of the process.

11. Staff and volunteers are trained in what to do if a child discloses abuse.

12. A crisis communication plan is in place. It identifies a crisis team and spokesperson, and includes message points, fact sheet, media relations, and so on.

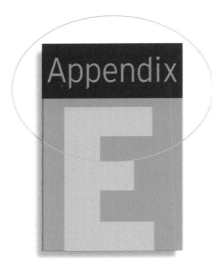

Health Precautions

for Swim Instructors

As a swimming instructor, you will be spending a lot of time in an aquatic environment.

This means that you will need to take a few daily precautions to avoid some common minor health problems affecting your eyes, hair, skin, and ears. You also should take care to ensure you don't strain your voice while teaching.

Care of Eyes

You may sometimes find that your eyes get red and irritated. This is not usually due to chlorine, but rather an improper pH level in the water. If this should occur, don't rub your eyes, but instead rinse them with water. When the pH level is corrected, the irritation should subside.

If you wear contact lenses, talk to your optometrist or ophthalmologist about whether they can be worn in the pool. Contacts can trap chemicals, bacteria, or foreign matter next to the eye, which may cause corneal swelling and microscopic abrasions that allow bacteria to enter the eye. If you wear your glasses, attach a safety strap so they don't fall off. Prescription goggles are also available.

When you teach in the sun, always wear sunglasses that filter 99 percent to 100 percent of UV-A and UV-B rays. Your eyesight can be damaged by prolonged sun exposure.

Care of Hair

Some people find that their hair can turn dry and brittle after being in pool water. To avoid this, wear a bathing cap when you swim. Rinse your hair as soon as you get out of the pool, and use a shampoo that can remove chemical buildup and impurities from the internal and external structure of the hair.

Care of Skin

If you swim in water that is properly treated, you generally don't have to worry about skin problems, other than dryness. However, it is possible for fungal diseases and other skin disorders to be transmitted in the pool area. The risk is greatly reduced when people with such skin disorders are not allowed into the pool. To protect yourself, though, be sure you shower with soap after you swim. Wearing slip-resistant water shoes or sandals in the shower areas will further help prevent the spread of fungal infections. Dry your skin well after showering, particularly between the toes, and apply a skin moisturizer if you have dry skin.

Remember that being in the water outdoors is no protection from the sun's rays; in fact, the water magnifies the intensity of the sun's rays. To avoid sunburn, put on sunscreen regularly. This also makes you a good model for your students, who also should be wearing sunscreen.

Care of Ears

Some instructors have a problem with frequent ear irritation or inflammation of the external ear. Infection of the inner ear is also possible.

To prevent such problems, dry your outer ear after each swim session. Gently dry it with a towel, and don't insert anything inside the ear. Tipping your head to let the water run out sometimes helps, too, and may make you feel less clogged. You may also want to use ear drops to help evaporate water in your ears. To prevent water getting inside the ears, you can wear silicone ear plugs and a tight swim cap, although this will also reduce your ability to hear.

Protection of Your Voice

Speaking to students in a pool environment can be difficult because you are always trying to talk over many other competing noises. Teaching consecutive classes, changing your voice pitch or volume suddenly, or not breathing properly while talking can also be hard on your voice.

If you experience throat or neck pain, a dry mouth or throat, hoarseness, temporary loss of voice or change of pitch, feel fatigued when talking, or constantly clear your throat, you may have injured your vocal cords. If these symptoms occur, consult your doctor or an otolaryngologist.

To help prevent injury, gradually warm up your voice, altering pitch, volume, and intensity. Build up to the necessary volume and pitch for teaching. Keep instructions short and direct, and don't talk unnecessarily (other than in a conversational tone). Drink water before, during, and after classes.

Observation

C h e c k s h e e t s

In this appendix we provide an observation checksheet for each of six common strokes:

→ Front crawl

→ Back crawl

→ Breaststroke

→ Butterfly

→ Sidestroke

→ Backstroke

Each checksheet lists components of the stroke and how they can best be performed. You can use these checksheets to help you decide which components to focus on when you observe a student, and you can record your observations on the sheets. Using these sheets will help you to guide students to better performance and to keep track of their progress over time.

Front Crawl Observation Checksheet

Class: _____ **Time and Date:** _____ **Instructor:** _____

YSWIM LESSONS

Component Observed	Observation Criteria	N	A	M	E					
BODY POSITION	Is the body in a prone position?									
	Are the body and legs vertical?									
	inclined?									
	level?									
	Are the hips high in the water, slightly below the surface?									
	Does body not wiggle side-to-side?									
	Is there a natural body roll on the long axis equally to both sides?									
	Do the legs roll with the body?									
	Does the waterline cross the forehead?									
ARM ACTION	Do the arms alternate their action?									
Recovery phase	Do arms recover out of water?									
	Are arms bent and high at elbow?									
	Does the pinkie leave the water first?									
Propulsion phase	Do fingers enter the water first, thumb side down and in line with and directly in front of the shoulder?									
	Do arms fully extend after entry?									
	Does each arm make an "S" curve?									
	Does the catch sweep outward first?									
	Are the elbows bent high during midpull?									
	Do arms accelerate consistently throughout the pull and push?									
LEG KICK ACTION	Do legs alternate up and down 10 to 16 inches?									
	Does the kick come from the hips?									
	Do heels come to the surface of the water with minimum splash?									
	Are feet pointed but relaxed?									

Front Crawl Observation Checksheet (cont.)

Class:

Time and Date:

Instructor:

NAME

Component Observed	Observation Criteria										
	Is the leg straight during the upward kick?										
	Do knees bend less than 30 degrees?										
	Do legs make two or four or six kicks/cycle?										
	Is the downbeat emphasized?										
	Is the kick continuous?										
	Is the kick symmetrical?										
BREATHING/ TIMING	Does the head/face enter the water for exhalation?										
	Does the head rotate to the side with body roll for inhalation, rather than lift forward?										
	Does head motion appear smooth?										
	Does inhalation come during recovery of the arm on the same side?										
	Does inhalation come without a pause?										
	Are bubbles visible before head turn?										
	Does exhalation occur during the pull and push of one arm?										
	Does the head move during exhalation to a central position with eyes looking forward (waterline at hairline)?										
	Is rotary breathing to the right or left, or is it to both sides?										
OTHER	Is kicking and pulling continuous?										
	Does the stroke appear fluid, graceful, smooth?										

Observation checksheets developed by Stephen J. Langendorfer based in part on information from the following books: Torney, John A., Jr., and Robert D. Clayton. 1981. *Teaching Aquatics*. Minneapolis: Burgess. YMCA Canada. 1993. *YMCA Advanced Swimming Instructor's Guide*. Toronto, Canada: YMCA Canada.

YSWIM LESSONS.

Back Crawl Observation Checksheet

Class: _____   Time and Date: _____   Instructor: _____

Component Observed	Observation Criteria	N	A	M	E			
BODY POSITION	Is the body in a supine position?							
	Are the body and legs vertical?							
	inclined?							
	level?							
	Are the hips high in the water, slightly below the surface?							
	Does the chest break the surface?							
	Is there a naturally occurring body roll on the long axis equally to both sides?							
ARM ACTION	Do the arms alternate their action?							
Recovery phase	Do arms recover out of water?							
	Does shoulder lift above water before arm?							
	Are elbows straight during recovery?							
	Are arms relaxed during recovery?							
	Do hands/arms not cross midline upon entry?							
	Does the pinkie finger enter the water first (fingers together)?							
	Is hand entry forward of the shoulder at 1 or 11 o'clock?							
	Do arms fully extend at entry?							
Propulsion phase	Is the catch deep?							
	Is the arm bent, fingers pointing to the side of the pool and elbow pointing toward the bottom of the pool through the pull?							
	Do elbows bend approximately 120 degrees during midpull?							
	Does the stroke continue past the thigh in an "S" or question mark pattern?							
	Do arms accelerate through the pull phase?							

Y SWIM LESSONS

Back Crawl Observation Checksheet (cont.)

Class:

Time and Date:

Instructor:

Component Observed	Observation Criteria	N	A	M	E						
LEG KICK ACTION	Do legs alternate up and down 12 to 15 inches?										
	Does the kick start from the hips, legs rolling with the body?										
	Do toes come near the surface of the water?										
	Are feet pointed?										
	Do knees not appear above water surface?										
	Is knee flexion = or < 45?										
	Do the legs make two or four or six kicks per cycle?										
	Is the kick shallow or continuous?										
	Is the kick symmetrical?										
BREATHING/ TIMING	Does face remain out of the water at all times?										
	Is head position back with ears skimming the surface and waterline crossing the back of the head?										
	Is breathing rhythmic, inhaling during recovery of one arm and exhaling during recovery of other arm?										
	Is inhalation through the mouth?										
OTHER	Does stroke appear fluid/graceful/smooth?										
	Is the stroke continuous?										
	Does swimmer's head not bounce up/down?										
	Does swimmer not roll head side to side?										

Observation checksheets developed by Stephen J. Langendorfer based in part on information from the following books: Torney, John A., Jr. and Robert D. Clayton. 1981. *Teaching Aquatics*. Minneapolis: Burgess. YMCA Canada. 1993. *YMCA Advanced Swimming Instructor's Guide*. Toronto, Canada: YMCA Canada.

Y SWIM LESSONS

Breaststroke Observation Checksheet

Class: **Time and Date:**   **Instructor:**

Component Observed	Observation Criteria	N	A	M	E					
BODY POSITION	Is the body in a prone position?									
	Are the body and legs vertical?									
	inclined?									
	level?									
	Does the swimmer glide with arms extended?									
	Is the body near the surface during the glide?									
	Does swimmer not move consistently left or right?									
ARM ACTION	Is the arm action symmetrical and simultaneous?									
	Do the forearms scull out, in, and back, tracing an inverted heart-shape underwater?									
Recovery phase	Do arms recover underwater?									
	Do elbows tuck to chest during recovery?									
	Does a glide follow the arm recovery?									
	Do arms and body stretch and streamline during the glide?									
Propulsion phase	Does catch sweep outward first?									
	Do palms turn slightly outward?									
	Do the elbows stay high until the hands are aligned with the shoulders?									
	Does the arm pull not travel back below shoulders?									
	Do elbows tuck inward at finish?									
	Do arms accelerate during finish?									
LEG KICK ACTION	Do legs kick symmetrically and simultaneously?									
	Are the knees about shoulder-width apart prior to the start of the kick, with feet flexed toward the shin (not pointed)?									
	Do legs circle up, out, backward?									

Y SWIM LESSONS

Breaststroke Observation Checksheet (cont.)

Y SWIM LESSONS

Class: _____ Time and Date: _____ Instructor: _____

Component Observed	Observation Criteria	N	A	M	E								
	Are heels drawn up toward the buttocks during kick recovery?												
	Are heels and knees relatively close together during kick recovery?												
	Do ankles recover wider than knees?												
	Do both ankles move toward the shins as the feet rotate outward?												
	Do toes come together after the kick, with body fully extended?												
	Does swimmer move forward after the kick?												
	Does leg kick follow the pull and breath?												
BREATHING/ TIMING	Is breathing forward, rather than to the side?												
	Does head/face go partially, rather than fully, underwater?												
	Does head breathing motion appear smooth?												
	Does face rise just before the breath?												
	Does face submerge just before arms reach full extension?												
	Does the swimmer hold his or her breath during the kick and glide phase?												
	Does exhalation occur underwater as the arm begins to pull?												
	Are bubbles visible before the breath?												
	Is there a breath every cycle?												
	Is pull and breathe-kick-glide timing used?												
OTHER	To glide, do arms pause straight ahead, or are they along the side or out to the side?												
	Does glide lengthen during slower swimming?												
	Is a long underwater pullout used for turns?												

Observation checksheets developed by Stephen J. Langendorfer based in part on information from the following books: Torney, John A., Jr., and Robert D. Clayton. 1981. *Teaching Aquatics*. Minneapolis: Burgess. YMCA Canada. 1993. *YMCA Advanced Swimming Instructor's Guide*. Toronto, Canada: YMCA Canada.

Butterfly Stroke Observation Checksheet

Class: Time and Date: Instructor:

Component Observed	Observation Criteria	NAME						
BODY POSITION	Is the body in a prone position?							
	Are the body and legs vertical?							
	inclined?							
	level?							
	Does body undulate or "porpoise" continuously?							
	Are the hips close to the surface?							
	Is the forehead at the waterline when swimmer is not breathing?							
ARM ACTION	Is arm action simultaneous and symmetrical?							
Recovery phase	Do arms recover out of water?							
	Are arms bent and high at elbow?							
	Does pinkie leave water first?							
Propulsion phase	Do arms fully extend at entry?							
	Do the index finger and thumb enter first rather than the palm?							
	Are elbows held high throughout propulsion?							
	Do arms make "keyhole" pull?							
	Does catch sweep outward first?							
	Do elbows bend high during midpull?							
	Do arms accelerate out during finish?							
	Do thumbs finish near the thigh?							
LEG KICK ACTION	Does the kick begin in the hips?							
	Do legs go up and down together?							
	Do the knees lead the legs on the downbeat of the kick?							
	Do heels come to surface of water?							
	Do feet point in downbeat?							

Y SWIM LESSONS

Butterfly Stroke Observation Checksheet (cont.)   ▼SWIM LESSONS

Class: Time and Date: Instructor:

Component Observed	Observation Criteria	N	A	M	E					
	Do knees bend 30 degrees to 45 degrees?									
	Do legs make zero, one, or two kicks/cycle?									
	Is the kick a big-kick, little-kick order?									
	Is the leg kick symmetrical?									
	Do the legs not come apart or flutter?									
BREATHING/ TIMING	Does head/face go in the water?									
	Does head tilt up and chin thrust forward for breathing?									
	Is breathing forward, rather than to the side?									
	Does the back arch when head surfaces to breathe?									
	Is forward head motion smooth?									
	Do bubbles appear before breath?									
	Does the head enter and exit before hands do?									
	Is a breath taken each stroke cycle?									

Observation checksheets developed by Stephen J. Langendorfer based in part on information from the following books: Torney, John A., Jr., and Robert D. Clayton. 1981. Teaching Aquatics. Minneapolis: Burgess. YMCA Canada. 1993. YMCA Advanced Swimming Instructor's Guide. Toronto, Canada: YMCA Canada.

Sidestroke Observation Checksheet

YSWIM LESSONS®

Class: **Time and Date:** **Instructor:**

Component Observed	Observation Criteria	NAME							
BODY POSITION	Is the body on the side in a streamlined position?								
	Are the body and legs vertical?								
	inclined?								
	level?								
	Does body move in straight line?								
ARM ACTION	Do arms alternate pull and recovery actions?								
Recovery phase	Does the hand of the leading arm stay underwater at all times?								
	Do arms recover under the water?								
	Are arms streamlined in recovery?								
	Does the leading arm extend after recovery, in line with body and parallel to water's surface?								
	Does the trailing arm lie against trunk with the hand against the thigh after recovery?								
Propulsion phase	Does the leading arm bend during pull?								
	Does the trailing arm bend during pull?								
LEG KICK ACTION	Do legs use a scissors kick?								
	Is there one leg-kick/stroke cycle?								
	Do hips and knees bend 90 degrees before "step"?								
	Does kick begin with "step" by both legs?								
	Do legs pull together simultaneously following wide stride, causing forward propulsion?								
	Do feet point during propulsion?								
	Do legs meet, but not cross, during glide?								
BREATHING/ TIMING	Is breathing fairly rhythmic?								
	Does the swimmer breathe through the mouth?								

TEACHING SWIMMING FUNDAMENTALS

180

Sidestroke Observation Checksheet (cont.)

Class: _____   Time and Date: _____   Instructor: _____

Component Observed	Observation Criteria	N	A	M	E						
	Does the swimmer inhale during leg recovery and exhale during the kick?										
	Does the head/bottom ear lay in the water?										
	Does the head hold still, looking toward the side?										
	Do legs recover during leading arm pull?										
	Do legs scissors during trailing arm pull?										
GLIDE	Is there a pronounced glide of one to three seconds?										
	Does the glide occur after the kick?										
	Is the body streamlined during the glide?										

Observation checksheets developed by Stephen J. Langendorfer based in part on information from the following books:
Torney, John A., Jr., and Robert D. Clayton. 1981. *Teaching Aquatics.* Minneapolis: Burgess.
YMCA Canada. 1993. *YMCA Advanced Swimming Instructor's Guide.* Toronto, Canada: YMCA Canada.

Elementary Backstroke
Observation Checksheet

Class: _____   Time and Date: _____   Instructor: _____

Component Observed		Observation Criteria	N	A	M	E				
BODY POSITION		Is the body in a supine position?								
		Are the body and legs vertical?								
		inclined?								
		level?								
		Does swimmer not go consistently left or right?								
ARM ACTION		Is the arm action symmetrical?								
	Recovery phase	Do arms recover underwater?								
		Do arms stay close to sides during recovery?								
		Is there a glide of two-three seconds before recovery?								
	Propulsion phase	Do the arms begin pull slightly above the shoulders?								
		Does the catch sweep outward first?								
		Do arms bend slightly at elbows?								
		Do arms accelerate throughout this phase?								
		Does the propulsion phase continue until the hands reach the thighs?								
LEG KICK ACTION		Do legs kick symmetrically?								
		Do legs lower downward toward the bottom until the knees bend almost 90 degrees?								
		Do feet make a semicircle during the kick, accelerating during the kick phase and coming together simultaneously at the fullest leg extension?								
		Are the knees about shoulder-width apart?								
		Do ankles recover wider apart than knees?								
		Do ankles turn outward?								
		Does swimmer move forward after kick?								

Y SWIM LESSONS

Y SWIM LESSONS

Elementary Backstroke Observation Checksheet (cont.)

Class: Time and Date: Instructor:

Component Observed	Observation Criteria	N	A	M	E						
BREATHING/ TIMING	Does head/face stay clear of water?										
	Is inhalation through the mouth?										
	Is breathing rhythmic?										
	Does the swimmer inhale during recovery and exhale during propulsion?										
	Does the head remain relatively still?										
	Is the leg kick simultaneous with the arm pull?										
	Does arm recovery usually start slightly before kick recovery?										
GLIDE	During glide, are arms straight ahead?										
	out to the side?										
	at the sides?										

Observation checksheets developed by Stephen J. Langendorfer based in part on information from the following books: Torney, John A., Jr., and Robert D. Clayton. 1981. *Teaching Aquatics.* Minneapolis: Burgess. YMCA Canada. 1993. *YMCA Advanced Swimming Instructor's Guide.* Toronto, Canada: YMCA Canada.

Bibliography

Allison, Pamela C. 1985. "Observing for Competence." *Journal of Physical Education, Recreation and Dance* (August): 50-51, 54.

Astrand, P.O., and K. Rodahl. 1986. *Textbook of Work Physiology: Physiological Bases of Exercises.* New York: McGraw-Hill.

Barrett, Kate R. 1979. "Observation for Teaching and Coaching." *Journal of Physical Education, Recreation and Dance* (January): 23-25.

Barrett, Kate R., Kathleen Williams, and Jill Whitall. 1992. "What Does It Mean to Have a 'Developmentally Appropriate Physical Education Program?'" *The Physical Educator*, 49:3, 114-118.

Behrman, Richard E., ed. 1987. *Nelson Textbook of Pediatrics.* Philadelphia: W.B. Saunders.

Birrer, R. 1989. "Prescribing Physical Activity for the Elderly." Pp. 75-93 in *Physical Activity, Aging and Sports: Scientific and Medical Research*, ed. R. Harris and S. Harris. Albany, NY: Center for the Study of Aging.

Bredekamp, Sue, and Carol Copple, eds. 1996. *Developmentally Appropriate Practice in Early Childhood Programs.* Rev. ed. Washington, DC: National Association for the Education of Young Children.

Christina, Robert W., and Daniel M. Corcos. 1988. *Coaches Guide to Teaching Sport Skills.* Champaign, IL: Human Kinetics.

Goodwill Industries of America, Inc. 1992. *People with Disabilities Terminology Guide.* Bethesda, MD: Goodwill Industries of America, Inc.

Horvat, Michael. 1990. *Physical Education and Sport for Exceptional Students.* Dubuque, IA: William C. Brown.

Kohlberg, L.A. 1971. "Development of Moral Character." Pp. 303-319 in *Developmental Psychology Today*. Del Mar, CA: Communications Research Machines.
———.1980. *The Meaning and Measurement of Moral Development.* Worcester, MA: Clark University Press.

Langendorfer, Stephen J., and Lawrence D. Bruya. 1995. *Aquatic Readiness: Developing Water Competence in Young Children.* Champaign, IL: Human Kinetics.

Langendorfer, Stephen, Elizabeth German, and Diana Kral. 1988. "Aquatic Games and Gimmicks for Young Children." *The National Aquatics Journal* (Fall): 11-14.

Logsdon, B.J., and K.R. Barrett. 1984. "Movement—the Content of Physical Education." Pp. 9-23 in *Physical Education for Children*. 2nd ed. Edited by B.J. Logsdon. Philadelphia: Lea & Febiger.

Miller, Freeman, and Steven J. Bachrach. 1995. *Cerebral Palsy: A Complete Guide for Caregiving.* Baltimore: Johns Hopkins University Press.

Mosston, Muska. 1966. *Teaching Physical Education.* Columbus, OH: Charles E.Merrill.

National Association for Sport and Physical Education, American Alliance for Health, Physical Education, Recreation and Dance. 19??. *Looking at Physical Education from a Developmental Perspective: A Guide to Teaching.* Reston, VA: National Association for Sport and Physical Education, American Alliance for Health, Physical Education, Recreation and Dance.

Roberton, Mary Ann. 1977. "Developmental Implications for Games Teaching." *Journal of Physical Education, Recreation and Dance*, September, 25.

Shepard, R.J. 1978. *Physical Activity and Aging.* London: Croom Helm.

Smith, Deborah Deutsch, and Ruth Luckasson. 1992. *Introduction to special education: Teaching in an age of challenge.* Needham Heights, MA: Allyn and Bacon.

Stevens, Suzanne H. 1985. *Classroom Success for the Learning Disabled.* Winston-Salem, NC: John F. Blair.

Torney, John A., Jr., and Robert D. Clayton. 1981. *Teaching Aquatics.* Minneapolis, MN: Burgess Publishing Company.

Index

A

abuse, child
    precautions 18, 21
    reporting 17-18
    signs of 17
    and YMCA's Code of Conduct 18-20
accident/incident reports 69
acquired immune deficiency syndrome 98
    National AIDS Information Clearinghouse 101
adolescent behavior and development 43-45
adult classes
    instructor/participant ratio for 68
    levels of 83
adult students
    versus children 80
    developmental characteristics of 83
    fear of water in 81, 82
    flotation devices for 84
    goal setting for 81, 87
    healthy lifestyle information for 85-86
    levels for 83
    motivating 87
    out-of-shape 81-82
    physical limitations of 83-84, 88-90
    psychological aspects of 81
    rewards for 87
    socializing among 82, 91
    tips for working with 90-91
age, as indicator of developmental progress 23
age group charts 26
    6 to 12 months old 27-28
    12 to 18 months old 29-30
    18 to 24 months old 31-32
    24 to 36 months old 33-34
    3 to 4 years old 35
    5 to 6 years old 36
    7 to 8 years old 37-39
    9 to 11 years old 40-42
    12 to 15 years old 43-45
agents of change, instructors as 7
aging and physical changes 88-90
AIDS 98

National AIDS Information Clearinghouse 101
American Association on Mental Retardation 101
Americans with Disabilities Act 93, 97
    ADA Technical Assistance phone number 101
amputations 97-98
analysis of student performance
    evaluation 76-79
    observation 9, 54, 55
aquatic assistants 68
aquatic body dimensions
    defined 47
    of water entry 50-52
aquatic effort dimension, defined 47
aquatic movement framework 47
aquatic patterns/formations 62-67
aquatic relationship dimension, defined 47
aquatic space dimension, defined 47
Archimedes' Principle 110, 111
arm movements
    back crawl 118-119
    backstroke 126
    breaststroke 120-121
    butterfly stroke 122-123
    front crawl 116-117
    propulsion patterns 106
    recovery patterns 107
    sidestroke 124-125
artificial limbs 97-98
assistants 68
asthma 98
Asthma and Allergy Foundation of America 101
athetoid cerebral palsy 96
Attention Deficit Disorder Association 101
attitude of instructors 3-4

B

back crawl 118-119
    flip turn 132
    open turn 131
    start 129-130
backstroke 126-127
backyard pool safety 85

balance in new swimmers 10
barbells 72
be-attitudes for instructors 3-4
beach safety 85
beginners level 60
beginning of classes 2-3
beginning swimmers
    adjustments for 10-11
    instructional flotation devices for 70-71, 72
behavior in children. *See also* age group charts
    correcting inappropriate 74-76
Bernoulli's theorem 115
bicycling 108
Bill of Rights for students 56
blindness 95
    terminology for describing 100
bloodborne pathogens, exposure to 69
boating safety 85
body positions in water 11, 106
books
    Developmentally Appropriate Practice in Early Childhood Programs 22
    The Parent/Child and Preschool Aquatic Program Manual 9, 60, 115
    People With Disabilities Terminology Guide 99
    Teaching Physical Education 5
    YMCA Swim Lessons Administrator's Manual 2, 60, 76, 79
    The Youth and Adult Aquatic Program Manual 9, 60, 115
brain injury 96
    National Head Injury Foundation 101
breaststroke 120-121
    start 129
    turn 132
breath control patterns 104, 105
breathing
    adjustments for beginners 10-11
    back crawl 118-119
    backstroke 127
    breaststroke 120-121
    butterfly 122-123
    front crawl 116-117
    problems in adult students 84
    sidestroke 125

bridging 5, 8
buoyancy
    center of 111
    negative 10
    patterns 105
butterfly
    start 129
    stroke 122-123
    turn 133

C

cardiorespiratory system of older adults 89
caring as a core value 12
cerebral palsy 95-96
    United Cerebral Palsy Association 101
Character Development Activity Box 15
character development of students
    activities for 15-16
    core values 12
    discussing values 14-15
    modeling YMCA's core values 13-14
    self-esteem and 11-12
    teachable moments for 15
checksheets, observation 54
chicken pox 70
child abuse
    precautions 18, 21
    reporting 17-18
    signs of 17
    and YMCA's Code of Conduct 18-20
Child Abuse Prevention YMCA Checklist 21
child development
    age group charts 26
        6 to 12 months old 27-28
        12 to 18 months old 29-30
        18 to 24 months old 31-32
        24 to 36 months old 33-34
        3 to 4 years old 35
        5 to 6 years old 36
        7 to 8 years old 37-39
        9 to 11 years old 40-42
        12 to 15 years old 43-45
    concepts on how children learn 25-26
    factors affecting motor development 24
    principles of 22-23
child-centered environments 26
childhood diseases 70

children. *See also* child development
    abuse of 17-21
    character development of 11-13
    misbehavior in 74-76
    moral reasoning of 14-15
circle swim pattern 65
class assistants 68
class management techniques 74-76
class organization
    lesson plans 60-62
    patterns and formations 62-67
    procedures 62
    session planning 58-59
class safety
    adult 85
    first-day orientation safety information 68
    health issues 69-70
    instructor/participant ratios 67-68
    policies 69
    risk management 69
climate, class 5, 56-57
closed-end classes 58
Code of Conduct 18-20
Code of Ethics 4
cognitive barrier 6
cognitive development of children
    from 6 to 12 months old 28
    from 12 to 18 months old 30
    from 18 to 24 months old 32
    from 24 to 36 months old 34
    from 3 to 4 years old 35
    from 5 to 6 years old 36
    from 7 to 8 years old 38
    from 9 to 11 years old 41
    from 12 to 15 years old 43
colds and allergies 70
command teaching style 6
conjunctivitis 70
consequences for children who break rules 74-75
    natural 76
    time-outs 76
core values
    checking your own 13-14
    teaching 12
corner swim pattern 63-64
crawlstroke 109, 116-117
critical features, defined 54
cultural diversity 100

D

day-care groups 101
deafness 95
development of children
    age group charts 26
        6 to 12 months old 27-28
        12 to 18 months old 29-30
        18 to 24 months old 31-32
        24 to 36 months old 33-34
        3 to 4 years old 35
        5 to 6 years old 36
        7 to 8 years old 37-39
        9 to 11 years old 40-42
        12 to 15 years old 43-45
    concepts on how children learn 25-26
    factors affecting motor development 24
    principles involved in 22-23
developmental stages of swimming 103-109
Developmentally Appropriate Practice in Early Childhood Programs 22
disabilities
    learning 94
    legislation on 92-93
    medical conditions 98-99
    mental retardation 93-94
    physical 95-98
    sensory 94-95
    terminology for describing 99-100
    tips for working with people with 99-100
Disability Rights Education and Defense Fund 101
diseases, childhood 70. *See also* health issues
distance to swim 102, 103
dog paddle 108
drowning, fear of
    in adults 81, 82
    in beginners 11

E

ear pain 70
ear tubes 70
Easter Seal Society, National 101
Education for All Handicapped Children Act 92
eels 60
emotional abuse of children 17
emotional development of children
    from 6 to 12 months old 28
    from 12 to 18 months old 30
    from 18 to 24 months old 32

from 24 to 36 months old 34
from 3 to 4 years old 35
from 5 to 6 years old 36
from 7 to 8 years old 39
from 9 to 11 years old 41-42
from 12 to 15 years old 44
encouragement, giving 3
enthusiasm, showing 10
environment, effective class 56-57
epilepsy 98-99
Epilepsy Foundation of America 101
Ethics, Code of 4
evaluation
    class 76
    of students 76-79
eye infections 70
eyesight, poor 84, 95

F
Family Huddles 79
family involvement in student evaluations 78-79
fear of water
    in adults 81, 82
    in beginners 11
    stages of water adjustment 103
feedback
    to adult students 81
    from parents 78
    to students 9, 55-56
feet, warts on 69
feet-first water entry 104
fins 84
first impressions 2
first-day orientation 68
fish 60
flip turns
    back crawl 132
    in competitive swimming 113
    crawlstroke 130-131
float belts 72, 84
floating 10, 105
flotation (Archimedes' Principle) 110
flotation devices 70-72
    for adults 84
flutter kick
    bent-knee 108
    rudimentary 108
    straight-leg 109

flying fish 60, 83
formations and patterns
    choosing 62
    circle swim pattern 65
    for class demonstrations 65, 66
    corner swim pattern 63-64
    for group discussions 65, 66
    long course practice swim pattern 64-65
    for series swimming and instruction 65, 67
    short course practice swim pattern 64
    single line pattern 65
    stagger pattern 63
    for water practice 65, 66
    wave formation 63
front crawl 109
    sequence 116-117
    start 129
    turns 130-131

G
games, aquatic
    choosing 73-74
    at conclusion of classes 60
    leading 74
    as part of learning 25
    during practice time 9
goggles
    prescription 84
    for short course practice swim 64
greetings at beginning of class 60
guided discovery teaching style
    defined 7
    skill themes for 47-49
gum 68
guppy level 60, 83

H
handouts, parent 79
hands-on experience for students 25
head-first water entry 104, 105
health issues 69-70
healthy lifestyle information 85-86
hearing, students' 11, 95
Hearing Information Center 101
home
    at-home activities 60
    pool safety at 85
honesty as a core value 12

hygiene rules 68
hypotonic cerebral palsy 96

I
impressions, first 2
indirect teaching methods
    guided discovery 7, 47-49
    problem-solving 7, 47-49
individual program teaching style 6
individual style of swimming 114
inertia 113
inias 60
instructional flotation devices 70-72
    for adults 84
Instructor Code of Ethics 4
instructor/participant ratios 67-68
instructors
    as agents of change 7
    be-attitudes for 3-4
    Code of Conduct for 18-20
    Code of Ethics for 4
    as guides and facilitators 46
    as health information sources 85-86
    responsibilities of 3-5, 69
    as role models for children 13
intervening, defined 5
intestinal disorders 69

K
kick
    backstroke 126-127
    breaststroke 120, 121
    dolphin 122
    flutter 108, 109
kickboards 72, 84, 115
kippers 60

L
L formation 66
Laban, Rudolph 47
language barriers 100
language development of children
    from 6 to 12 months old 27
    from 12 to 18 months old 29
    from 18 to 24 months old 31
    from 24 to 36 months old 33
    from 3 to 4 years old 35
    from 5 to 6 years old 36

from 7 to 8 years old 37
from 9 to 11 years old 40
from 12 to 15 years old 43
Learn to Swim Month 84
learning. *See also* child development; student-centered
  teaching styles
    concepts on how children learn 25-26
    environment for 56-57
    stages of 26
    student-centered 7-8
    teacher-centered 7
learning disabilities 94
leg actions
    backstroke 126-127
    breaststroke 120-121
    butterfly stroke 122
    front crawl 116-117
    sidestroke 125
    stages of 108-109
leg floats 72
legislation on people with disabilities 92-93
lesson plans
    as adaptable guides 10, 60
    components of 60
    form for 61
    safety factors in 62
levels, YMCA
    instructional flotation devices for 72
    names of 60, 83
levers, law of 112
life jackets 84
Lifestyle Assessment for adult students 86
long course practice swim pattern 64-65

M
mental retardation 93-94
    American Association on Mental Retardation 101
minnow level 60, 83
moral reasoning, children's 14-15
Mosston, Muska 5
motivational techniques
    for adult students 86-87
    creating effective class environment 56-57
    giving encouragement 3
    giving praise 47
motor development of children
    factors affecting 24
    from 6 to 12 months old 27

from 12 to 18 months old 29
from 18 to 24 months old 31
from 24 to 36 months old 33
from 3 to 4 years old 35
from 5 to 6 years old 36
from 7 to 8 years old 37
from 9 to 11 years old 40
muscle cramping 90
musculoskeletal system of older adults 89-90

N
names, students' 3
nasal discharge 70
negative buoyancy 10
neglect, child 17, 19
Newton's First Law of Motion 113
Newton's Second Law of Motion 114
Newton's Third Law of Motion 110-111

O
observation
    checksheets 54
    factors affecting 55
    during practice sessions 9
older adults
    physical limitations of 83-84, 88-90
    tips for working with 90-91
organizational patterns/formations
    choosing 62
    circle swim pattern 65
    for class demonstrations 65, 66
    corner swim pattern 63-64
    for group discussions 65, 66
    long course practice swim pattern 64-65
    for series swimming and instruction 65, 67
    short course practice swim pattern 64
    single line pattern 65
    stagger pattern 63
    for water practice 65, 66
    wave formation 63
orientation
    first-day 68
    parent 2, 3, 79
overweight adult students 81-82

P
*The Parent/Child and Preschool Aquatic
  Program Manual* 9, 60, 115
parents
    feedback from 78-79
    handouts for 79
    orientation for 2, 3, 79
part-whole teaching method 53
partner teaching style 6
patterns and formations
    choosing 62
    circle swim pattern 65
    for class demonstrations 65, 66
    corner swim pattern 63-64
    for group discussions 65, 66
    long course practice swim pattern 64-65
    for series swimming and instruction 65, 67
    short course practice swim pattern 64
    single line pattern 65
    stagger pattern 63
    for water practice 65, 66
    wave formation 63
People With Disabilities Terminology Guide 99
perch 60
personal touch 91
personal values worksheet 14
physical abuse of children 17, 19
physical development of children
    factors affecting 24
    from 6 to 12 months old 27
    from 12 to 18 months old 29
    from 18 to 24 months old 31
    from 24 to 36 months old 33
    from 3 to 4 years old 35
    from 5 to 6 years old 36
    from 7 to 8 years old 37
    from 9 to 11 years old 40
    from 12 to 15 years old 45
physical limitations of older adults
    adaptations for 83-84
    changes accompanying aging 88-90
physics of swimming 109-110
    acceleration 114
    action and reaction 110-111
    Bernoulli's theorem 115
    center of buoyancy 111
    flotation 110
    individual physical differences 114

inertia 113
law of levers 112
symmetrical movement 112
volume 111
water resistance 112
Piaget, Jean 25
pikes 60
pink eye 70
plantar warts 69
play
    aquatic games 73-74
    learning through 23, 25
poison ivy 69
polliwog level 60, 83
pool area, familiarization with 68
pool entry
    head-first 104, 105
    question tree 49-52
    stages of 104
pool safety, backyard 85
porpoise level 60
practice sessions 9
preparation for each lesson 8
preschool classes, instructor/participant ratio for 68
problem-solving teaching style
    defined 7
    skill themes for 47-49
profanity 20
professionalism 4
progress of students
    discussions with parents about 78-79
    skill sheets for charting 76-78
progressive part teaching method 53
propulsion 11
    arm 106
prostheses 97-98
pull buoys 72
punishment for misbehavior 74-76

Q

question stems 8
question trees
    defined 49
    sample question tree for water entry 50-52
questions
    get-acquainted 3
    in skill presentations 8-9

R

rashes 69, 70
ratio of instructor to participants 67-68
rays 60
reading, related
    Developmentally Appropriate Practice in Early Childhood Programs 22
    The Parent/Child and Preschool Aquatic Program Manual 9, 60, 115
    People With Disabilities Terminology Guide 99
    Teaching Physical Education 5
    YMCA Swim Lessons Administrator's Manual 2, 60, 76, 79
    The Youth and Adult Aquatic Program Manual 9, 60, 115
reciprocal teaching style 6
recovery, arm 107
    back crawl 119
    front crawl 117
registration
    first impressions at 2
    parents' orientation packet 2
Rehabilitation Act 92
repetition, reinforced 25
resistance, water 11, 112
respect as a core value 12
responsibilities of instructors
    Be-Attitudes 3-5
    Code of Conduct outlining 18-20
    risk management 69
responsibility as a core value 12
risk management 69
rules
    consequences for children who break 74-75, 76
    explanation of rules at orientation 2, 68

S

safety
    factors in lesson plans 62
    first-day orientation safety information 68
    health issues 69-70
    instructor/participant ratios 67-68
    policies 69
    risk management 69
Scott, Ron 5
seizures, epileptic 98-99
self-esteem and values 11-12
sensory disabilities 94-95
sensory perceptions in older adults 88
series swim, defined 60
series swimming patterns 65, 67
session and lesson plans 58-62

sexual abuse 17, 19
shark level 60, 83
short course practice swim pattern 64
shrimps 60
sidestroke 124-125
sign language 95
single line formation 66
single line pattern 65
skill sheets 76-78
skill themes 47-49
skin rashes 69, 70
small group teaching style 6
smoking 20
social development of children
    from 6 to 12 months old 28
    from 12 to 18 months old 30
    from 18 to 24 months old 32
    from 24 to 36 months old 34
    from 3 to 4 years old 35
    from 5 to 6 years old 36
    from 7 to 8 years old 39
    from 9 to 11 years old 41-42
    from 12 to 15 years old 44
socializing in adult classes 83, 90-91
spastic cerebral palsy 96
speed/tempo of strokes 102, 103
spina bifida 97
Spina Bifida Association of America 101
spinal cord injury 96-97
    National Spinal Cord Injury Association 101
stages of learning for swimming 26
stagger pattern 63
starfish 60
starts 128-130
stiffness, back and neck 84
strokes
    back crawl 118-119
    backstroke 126-127
    breaststroke 120-121
    butterfly stroke 122-123
    front crawl 116-117
    sidestroke 124-125
    stroke progression 102-103
    turns for different strokes 130-133
student evaluations
    family involvement in 78-79
    skill sheets for 76-78
student-centered learning 7-8

student-centered teaching styles 5
  defined 46-47
  feedback 9, 55-56
  framework for aquatic movement 47
  guided discovery style 7, 47-49
  practice for 9
  preparation for 8
  presentation of 8-9
  problem-solving style 7, 47-49
  question trees 49-52
  skill themes for 47-49
students
  acquainting yourself with 3
  adolescent 43-45
  adult 80-91
  with AIDS 98
  with amputations 97-98
  with asthma 98
  Bill of Rights for 56
  blind 95
  with brain injury 96
  with cerebral palsy 95-96
  character development of 11-16
  children and toddlers as 22-42
  from cultures other than your own 100
  in day camp and day-care groups 101
  deaf 95
  with epilepsy 98-99
  with learning disabilities 94
  with mental retardation 93-94
  older adult 88-91
  out-of-shape 81-82
  with spina bifida 97
  with spinal cord injury 96-97
  using names of 3
summaries at end of each class 5
symmetrical movement 112

T
tasks, assigning 5
teachable moments
  defined 15
  in games 73
teacher-centered learning 7
teacher-centered teaching styles 6
Teaching Physical Education 5
teaching styles
  choosing a style 5-6
  command style 6

guided discovery style 7, 47-49
individual program style 6
problem-solving style 7, 47-49
reciprocal style 6
small group style 6
task style 6
teaching values 11-13
teaching water skills
  giving feedback 9, 55-56
  guided discovery method for 7, 47-49
  knowledge of child development for 22
  observation of skill performance 54-55
  problem-solving method for 7, 47-49
  question trees for 49-52
  skill themes for 47-49
  student-centered approach to 5, 8-10
  styles of 5-7
  tasks involved in 5
  tips on 100
  whole or part instruction for 53-54
tendons, tight 84
terminology for describing disabilities 99-100
three-jointed bubble 72
time-outs for young children 76
turns
  back crawl flip turn 132
  back crawl open turn 131
  breaststroke turn 132
  butterfly turn 133
  crawlstroke flip turn 130-131
  crawlstroke open turn 130

V
values
  activities 15-16
  core 12
  discussing 14-15
  modeling 13-14
  and self-esteem 11-12
verbal abuse 19
vision
  poor 84, 95
  in water 10-11
volunteers 81

W
warm-up (series swim) 60, 65, 67
warts 69
water adjustment and orientation 103

water entry
  head-first 104, 105
  question tree 49-52
  stages of 104
water logs 72, 84
water resistance 11, 112
water wings 72
wave formation 63
whole teaching method 53, 54
whole-part-whole teaching method 53

Y
YMCA Instructor Code of Ethics 4
YMCA Swim Lessons Administrator's Manual
  family handouts from 60, 79
  parent orientation agenda in 2
  skill sheets in 76
The Youth and Adult Aquatic Program Manual 9, 60, 115

YMCA Swim Lessons Level Logos

Shown on this and the next page are the logos for each of the levels in the YMCA Swim Lessons program. They can be used on information sheets, handouts, and flyers, even on t-shirts.

Parent/Child and Preschool Program

perch

inia

Shrimp

eel

Kipper

Pike

Ray

Starfish

Youth and Adult Program

Polliwog

Guppy

Fish

Minnow

Flying Fish

Shark

Porpoise

Additional Resources for Your Aquatics Program

For details about these additional items, current prices, and a complete listing of available accessories, contact the Y Program Store, P.O. Box 5076, Champaign, IL 61825-5076, phone (800) 747-0089. To save time, order by fax: (217) 351-1549. Please call if you are interested in receiving a free catalog.

YMCA Swim Lessons manuals

5412	YMCA Swim Lessons Administrator's Manual (Approx 416 pp)
5419	The Youth and Adult Aquatic Program Manual (208 pp)
5420	The Parent/Child and Preschool Aquatic Program Manual (Approx 208 pp)

YMCA Swim Lessons training videos

5434	Teaching Swimming Fundamentals Video
5435	The Youth and Adult Aquatic Program Video
5436	The Parent/Child and Preschool Aquatic Program Video

Aquatics

5285	Principles of YMCA Aquatics (144 pp)
5243	Everybody Swims, Everybody Wins (11-minute video)
5322	Water Fun and Fitness (176 pp)
5296	Aquatic Games (144 pp)
5229	YMCA Pool Operations Manual (Second Edition, 160 pp)

Aquatic Safety

5328	YMCA Splash (150 pp)
5428	Aquatic Safety Training Video (9-minute video)

Lifeguarding

5334	On the Guard II (Third Edition, 272 pp)
5342	Instructor Manual for On the Guard II (Third Edition, 568-page notebook and 93-minute video) ***Note:** *This manual may only be purchased by certified YMCA lifeguard instructors with a sanction number.*

Competitive Swimming and Diving

5302	Principles of YMCA Competitive Swimming and Diving (152 pp)
5287	Rookie Coaches Swimming Guide (80 pp)
5290	Coaching Swimming Successfully (200 pp)
5423	Swimming Drills for Every Stroke (208 pp)
5258	Swimming Into the 21st Century (272 pp)

Water Polo

5271	United States Water Polo Level One Coaching Manual (78 pp)